MW01502861

THE
ENIGMATIC
SOUTH

THE
ENIGMATIC
SOUTH

TOWARD CIVIL WAR
AND ITS LEGACIES

EDITED BY

SAMUEL C. HYDE, JR.

WITH A FOREWORD BY
JAMES M. MCPHERSON

AND AN AFTERWORD BY
GAINES M. FOSTER

LOUISIANA STATE UNIVERSITY PRESS
BATON ROUGE

PUBLISHED WITH THE ASSISTANCE OF THE V. RAY CARDOZIER FUND

Published by Louisiana State University Press
Copyright © 2014 by Louisiana State University Press
All rights reserved
Manufactured in the United States of America
FIRST PRINTING

DESIGNER: *Mandy McDonald Scallan*
TYPEFACE: *Whitman*
PRINTER AND BINDER: *Maple Press, Inc.*

Library of Congress Cataloging-in-Publication Data
The enigmatic South : toward Civil War and its legacies / edited by Samuel C. Hyde Jr. ; with a foreword by James M. McPherson and an afterword by Gaines M. Foster.
pages cm
ISBN 978-0-8071-5694-0 (cloth : alkaline paper) — ISBN 978-0-8071-5695-7 (pdf) — ISBN
978-0-8071-5696-4 (mobi) — ISBN 978-0-8071-5697-1 (epub) 1. Southern States—Civilization—1775–1865. 2. Southern States—History—1775–1865. 3. Southern States—Social
conditions—19th century. 4. Slavery—Southern States—History. 5. Secession—Southern States. I.
Hyde, Samuel C., 1958–
F213.E535 2015
975'03—dc23

2014011364

The paper in this book meets the guidelines for permanence and durability of the Committee on
Production Guidelines for Book Longevity of the Council on Library Resources.♾

CONTENTS

FOREWORD

James M. McPherson

This collection of essays offers a fitting tribute to Bill Cooper's career spanning nearly half a century as scholar, teacher, and mentor. Written by former students plus a colleague at Louisiana State University, these articles deal with many of the same themes that Bill's books and essays focused on: the politics of slavery in the antebellum South; education and intellectual life in the region; problems faced by Jefferson Davis and the Confederacy during the Civil War; class structure and the degree of social cohesion in the Old and New South; and the question of continuity versus discontinuity in the South across the great divide of the Civil War.

Chris Childers shows how the Missouri Compromise debate shocked southerners into an awareness of northern hostility to slavery, which produced in turn a preoccupation with creating a bulwark of state rights and national political power to defend the institution. Southern churches and clergy became part of that defense, as demonstrated by Julia Huston Nguyen, who depicts the important role prominent preachers played in supporting secession to preserve slavery from the perceived threat posed by Lincoln's election. Sarah Hyde convincingly challenges the stereotype of educational backwardness in the antebellum South but also hints at the way in which the intensifying conflict over slavery's expansion weakened southern Whigs and their support for expanded public education in the 1840s and 1850s.

Jefferson Davis believed that the Confederacy could win its independence only through victory on the battlefield, which could be achieved by a full mobilization of the South's manpower and resources. Although Davis failed to explain fully to the southern people the need for conscription as a key element of mobilization, John Sacher maintains that the Confederate president did a reasonably good job of overseeing that controversial policy, which brought an extraordinary proportion of the eligible population into the army. And in spite of apparent class discrimination in the application of the draft—exemplified by substitution, the Twenty-Negro law, and certain occupational exemptions—Paul Paskoff's findings confirm other recent research showing that at least as large a proportion of men from the slaveholding class served in the armed forces as those from poorer classes; it was not disproportionately "a poor man's fight." How much help the Confederacy might expect from northern antiwar "Copperheads" like Clement Vallandigham presented southern leaders with a dilemma, as delineated by George Rable. Vallandigham's opposition to the war had the potential to divide the northern people, which could have benefited the South, but he also professed to support the goal of preserving the Union. Thus, to Jefferson Davis and other southern leaders, faith in Vallandigham as an ally represented a will-o'-the-wisp for the cause of Confederate independence.

Was the Old South a seigniorial society based on the premodern institution of slavery or a capitalist society featuring modernizing tendencies? Richard Follett analyzes this question with respect to Louisiana's capital-intensive sugar plantations and concludes that they combined elements of premodern and modern social and economic relations, which persisted into the postwar era. Focusing on the case study of a wealthy cotton planter in Mississippi, Samuel Hyde comes to a similar conclusion. His study of Edward McGehee suggests that the answer to the much-debated question of the degree of continuity or discontinuity between the Old and New South is not an either-or proposition; the Civil War marked a sharp change in many respects, abolishing slavery and the plantation economy, but sometimes it seemed as if the more things changed the more they stayed the same. That was certainly the purpose of the progenitors of the "Lost Cause" crusade in the postwar South, of which John Witherspoon Du Bose's hagiographic biography of William Lowndes Yancey was a conspicuous part. Eric Walther skillfully makes the case that Du Bose consciously sought to use this biography as an opportunity to perpetuate "that civilization for the preservation of which the Confederacy was formed."

The nine essays in this book enrich our understanding of all of these themes in southern history. Bill Cooper can be proud of his legacy as a teacher and scholar embodied in the pages that follow.

ACKNOWLEDGMENTS

Initial conversations about putting together a compilation of articles on southern history to honor our friend and mentor Bill Cooper began nearly fifteen years ago. While everyone agreed it would be a worthy project, some of us thought it was too soon. With Bill continuing to produce book after book it seemed too early to offer a statement on his career. Years later with no evidence of abatement in Bill's productivity, rumors of his impending retirement from Louisiana State University prompted us to move the project forward.

The resulting volume, *The Enigmatic South: Toward Civil War and its Legacies,* accordingly serves several purposes. It is a physical manifestation of our affection and gratitude for Bill. Each of the eleven scholars whose work appears in this book has in one form or another been positively impacted by their association with him. The contributors include three colleagues and eight of his former students, all of whom have benefitted from Bill's insight, professionalism, friendship, and patience in our varied paths to becoming the scholars we are today. This book functions as a painfully inadequate *thank you* to Bill for the guidance he has provided in our lives and, perhaps more importantly, for his nurturing a more meaningful appreciation of southern history in each of us.

Appreciating southern history serves as the second purpose of this book. The ever-expanding mechanisms of popular culture have created new challenges for students of southern history that frequently burden our efforts to educate. Expanding awareness of our past serves as a positive contribution of film and other popular media outlets. It has long been known that Hollywood is nonetheless frequently guilty of shaping the historical record either to add drama or to conform to a particular political perspective, and in the minds of the unsuspecting the result can be a distortion of the truth.

Equally troubling is the tendency of some to interpret events through the lens of modern society. As professional historians we have an obligation to understand all aspects of the past, even those with which we profoundly disagree. Accordingly, we must come to terms with the past as the people of the period we are researching understood it. Today no one would deny that slavery is inherently evil or secession from the Union illegal. In the antebellum era such certainties of conviction were not everywhere apparent even among the most educated men of the age. Without ignoring the ills of the past, we must strive to keep our understanding of history consistent with time and space by accounting for those opinions that differ from our own. Interpretations that depart from the reality of the time period obfuscate the motives that stimulated the behavior of individuals and groups from our past. Our readers and students deserve the most accurate portrait of the past we can provide and the integrity of the historical record demands it!

Despite mounting interpretational obstacles, revealing the true South is a burden the contributors to this volume happily embrace. The opportunity to rescue John C. Calhoun, Sarah Grimke, or Osceola from the dustbin of popular history is an exciting component of our profession—one that has been cultivated by our association with Bill. It is our purpose in this volume to report the historical record as it was and not how it has been interpreted, or better recast, through the lens of contemporary popular culture. We strive to portray characters and events in the context of their time. These are lessons many of us acquired from Bill and it is a guiding principle of this volume.

Finally, the articles included in this volume do not reflect the gamut of southern history. None of the articles exclusively focus on slavery, women, or other issues central to understanding the South. Rather than offer a diffuse compilation of varied topics, we instead focused on creating a book that highlights the time and subject matter of Bill's primary research interests. Even within such a framework the contributions to this volume reflect broad diversity. The articles included reveal the range of scholarship Bill directed through the work of his students, as well as his influence on the work of colleagues, and they remind us that there were indeed many Souths. Or, perhaps better stated, that the South defies easy compartmentalization—hence the title. *The Enigmatic South.*

Many individuals contributed to bringing this project to fruition. Other Cooper students including Brad Bond, Larry Hewitt, Chad Vanderford, and Chris Leahy were involved in the discussion at various points during the process. Charles M. Morse generously responded to calls for assistance, and Keith M. Finley kindly critiqued portions of the manuscript. Rand Dotson and Lee Sioles masterfully guided the process at LSU Press, and Julia Smith proved an excellent copy editor. The result we hope will both entertain and educate—just as would be expected by anyone who enjoyed the opportunity to attend a Bill Cooper class.

PART I

POLITICS, EDUCATION, AND SECESSION

CHAPTER ONE

The Old Republican Constitutional Primer

States Rights After the Missouri Controversy and the
Onset of the Politics of Slavery

Christopher Childers

P resident James Monroe summoned the members of his cabinet to the Executive Mansion on March 3, 1820, to discuss a matter of utmost urgency: Congress had crafted legislation that promised to settle the bruising dispute over slavery and Missouri statehood. Their compromise, however, involved prohibiting slavery in all American territory north of 36° 30' latitude, and the president could not decide for himself whether the provision was constitutional. Therefore, he asked the cabinet members to state their opinion, in writing, on two issues: First, did Congress have the right to prohibit slavery in a territory? Second, did the slavery prohibition in the bill pertain only to a territory or did its force extend into statehood? On the latter question, the cabinet found consensus only after Monroe reworded his query (and hedged on its meaning) to ask whether the interdiction was compatible with the Constitution. On the former question, all agreed that Congress could indeed prohibit slavery in a territory. Satisfied with the responses proffered by his cabinet, Monroe signed the legislation into law on March 6.[1]

Monroe's indecision in no small part reflected his position as a Virginia Republican, though in keeping with his characteristic old-fashioned sensibility, the president shunned party labels. Nevertheless, Monroe knew that his friends and colleagues in the Old Dominion strongly opposed the compromise. The Old Republicans of Virginia would not soon forgive the president for giving ground on a question they saw as directly related to Jeffersonian states rights and localism: the right of self-determination on the slavery question and the sanctity of self-government for any state in the Union. Thomas Ritchie, editor of the *Richmond Enquirer* and a leader of the so-called Richmond Junto that controlled Virginia politics, decried the compromise. "A constitution warped from its legitimate bearings, and an immense region of territory closed for ever against the Southern and Western people—such is the 'sorry sight' which rises to *our* view," he lamented in his newspaper. To

Ritchie's mind, "What is a territorial restriction to-day becomes a state restriction to-morrow." In the aftermath of the Missouri Compromise becoming law, Ritchie and the Old Republicans would develop a case—and indeed an ideology—that ceding local authority over slavery had struck a mighty blow against states rights and local self-government. Their statements, radical in American political discourse of the 1820s, would become an integral part of the southern defensive position against growing nationalist sentiment and the progression of antislavery thought.[2]

———————★———————

The seemingly inexorable westward march of Americans from the Atlantic to the Pacific shaped and formed the nature of the early American republic in ways that surpassed the process of mere territorial enlargement. Westward expansion helped define the social character, the economic profile, and the political development of the United States in much of its first century. But in a development that bade ill for the future of the Union, territorial expansion added a new dimension to the persistently vexing issue of slavery. That institution had troubled the founders, and it would trouble their descendants until the nation sundered in 1861 and descended into four years of civil war. By linking the expansion of slavery with the extension of the Stars and Stripes over new territories purchased and conquered from foreign powers, America's settlers and adventurers—along with the politicians who represented them in the nation's capital—unleashed an issue that proved detrimental to intersectional unity between the free North and slaveholding South and ultimately led to the secession of thirteen states from the Union of their forefathers.

The Missouri controversy marked the fulcrum of the debate over slavery in the territories; for southern slaveholders, it signified a transition point for the status of their peculiar institution and for their power within the Union. Slavery extension had surely roiled American political discourse before James Tallmadge introduced an amendment to a Missouri statehood bill that provided for the gradual end of slavery within the prospective state's borders. But after the Missouri crisis had passed and in spite of the compromise that leaders from both sections had brokered, southerners would never again completely trust their northern brethren. After the Missouri controversy, southern leaders regretted the compromise that had tacitly accepted federal authority over slavery in the territories. Accordingly, they sought to remove the issue of slavery extension from congressional purview and enshrine it as a purely southern institution governed by slaveholders themselves. They did so by linking authority over slavery to the Jeffersonian tradition of states rights and local self-government. The legality of slavery in any given place, they argued, should rest with the people who lived there. Thirty years later, political leaders would coin the term *popular sovereignty* to describe this doctrine. If southerners removed to western territories, so the slaveholders' logic went, they and they alone should have the right to extend slavery to their new home—free from the interference of the growing cadre of antislavery congressmen in Washington, D.C.

Political leaders derived the idea of popular sovereignty from the revolutionary era ideal of consent of the governed. In the first decade of the American republic, the Jeffersonians embraced the concept of local self-government as political and ideological dogma. American citizens, through their collective identity as individual states, possessed the right to determine the boundaries of slavery state by state, territory by territory. And throughout the eighty-five years preceding the Civil War, staunch Jeffersonians and Jacksonians—as intellectual descendants of the third president—upheld the belief that nascent political communities, or territories, had the right to create their own organic law and enter the Union on an equal footing with the original states. That included determining whether slavery would exist within a territory or state gaining admission to the Union. Indeed, one of the major constitutional dilemmas of the early American republic centered on the interpretation of popular sovereignty itself: Did a political community gain sovereignty at the beginning of its existence as a territory, when it reached a certain population, or when it drafted a constitution prior to admission as a state?[3]

Popular sovereignty bore a close link to the states rights doctrine that since 1798 southerners had cherished as their section's saving grace. And between 1819 and 1821, states rights seemed under assault by a northern congressional delegation flexing its political muscle against the Virginia dynasty and southern domination of national politics. Restrictionists seemed bent on prohibiting slavery in Missouri as a condition of statehood. So did a Supreme Court that in the cases of *McCulloch v. Maryland* (1819) and *Cohens v. Virginia* (1821) had broadened national authority by invoking the constitutional doctrine of implied powers. The Missouri issue and the decisions of the nationalist high court led by John Marshall provoked a conservative reaction in the southern states, especially in Virginia where the Old Republicans held sway. The Richmond Junto and particularly Spencer Roane railed against the nationalizing tendency and tried unsuccessfully to encourage James Madison to lead the charge against the court by reinvigorating the principles of 1798. Roane, who was a relative of Thomas Ritchie, frequently contributed to the editorial pages of the *Enquirer* in opposition to nationalism and in defense of the "glorious revolution of 1799"—the Kentucky and Virginia Resolutions. An apoplectic Ritchie joined him, decrying the pernicious influence of the Supreme Court and calling for circumscribing its jurisdiction only to settling disputes over express powers within the Constitution itself.[4]

The states rights reaction came after several decades of loose construction on the part of southerners concerning slavery in the territories. Before the Missouri crisis, southerners had generally accepted—if not pledged their outright support—to federal authority over slavery. They did so with good reason; southern politicians and southern presidents had generally upheld slavery in a substantive portion of the national domain where geography and climate would allow it to flourish. At the extreme, in 1784 Thomas Jefferson himself had crafted a plan to prevent the extension of slavery to any territory. His Ordinance of 1784 failed for want of a single vote in the Confederation Congress, but in an era where slaveholders spoke apologetically about their peculiar institution, the ordinance betrayed ambivalence about slavery in the new republic. At the same time, northerners seemed willing to accept compromise with their southern brethren on the slavery issue. Through a series of political compromises beginning with the Northwest Ordinance of 1787 and extending to the Louisiana Purchase era, northern and southern congressional leaders had effectively divided the American territorial domain into free and slave sections. The Northwest Ordinance forbade slavery in territory north of the Ohio River. Three years later, the Southwest Ordinance granted settlers south of the Ohio in present-day Tennessee, Kentucky (after 1792), and areas of Georgia the right to permit or prohibit slavery as they pleased. This practice continued with minimal resistance for over twenty-five years.[5]

During the Missouri crisis, however, northerners made clear that they intended to use federal authority to circumscribe the limits of slavery in a territory where it already existed. Resentful of southern domination of federal politics and fearing the further augmentation of sectional supremacy, northern politicians sought to halt the unequal advantage that the three-fifths compromise gave to southern representation in Congress. Politics, coupled with a growing moral indignation against slavery, spurred the growth of antislavery politics in the North during the twilight of America's first system of political parties. With northern intentions revealed, southern slaveholders had to retreat from their support of federal authority and instead develop a states rights interpretation of the Constitution rooted in the Jeffersonian "principles of '98," referring to the Kentucky and Virginia Resolutions of 1798 that had introduced an initial version of the compact theory of the American Union.

In developing their mode of attack against the northern restrictionists, southern leaders linked the doctrines of state sovereignty and self-government, once distinct ideas but now unified in the southern defense of slavery. Southerners accused Tallmadge and his northern allies of legislating against the wishes of Missourians—and overruling the action of a previous Congress—by restricting slavery in a future state in which slavery had thrived during its territorial years. Proslavery critics accused the restrictionists of rescinding the latitude of self-government over the slavery issue that Congress had granted the Missourians in the law creating the territory. Tallmadge's amendment not only ignored the fact that slavery already existed in Missouri but also interfered with the right of Missourians to draft a constitution according to their own wishes.

The issues raised in previous discussions over the extension of slavery and territorial policy—whether Congress or the people of the territories had the right to permit or prohibit slavery—became linked in the Missouri debate, producing a true crisis of the Union. Tallmadge and his fellow restrictionists had asserted federal authority over the extension of slavery, while southerners rooted in the Jeffersonian tradition argued that the Constitution forbade Congress from reaching beyond its positive mandate to ensure that any incoming state's constitution provided a republican form of government. Faced with an antislavery front using congressional authority to limit the boundaries of slavery, southerners responded with the concepts of states rights and self-government to circumscribe federal authority over slavery.[6]

Proslavery southerners denied the constitutionality of a ban on the institution and the right of Congress to impose it, in spite of the fact that the federal government had clearly exercised such authority in the past—and with southern assent. The historical record, when fully examined, only weakened their doctrinaire case for states rights. Heretofore, southerners had weakly resisted congressional authority over slavery in the territories and in some cases had overtly supported it when such action produced a proslavery outcome. Now that an emerging northern antislavery bloc resolved to use congressional authority to prohibit slavery in a territory where it had existed, proslavery leaders vowed a spirited attack against overweening federal power. They began to question the wisdom of federal authority once it became clear that northern congressmen could and would act to restrict slavery.

In what one historian has called "the most candid discussion of slavery ever held in Congress," northerners rallied behind the Tallmadge effort, while southerners battled against what they saw as a bold usurpation of local power and states rights and an unabashed expansion of federal authority. The opponents of restriction insisted that Congress "had no right to prescribe to any State the details of its government, any further than that it should be republican in its form." Furthermore, any territory admitted to statehood possessed the "unquestioned right" to amend its constitution, therefore rendering the entire debate moot. Restrictionists refuted this claim by arguing that "Congress had the right to annex conditions" to the admission of a new state and that slavery "was incompatible with our Republican institutions." According to the antislavery faction, Congress had a duty to impose the ban on slavery in Missouri.[7]

The debate over slavery that emerged from Missouri's bid for statehood provoked a schism within the Jeffersonian Republican party when northerners took up the antislavery cudgels and southerners united across party lines in resistance to federal authority over slavery in the territories and states seeking admission to the Union. In the middle, a small but influential group of northern and southern nationalists committed to preserving the Union worked diligently to quiet the rhetoric on both sides of the issue. Speaker of the House Henry Clay of Kentucky led the moderate nationalists, staking a middle ground between the most extreme viewpoints emerging in the tense congressional debates. Embracing the Jeffersonian rhetoric of local self-government, Clay argued that Congress had "no right to prescribe any condition whatever to the newly organized States, but must admit them by a simple act, leaving their sovereignty unrestricted."[8] Yet Clay felt deep misgivings about the peculiar institution even as he owned slaves himself, and his feelings would emerge throughout the Missouri debates.

Even given Clay's efforts to quiet sectional discord, northern Republicans had touched a raw nerve in the South by questioning local authority over slavery. The tenor of the debate on Missouri intensified, and concern grew among southerners that the safety of slavery rested in the political supremacy of slaveholder interests at the federal level. Federalists did what a decade before would have been unthinkable. Seeking to earn desperately needed political capital and perhaps revivify their moribund party, they united with northern Republicans like Tallmadge and the influential New York representative John Taylor, who likewise opposed southern power, by using the Missouri statehood bill as their rallying point. "The attempt to extend slavery to the new States," a Massachusetts Federalist stated, "is in direct violation of the clause which guaranties [sic] a republican form of government to all the States."[9] Interestingly, if erroneously, many southerners "insisted at every turn that Federalists were the principal *provocateurs*."[10] Federalists certainly exploited the slavery issue in an effort to regain lost political power, yet more ominously for the adherents of party politics, northern Republicans led the restriction vanguard. The Era of Good Feelings may have marked the eclipse of interparty conflict on significant economic issues that had concerned Jeffersonians and Federalists, but the Missouri controversy revealed that the politics of slavery could fill the void, thereby dividing the nation along sectional lines.

Southerners rooted their response to restriction in an emerging interpretation of the Constitution that drew on the section's states rights heritage while responding to the political realities emerging in a period of discord over slavery itself. Since Thomas Jefferson and James Madison had responded to Federalist abuses of power during the John Adams administration—especially the Alien and Sedition Acts of 1798—the Virginia and Kentucky Resolutions had come to embody the southern constitutional mantle of states rights and local self-government giving birth to an antifederal persuasion that strengthened over time. Resistance to federal authority over local affairs such as slavery— and to southerners in this period slavery was indeed a local matter—became the logical response to the restrictionist agenda. To protect slavery's future, it had to become a purely local matter and federal authority must itself be restricted. In 1819 and 1820, southern political leaders quickly countered that the nation's organic law forbade infringing on the rights of a people to draft a state constitution free from federal interference. The Missouri crisis, however, led them to take a new step in their reasoning: southerners now argued that the sanctity of state sovereignty extended to the people of a territory drafting a constitution and seeking admission to the Union.[11] Heretofore, few southerners had objected to federal control over the territories because Congress, with southern votes providing the key, had always protected slaveholder interests where the institution would most likely flourish.

Once northern congressmen initiated an antislavery movement in Congress, however, the South began to reconsider its position on federal authority. Inching toward a defense of slavery in the territorial phase but stopping well short of the position that the federal government had a duty to protect slavery in the territories that John C. Calhoun would advance twenty years later, Philip P. Barbour of Virginia, asserted that if Congress had wished to ban slavery in Missouri, it should have done so when creating the territory itself. The Old Republican asserted, however, that Congress should consult the people of Missouri to discern their opinions on the issue, "because [otherwise] we should be legislating directly against the wishes of a people who were competent to legislate for themselves."[12]

The debate concerning federal authority over slavery in the territories—a case of conflict between the core versus periphery that Americans imbued with the spirit of the Revolution would have clearly recognized—spread beyond the walls of the Capitol. People across the country took up the Missouri debate where their representatives had left off. Public opinion, as expressed in newspapers throughout the nation, revealed the salience of slavery extension outside of Washington. Missourians, who had the most at stake in the controversy, in particular argued their case with great force. The Virginian Nathaniel Beverley Tucker, writing under the pseudonym "Hampden," mixed Old Republicanism with the frontier desire of self-government, labeling restriction as an insult to the citizens of Missouri Territory who had proven their loyalty in the War of 1812. Tucker, half-brother to eminent jurist St. George Tucker and cousin of John Randolph of Roanoke, had settled in Missouri in 1816 and had been appointed as a judge in St. Louis. Leading the charge against restriction, he reminded his audience that as American citizens, the Missourians possessed the right to legislate their own local affairs. Taking aim at those who interpreted the needful rules and regulations clause of the Constitution as sanctioning broad federal authority over the territories, Hampden articulated an opinion that would become a staple of the southern movement against congressional interference with slavery: the clause had nothing to do with congressional authority over local law but solely addressed the purchase and disposition of federal property in the territories.[13]

As a follower of Old Republican principles, Hampden developed an organic theory of constructing a political community that preserved and upheld localism—and protected the institution of slavery from the antislavery vanguard. He relied on the tenth amendment, the bulwark of states rights ideology, in asserting that self-government "is inherent in, and is moreover expressly 'reserved to the states respectively, or to the people.' The state of Missouri then, can derive none of its *powers* from Congress; all it needs from that quarter is the *means of organization.*" Retreating from any notion of federal authority in territory making, except that Congress ensure a republican form of government for the territories-cum-states, Tucker's writings suggest that certain proslavery leaders wished to extend to territories a modicum of the sovereignty that states possessed.

Indeed, the Hampden essays suggest a new step in the slavery extension dialectic that the right of a state to create and exercise sovereign authority rested in its ability to use such sovereignty at some point preceding statehood, particularly with respect to slavery. "Is it not insulting to our common sense, to be told that a constitution not only permitting, but partly based on domestic slavery" would allow for federal interdiction of the institution, Hampden asked. "But it is just such a doctrine as I should expect to hear" from those who believed that "*Congress have power to make laws to bind the territory in all cases whatsoever.*" Other Missourians likewise denounced the Tallmadge amendment. A citizens' meeting in Montgomery County attacked the congressional hypocrisy in admitting the Alabama Territory without restriction, "while the people of this territory have been refused, unless they would stoop to a condition, which degrades them below the rank of free men, and lays the foundation of a slavery more abject than that which congress pretends to be so zealous to reform."[14]

Hampden's logic represented a first step in the emergence of the Calhounite argument that placed slavery in the territories within a sort of extraconstitutional status that declared its existence beyond the purview of Congress or territorial legislatures that might prove hostile to the institution. Responding to rising antislavery sentiment during the Missouri crisis, southern politicians insisted that states rights began with the power to craft organic law. Each territory seeking admission had a right to create its own organic law, a constitutional theory of popular sovereignty steeped in Jeffersonian ideology that "became the centerpiece of the southern stand against restriction."

Beverley Tucker claimed that restriction would "establish a precedent that will sap the foundation of state authority and make this federal government a consolidated nation." Ignoring the Northwest Ordinance, a gigantic omission, he argued that Congress could not restrict the right of a citizen to move to any territory with his personal property—slaves certainly included. When a territory prepared for statehood, its inhabitants could decide in a constitutional convention whether to permit or prohibit slavery. This authority, according to a Kentucky writer who appealed to the logic of the Tenth Amendment, "is unquestionably one of those rights which the citizens did not surrender by the federal constitution."[15]

President James Monroe had remained silent on the matter in his State of the Union message to Congress in December 1819, but he expressed privately to friends and advisors his hope that restriction would fail. Though the Virginian had questioned the constitutionality of the Northwest Ordinance's prohibition of slavery, Monroe sought to avoid that constitutional thicket—and the enmity of his Old Dominion friends—and instead sided with the South on different grounds. Congress could not admit a new state on conditions different from the old states, according to the president, and it could not prohibit slavery in the territories. By implicitly questioning the force of the Northwest Ordinance, Monroe represented the prevailing opinion of his home state—and indeed the South at large—even as he tried to steer clear of offending northern allies. Other southerners proved less ambiguous in their disdain for the ordinance. Ignoring southern support for the Northwest Ordinance some forty years earlier, Thomas Ritchie cited the 1787 act as a "usurpation" of power and believed that it had gained passage "without adequate discussion and deliberation."[16]

By February 1820, negotiators from the North and South seemed close to devising a way out of the impasse. The plan of Illinois senator Jesse Thomas to admit Missouri as a slave state while declaring the remainder of the Louisiana Purchase north of 36° 30' free from slavery appealed to moderate northerners and southerners, especially the Republicans. Yet many restrictionists in the North and proslavery advocates in the South remained wary of compromise. The impetus for moderation in his home state forced Delaware senator Louis McLane to approach the debate warily. McLane affirmed his belief "that Congress does not possess the power to impose the contemplated restriction," but he assiduously avoided states rights rhetoric by maintaining that Congress had vacated its power to impose conditions on Missouri when it permitted slavery in the territorial enabling bill.[17]

Other southern leaders led the charge against restriction—and indeed against compromise—by attacking the Thomas proposal as a dangerous precedent for future federal interference with slavery. The Old Republicans emerged as the strongest defenders of southern interests and slavery extension, advancing arguments that portrayed compromise as a tacit admission of federal authority over slavery in the territories. "Can we compromise with the constitution of our country?" Ritchie asked his readers. Indeed, he argued, the Thomas compromise proposal did just that. Other Old Republicans concurred with Ritchie's assessment and charged that restriction threatened the safety of the Union. "If the Southern people yield," another Virginia Republican wrote to David Campbell, a politician from western Virginia, "the consequences will be serious—and unless the Northern people retrace their steps, the result will be equally so." The federal government could not legally restrict even a territory, according to some of the southern conservatives, for Congress was "no more authorized to inhibit slavery in the territory, than they are in the State—for, if they should have the power, it would indirectly effect the same thing."[18]

Politicians and the public, however, desired an end to the crisis, and by March 1820 the Thomas compromise would bring the debate to a close. The Missouri Compromise settled the issue of dividing the Louisiana Purchase into free and slave territory by drawing an arbitrary line between the two increasingly distinct societies. Moderates hailed the law's passage as a victory for the Union. Many southerners saw the compromise as an extension of a precedent endorsed by the previous generation of southern leaders and therefore acceptable. Strict constructionists, however, regretted that the moderate phalanx had compromised on the issue of federal authority over slavery in the territories. By endorsing the Thomas amendment, proslavery leaders argued, southerners had conceded that Congress could determine the status of slavery in the territories, at least north of 36° 30'. For a time, it had seemed that the Old Republicans would insist on congressional sanction of the right of settlers in the territories to determine the legality of slavery. The moderates prevailed, choosing instead to focus on strengthening slavery through promoting sound Jeffersonian doctrine in the future. To a South that remained overwhelmingly certain of its power and influence within the Union, compromise in 1820 seemed safe. In the future, as Ritchie and the Old Republicans predicted, southerners would come to regret their decision and insist that the maintenance of states rights and the institution of slavery also required an end to congressional interference with slavery in the territories.

The 1820s marked a new phase in the South's relationship with the federal government, especially regarding the extension of slavery. Many, if not most, Americans believed that the Missouri Compromise would usher in a period of tranquility on the contentious constitutional issues raised in the Missouri debates. Yet conflict appeared sooner rather than later as the nation extended its boundaries and organized territories and states in the twenty-five years following the denouement of the Missouri crisis. Over the course of the 1820s, antislavery forces became emboldened by an emerging moral reproach of slavery among the northern populace. In turn, the South rose in defense of its peculiar institution, accusing the antislavery movement of denying southerners equal status within the Union even after they had conceded to the terms of the Missouri Compromise.

Sectional divisions over slavery persisted despite the creation of a new political party system designed to remove the slavery issue from public discourse and focus the young nation on social issues and economic development. In the face of antislavery resistance, the South moved toward creating a political system that would ensure that southerners alone governed slavery and would protect slaveholders' rights to possess slaves in the territories. In the years between the Missouri controversy and the annexation of Texas, many southerners embraced the Old Republican critique of the Missouri Compromise which condemned compromise on the grounds that the South had conceded its Jeffersonian principles of localism by assenting to the solemn pact of 1820. "Thoughtful southern leaders recognized that they had suffered at least a partial defeat in the Missouri controversy," legal historian William Wiecek has argued, by acquiescing to give Congress power to legislate on the issue of slavery in the territories. And southern sectionalists predicted that the Missouri Compromise would never satisfy the North's "insatiable appetite" for the ultimate extinction of slavery.[19]

The Old Republicans did not let their southern brethren forget the lessons of 1820. Ritchie decried the concessions made in the Missouri Compromise and criticized the promoters of conciliation who had given so much territory to the antislavery interests by conceding the right of Congress to restrict the extension of slavery. The compromise had blocked the northward migration of slaveholders based on an artificial and arbitrary line. "If we are cooped up on the north, we must have elbow room to the west," Ritchie noted. But the Adams-Onís Treaty of 1821 blocked the westward migration of slavery as well by setting the southwestern boundary of the nation at the Sabine River. The South did gain the Territory of Florida, but the further westward expansion of slavery after 1821 seemed unlikely given the Missouri Compromise and the treaty with Spain. Domestic and foreign events had hemmed in the South, leaving no room for westward expansion after the states of the Old Southwest became populated. No slaveholder would move into a territory where his slaves could not follow. Not only did southerners wish to protect their right of expansion to the west, but they also sought to secure the economic fruits of selling surplus slaves from older states such as Virginia to settlers in new states and territories via the burgeoning domestic slave trade.[20]

The outcome of the Missouri debates led many southerners to believe that westward expansion provided the only way to safeguard slavery, local interests throughout the South, and southern power within the federal government in the future. During the 1820s, they renewed their defense of states rights, self-government, and the rights of slaveholders to move west with their human chattel. Even after the dust had settled from the Missouri controversy, Ritchie continued to chastise northerners for assaulting the right of territorial sovereignty north of the Missouri Compromise line. That "Congress should forever take from [the settlers of the territories] the privilege of self-government, under the pretence that it is a 'needful regulation,'" he argued, smacked of arbitrary government. In his remonstrances against congressional intervention over slavery in the territories, Ritchie represented a set of principles that became increasingly influential with southern conservatives. The Missouri controversy revitalized the notion of states rights and strict construction embodied in the 1798 Virginia and Kentucky Resolutions, those pillars of self-government and states rights. Yet their conservative vision looked to the future even as it celebrated the constitution of their fathers. Only by defending its interpretation of the nation's founding principles could the South protect its future. Ritchie and other southern conservatives cloaked themselves in the mantle of strict construction to decry the expansion of federal authority over domestic institutions in the territories. Southerners must choose to "stand in the breach between our native states and their assailants," Beverley Tucker opined, "and to call back our countrymen to the forgotten principles of their forefathers."[21]

The most forceful, and the most eccentric, explanation of the emerging southern position came from the mind of an exceptionally talented political theorist from Caroline County, Virginia. John Taylor had long espoused libertarian views on federal authority and a states rights interpretation of the constitution.[22] In November 1820, Ritchie's *Richmond Enquirer* press would publish Taylor's *Construction Construed, and Constitutions Vindicated,* in which the Virginian dismissed the Missouri crisis as an "absurd controversy," even as he alerted southerners to the danger of the precedent that it set for federal power. In inimitable rambling prose, Taylor posited that the Missouri Compromise's "balance of power contemplates two spacious territories, with the population of each separately integral, as conglomerated by an adverse interest, and though substantially federal in themselves, substantially anti-federal with respect to each other." In sum, Taylor argued that Congress and the compromisers had divided the nation into two antagonistic sections by dividing the nation's territorial domain into free and slave territory. Yet again, an influential southern political mind suffered from a case of historical amnesia, as Taylor made no concession for the fact that Congress had made just such a distinction between the Northwest and Southwest Territories in the 1790s. Southerners continued to dismiss or ignore that the previous generation had already compromised on the slavery issue and federal authority over the extension of the peculiar institution.[23]

Notwithstanding historical precedent, Taylor and other like-minded advocates for southern rights sought to reset the political match concerning federal authority over slavery in the territories by denying the right of Congress to legislate on the slavery issue thereafter. Accordingly, they adopted the notion that the Missouri Compromise represented a new dawn in the relationship between the federal government and the slavery issue. Casting themselves as the defenders of the framers' original intent in writing the Constitution, the Old Republicans and southern rights theorists denied congressional authority over slavery extension and state making. Repeating the argument expressed by many southerners during the Missouri debates, Taylor asserted that Congress could not *make* a state but only *admit* it once the people of a territory had written a republican constitution and petitioned for admission to the Union. "Do congress participate of this sovereignty with the people of Missouri," Taylor asked, or is the sovereignty of the people subservient to federal authority? Taylor and the southerners answered resoundingly in favor of local self-government as the surest means to protect slavery and southern rights in the Union. Crafting organic law in territories poised to become states "must be the work of the sovereignty of the people, associating by their title to self-government," according to Taylor and the southern rights vanguard. Popular sovereignty with respect to slavery in Missouri and Arkansas may have prevailed, but Congress had unconstitutionally established a different set of rules for the remainder of the Louisiana Purchase.[24]

Southern leaders sought to seize the initiative by advancing an ardently pro-southern, proslavery, states rights interpretation of the Constitution of 1787 by fighting the old battles over federalism versus local authority that had characterized the debate over ratification thirty years before, as well as the localist reaction that found its greatest manifestation in the Tenth Amendment. Seeking to capture the intent of the states that ratified the Constitution—and southerners like Taylor specifically referred to the states, not the people as individuals, as the true ratifiers of the constitutional compact—Taylor affirmed that no state had assented to the conveyance of congressional authority to enact local legislation.

Southern conservatives hearkened back to the principles of 1798 by insisting on states rights and strict construction, but they also advanced a corollary—territorial self-government—as another means of defense against rising antislavery sentiment. If the South could dominate the stream of westward migration, as it had in the Old Southwest states, it could use popular sovereignty as a vehicle to extend the boundaries of slavery. From the carefully reasoned arguments found in Taylor's writings to the essays found in newspapers such as the *Richmond Enquirer,* southerners asserted the primacy of self-government, a principle that had served as "the keystone of the South's entire constitutional defense system in 1819–1821." Asserting the right of self-government in the territories of Missouri and Arkansas seemed to vindicate southerners' claims, but the positive exclusion of slavery north of the compromise line had breached that principle. Why did Congress deem it safe to only allow self-government south of 36° 30'? Surely southern moderates had endorsed the compromise because it ensured that slavery could flourish where geography and climate favored slave-based agriculture. Conditions in the northern portion of the Louisiana Purchase, which Stephen Long labeled the "Great American Desert" in 1823, precluded the profitable use of slave labor. Even some southerners considered the land uninhabitable. Conservatives, however, concerned themselves not with the practical limits of slavery's extension but with the principles of federal power. Ironically, their conservative vision of nationhood had a progressive outlook, for only individuals who saw an ever-expanding Union would risk the perils of sectionalism to stand on the principle of self-government for present as well as, more importantly, future territorial acquisition. This explains why so many southerners scorned the Adams-Onís Treaty of 1821 and sought to uphold the right of slaveholders to carry their chattel to any potential territorial acquisitions in the future.[25]

Southern moderates emerged victorious from the Missouri debates, but a conservative reaction during the 1820s would sweep them from power and influence as moderates and conservatives sparred over the compromise. Indeed, the conservatives first won the rhetorical advantage and then the battle at the ballot box. The Thomas proviso had divided the South "between those who were more sensitive to the relationship of slavery to politics and those who were less so." Southern conservatives solidified their power by engaging in what William J. Cooper Jr. has called the politics of slavery. Conservatives persuaded the southern electorate that northern antislavery sentiment threatened the future of their peculiar institution and that only bold action—and not compromise—would save slaveholders from the antislavery onslaught and a consolidation of federal power that compromised the integrity of Jeffersonian political theory. The Missouri crisis revealed that opposition to southern power, especially as expressed in the three-fifths clause, had become "entwined with the humanitarian movement against slavery." Faced with eroding indifference to southern slavery among northern political allies, southern leaders sought to achieve sectional solidarity in defense of states rights and nonintervention with slavery. After 1820, "it became increasingly difficult for a defender of slavery to support the expansion of federal power." In 1822, southern voters sided with the conservatives by reelecting 70 percent of the congressman who had voted against compromise. Conversely, only 39 percent of the congressmen who supported the Thomas proviso gained reelection. The Missouri controversy had breathed new life into Old Republicanism as it maneuvered for political advantage in the 1820s.

To a degree, the Old Republicans had anticipated the southern political trajectory, but by the late 1820s and into the 1830s, the radical states rights ideologies of men like Ritchie would become rather moderate when placed aside the ideas of those surrounding Calhoun, who had transformed from an advocate of nationalism to the progenitor of nullification. Many southerners believed that their section would have to guard assiduously its rights in the future against further antislavery activism. Perhaps no other person better exemplifies the transformation many southerners underwent in the 1820s and 1830s than Calhoun. An ardent nationalist who had upheld the constitutionality of the Missouri Compromise in his role as Secretary of War in Monroe's cabinet, Calhoun now embarked on a conversion that would make him one of the most doctrinaire adherents of the states rights banner. Calhoun and the Old Republicans had shared a checkered relationship, which during the 1820s had as much to do with the labyrinthine party realignment process then occurring as it did with constitutional interpretation. His early paeans to the nationalist spirit had even won plaudits from Ritchie, who praised his political acumen and predicted he would become "one of the master-spirits who stamp their name upon the age in which they live."[26]

But by the early 1820s, Calhoun had begun to transform himself from economic nationalist to states rights doctrinaire. In 1824, the ambitious South Carolinian had become a presidential aspirant, and in a fluid political culture where parties had disintegrated and numerous factions filled the void, Calhoun ran afoul of Ritchie and the Old Republicans of Virginia, who supported William H. Crawford of Georgia. Crawford, they believed, could add the critical states of New York, Pennsylvania, and New Jersey to his considerable southern support, thereby securing victory. And a Calhoun candidacy stood in the way of that prospect.[27] Ritchie firmly believed in the north-south association of planters and plain republicans—as Martin Van Buren would so elegantly phrase it in 1827—while Calhoun would come to despise such intersectional comity and would later call for a rigid states rights doctrine that would make the Old Republicans of the early 1820s appear moderate.

Indeed, Calhoun would use the principles advocated by the Old Republicans as the bedrock on which he would build new theories of constitutionalism and nationhood that emphasized the Union as a compact of sovereign states—all of which was meant to protect the institution of slavery. But Calhoun's aims differed from the emerging party system that coalesced during the late 1820s and 1830s. The Jacksonian Democrats, which in some ways drew from the remnants of the Jeffersonian era parties, emerged as an alternative to the dangerous one-party politics that had engendered sectional discord and threatened the Union in 1820 and 1821. Men like Ritchie and Van Buren, as well as numerous other devotees of the old Jeffersonian alliance, sought moderation and conciliation by uniting the "planters of the South and the plain Republicans of the north" to replace (or at least overshadow) sectional tensions by reviving party distinctions. Southern moderates and conservatives alike became drawn to the new party—and to its standard bearer Andrew Jackson—because it rested on the premise that slavery fell entirely under southern control. This premise may have cemented the bond between southerners and northerners, but it also revealed that slavery had become a divisive issue that politicians must avoid. For a time, however, the sectional alliance within the party successfully bridged the Mason-Dixon line as southern Jacksonians allied with mid-Atlantic northerners to champion the principles of Jeffersonian republicanism in a new age. For southerners, the new party system seemingly portended an end to the nationalist politics of the Era of Good Feelings that had strengthened the federal government and threatened the institution of slavery.[28]

But for Calhoun, the new system provided insufficient protection for the South. Indeed, Calhoun and his allies considered compromise and conciliation a sign of weakness and a threat to southern interests. Whereas Old Republicans such as Ritchie saw the intersectional Democratic Party as a protector of southern interests precisely because it bound northerners and southerners together, the Calhounites looked to southern unity alone. The Nullification Crisis of the early 1830s became the first example of the quest for southern supremacy. Old Republicans like Ritchie and Beverley Tucker opposed nullification; indeed, Ritchie saw the principles of 1798 as an appropriate counterpoise between nationalism and what Ritchie called that "*Storm from the South.*" Calhoun, to Ritchie's mind, had perverted the Jeffersonian doctrine of interposition.[29]

For southerners, the fear of northern encroachment on slavery and its expansion became a reality as a more aggressive antislavery movement began to take shape over the next two decades. The argument over slavery in the territories may have calmed after 1821 but only because the Union had ceased momentarily to acquire new territory. By the end of the decade, however, the appearance of abolitionism and the impetus for territorial expansion portended a renewal of the slavery debate. Southerners who had sounded a clarion call in the early 1820s against the perils of federal authority over the extension of slavery now resolved to remain vigilant against any federal interference. Northerners responded in kind, expressing their own concerns about slavery and sectional power. But when the next crisis over the future of slavery arrived, southerners were armed with the refined doctrines of states rights, local authority over slavery, and an emphasis on the South retaining complete control over its peculiar institution. Only politicians who upheld these strictures deserved election to office. The politics of slavery had arrived.

NOTES

1. Noble E. Cunningham Jr., *The Presidency of James Monroe* (Lawrence: University Press of Kansas, 1996), 103–4.

2. *Richmond Enquirer*, March 7, 1820.

3. See George William Van Cleve, "Founding a Slaveholders' Union, 1770–1797," in John Craig Hammond and Matthew Mason, eds., *Contesting Slavery: The Politics of Bondage and Freedom in the New American Nation* (Charlottesville: University of Virginia Press, 2011), 121–24; Peter S. Onuf, *Statehood and Union: A History of the Northwest Ordinance* (Bloomington: Indiana University Press, 1987), 46–66.

4. See Norman K. Risjord, *The Old Republicans: Southern Conservatism in the Age of Jefferson* (New York: Columbia University Press, 1965), 222–27. For Ritchie and the Supreme Court, see *Richmond Enquirer*, January 22, 1822; Charles Henry Ambler, *Thomas Ritchie: A Study in Virginia Politics* (Richmond: Bell Book & Stationery, 1913), 80–81. For Spencer Roane's role, see Andrew Burstein and Nancy Isenberg, *Madison and Jefferson* (New York: Random House, 2010), 581–84.

5. For a thorough discussion of the Ordinance of 1784, see Arthur Bestor, "Constitutionalism and Settlement of the West: The Attainment of Consensus, 1754–1784," in John Porter Bloom, ed., *The American Territorial System* (Athens: Ohio University Press, 1973): 13–44.

6. See Robert Pierce Forbes, *The Missouri Compromise and Its Aftermath: Slavery and the Meaning of America* (Chapel Hill: University of North Carolina Press, 2007), 33–41; Matthew Mason, *Slavery and Politics in the Early American Republic* (Chapel Hill: University of North Carolina Press, 2007), 177–88.

7. Forbes, *The Missouri Compromise and Its Aftermath*, 36; Annals of the Congress of the United States, House, 15th Cong., 2nd Sess. (1819), 1170.

8. Remarks on the Tallmadge Amendment, February 15, 1819, in James F. Hopkins, ed., *The Papers of Henry Clay*, 11 vols. (Lexington: University of Kentucky Press, 1959–92), 2:670.

9. Annals of Cong., House, 15th Cong., 2nd Sess. (1819), 1182.

10. Shaw Livermore Jr., *The Twilight of Federalism* (Princeton: Princeton University Press, 1962), 90.

11. Forbes, *The Missouri Compromise and Its Aftermath*, 41; Sean Wilentz, *The Rise of American Democracy: Jefferson to Lincoln* (New York: W. W. Norton, 2005), 227–28. The first scholar to

make this distinction was Hermann von Holst, *The Constitutional and Political History of the United States*, 8 vols. (Chicago: Callaghan and Company, 1876–92), 1:364–65.

12. Annals of Cong., House, 15th Cong., 2nd Sess. (1819), 1185, 1191.

13. See Robert J. Brugger, *Beverley Tucker: Heart over Head in the Old South* (Baltimore: Johns Hopkins University Press, 1978), 49–57; *St. Louis Enquirer*, April 7, 1819.

14. *St. Louis Enquirer*, April 7, 28, 1819, May 12, 1819. Italics in the original.

15. Forbes, *The Missouri Compromise and Its Aftermath*, 40; *St. Louis Enquirer*, April 28, 1819; *Kentucky Reporter*, quoted in *St. Louis Enquirer*, June 9, 1819.

16. James Monroe to George Hay, December 20, 1819, quoted in Noble E. Cunningham, *The Presidency of James Monroe* (Lawrence: University Press of Kansas, 1996), 94; *Richmond Enquirer*, December 21, 1819.

17. Annals of Cong., House, 16th Cong., 1st Sess. (1820), 1140.

18. *Richmond Enquirer*, February 10, 1820; C. W. Gooch to David Campbell, February 16, 1820, box 4, Campbell Family Papers, Rare Book, Manuscript, and Special Collections Library, Duke University, Durham, North Carolina; Annals of Cong., House, 16th Cong., 1st Sess. (1820), 1327.

19. William M. Wiecek, *The Sources of Antislavery Constitutionalism, 1760–1848* (Ithaca: Cornell University Press, 1977), 126; *Richmond Enquirer*, March 17, 1820.

20. *Richmond Enquirer*, March 7, 1820; Samuel Flagg Bemis, *John Quincy Adams and the Foundations of American Foreign Policy* (New York: Alfred A. Knopf, 1949), 309–10; 321–22; for the interstate slave trade, see Steven Deyle, *Carry Me Back: The Domestic Slave Trade in American Life* (New York: Oxford University Press, 2005), 42–46 and passim.

21. *Richmond Enquirer*, March 7, 1820; Nathaniel Beverley Tucker to James Monroe, August 4, 1819, quoted in Brugger, *Beverley Tucker*, 57.

22. For a brief sketch of Taylor's intellectual heritage, see Michael O'Brien, *Conjectures of Order: Intellectual Life and the American South, 1810–1860* (Chapel Hill: University of North Carolina Press, 2004), 785–99.

23. John Taylor, *Construction Construed, and Constitutions Vindicated* (Richmond: Shepherd & Pollard, 1820), 229, 292–93.

24. Ibid., 304 (first and second quotes).

25. Glover Moore, *The Missouri Controversy, 1819–1821* (Lexington: University of Kentucky Press, 1953), 123.

26. *Richmond Enquirer*, December 24, 1811. For the relationship between Ritchie and Calhoun, see Merrill Peterson, *The Great Triumvirate: Webster, Clay, and Calhoun* (New York: Oxford University Press, 1987), 26–27, 118–21.

27. See Ambler, *Thomas Ritchie*, 87–95.

28. Richard H. Brown, "The Missouri Crisis, Slavery, and the Politics of Jacksonianism," *South Atlantic Quarterly* 65 (Winter 1966): 60, 69; Charles S. Sydnor, *The Development of Southern Sectionalism, 1819–1848* (Baton Rouge: Louisiana State University Press, 1948), 132; Don E. Fehrenbacher, *Sectional Crisis and Southern Constitutionalism* (Baton Rouge: Louisiana State University Press, 1995), 22. For the rise of southern Jacksonian Democrats, see William J. Cooper Jr.,

The South and the Politics of Slavery, 1828–1856 (Baton Rouge: Louisiana State University Press, 1978), 5–11.

29. Thomas Ritchie to Archibald Ritchie, June 8, 1830, in *The John Branch Historical Papers of Randolph-Macon College* 2 (June 1902): 148; see also *Richmond Enquirer,* March 13, 1832, for Ritchie's condemnation of the Calhoun version of nullification.

CHAPTER TWO

Punctuated Progress
Education Developments in the Antebellum Gulf South
Sarah L. Hyde

Misconception may very well serve as the defining characteristic of popular perceptions of the South. Opinions of political conditions, social structure, and relative wealth are often influenced more by generalities based on prevailing political trends of popular culture than by fact, especially when considering the antebellum period. The status of education in the antebellum South serves as a case in point. Most of the historical literature that even briefly considers the topic tends to suggest that southerners valued learning less than people in other regions of the country, a finding supposedly evidenced by the presence of fewer schools and less-developed public education systems. Such conditions, the thinking frequently goes, allowed the slaveholding elite, who enjoyed a virtual monopoly on educational services, to further their regional dominance and lead the ignorant masses of the South to civil war and disaster.[1] Contrary to this perception, however, learning absorbed the lives of southern youth prior to the Civil War in substantial ways. In the Gulf South states of Louisiana, Mississippi, and Alabama, parents generally availed themselves of any opportunity to have their children taught, sacrificing financially in order to secure the blessings of a well-rounded education for their offspring. Lessons and learning played a central role in the culture of the antebellum Gulf South.

Since before formal schools appeared in the South and long after such institutions were established, some of the earliest instruction children received came in the comfort of their own homes, where a mother or older sibling offered lessons to younger members of the family. Such schooling, though it did not take place in a traditional schoolroom with a certified teacher, formed an educational foundation for generations of southerners. Some children simply learned the basics that might later be expanded upon through formal schooling and independent study, while other children received an intense immersion into complex subject matter. In addition to cleaning, sewing, cooking, and caring for children, many mothers in the Gulf South also considered it their obligation to educate their sons and daughters. In *The Plantation Mistress: Woman's World in the Old South*, Catherine Clinton first mentions the duty of educating children when discussing the threefold responsibility of mothers in the antebellum South. Many mothers took this task quite seriously and expended considerable time and effort instructing their young.[2]

In a memoir about her childhood in south Louisiana, Celine Fremaux recounts how, much to the children's chagrin, her mother provided the initial education for Fremaux and her siblings before they entered formal schools. Fremaux explains that "if it had not been for Ma's idea that her duty to us rested mainly in educating us herself, we would have been as happy as other children. But she *would* teach us, and teach us incessantly . . . Our lessons were as regular as clockwork." While one might assume that the lessons offered by a family member would be less rigorous or disciplined than a hired teacher's, the instruction that the Fremaux children received from their mother proved academically advanced and strict. Reading Fremaux's account of the harsh discipline that accompanied her mother's lessons, one is left hoping other children fared better with their instructors. During his French lessons, her brother "had his ears pulled so often that he was hardly ever without little scabs at the back of them and his head would be bumped against the wall so often that he used to say, 'As soon as I am big enough, I will run away.'"[3]

Aside from parents who taught their children, older siblings who themselves had received some schooling often took on the responsibility of educating younger brothers and sisters. Such was the case for the Ellis Family of East Feliciana Parish, Louisiana. After attending Centenary College in Jackson, Louisiana, and before moving to New Orleans to study law, older brother Thomas returned to his family home in Clinton, where he took on the responsibility of educating his younger sisters and brothers, one of whom later became a United States congressman. Interspersed among his notes about politics, hunting, and reading law, Thomas records in his diary for 1855 and 1856 "hearing the lessons of the 'young'uns'" and says that he "stayed at home, all day . . . acting the pettifogger and the pedagogue." Although Thomas did not always offer lessons daily, his instruction no doubt afforded his younger siblings a basic education that could be expanded and enhanced in later years.[4]

While some children received instruction from family members at home, eliminating the cost of hiring a teacher, the ubiquitous presence of private tutors in the antebellum Gulf South reveals another important form of schooling available outside the conventional schoolroom. Tutors, like antebellum teachers more generally, tended to be male and usually undertook teaching temporarily before embarking on a more permanent and lucrative profession. After completing his studies at Princeton College, Abraham Hagaman, a New Jersey native, took on tutoring jobs in Virginia, Mississippi, and Louisiana before becoming a minister and entrepreneur in Jackson, Louisiana. Hagaman's account is typical in that it shows the precarious position of tutors in charge of another's children. The expectations for a tutor differed drastically from one family to another, with some parents looking to the tutor as a hired hand and expecting his assistance with chores and crops as the need arose. Tutors found themselves in an especially delicate situation when it came to disciplining their students. While Hagaman's first employer insisted that he was too gentle with his pupils and assured him the only remedy for their unruliness was free use of the rod, his next employment ended abruptly for, according to Hagaman, "I had given offense to Mr. Longhorn by exercising what he regarded as too strict discipline towards one of his children."[5]

Not only did the expectations for a tutor differ from home to home, but the quality of instruction provided by hired teachers differed drastically. Louisiana historian Joseph Tregle writes that tutors in Louisiana "generally proved a disgrace to the profession, intellectual mountebanks with a reputation for drunkenness and dissoluteness exceeded by hardly any other group in the community." Despite Tregle's disparaging comments, many tutors excelled at their calling and became an integral part of plantation life, providing children with the crucial instruction needed to ready them for the world.[6]

Although different from the formal graded schools most of us recognize today, instruction from family members and private tutors played no less an important role in educating young southerners. Whether provided by a strict disciplinarian like Ma Fremaux—who had her children recite lessons even as the Union army bombarded their city—or a gentle older brother like Thomas Ellis—who took time off from teaching to visit friends and hunt the piney woods—instruction provided in the home often laid the foundation for later educational pursuits.

Lessons offered at home proved beneficial to younger generations in the South for many reasons. The pecuniary benefits associated with lessons given by a family member rather than a hired teacher allowed families who could not afford school for extended periods to impart to their children a basic level of literacy. In a letter to her son Albert at the Kentucky Military Institute in 1861, Martha Batchelor warned of the family's declining fortunes and urged him to make the most of his time at school, noting "you may even have to help educate your younger brother and sister."[7]

Home instruction also eliminated problems associated with the scattered settlement of rural society. Since southern families lived spread out on farms and far from neighbors, it proved nearly impossible to situate a school where more than a few children could attend without considerable hardship. Rather than leaving home to travel some distance to a formal school, children instructed in their own homes did not have to worry about transportation or boarding. Parents often were happy to be able to directly supervise their children's instruction at home, where they didn't have to worry about the children's activities or the quality of instruction offered at faraway schools.

The informality of home schooling also allowed total synchronization with the rhythms of family and agricultural life. Lessons could easily be put on hold when young girls were needed to help with a new baby or boys were needed in the fields. Such accommodations fit the needs of the agricultural South. It is therefore inaccurate to characterize the antebellum South as uninterested in education simply because the public school system took hold there later, as many scholars have done. Some have gone so far as to postulate that the presence of home schooling evidenced a disregard for education, but that conclusion is inaccurate. The system of home schooling from which southerners benefitted for generations perfectly suited an agricultural society and was not deficient or substandard to any large degree.

There were also many private schools and academies throughout the Gulf South. These institutions were less permanent than modern schools, in part because teachers, like private tutors, often saw instruction as a temporary occupation. Teachers moved frequently in search of better conditions and higher pay, and they usually left the profession altogether after a few years if more lucrative work could be found. These conditions combined to create a fluid educational structure. Many students availed themselves of different forms of instruction as they became available, so that a child might study under the watchful eye of both a relative and private tutor at different times before moving on to a public school or private academy.

Like tutors, who held a precarious position in southern society, private school teachers endured many challenges. William Lacey, the principal of the Southern Institute in Jackson, Louisiana, had two girls removed from his school after one of the girls reported that Lacey had called her and her mother "fools." Lacey went to great lengths to explain the origins of the conflict to the girls' uncle, Judge Thomas Butler, a man of considerable prominence in the local community. Schoolteachers were often at the mercy of their pupils, whose reports to their parents or guardians could mean the difference between profitable employment or pauperism. A married couple who ran a school in Florence, Alabama, in the 1830s were interrupted at supper one evening by a rider bringing an aggressive note from the uncle of one of their pupils based on the "false statements of his niece." Teachers regularly found themselves in these sorts of disputes and often proved unsuccessful in their attempts to assuage offended parents.[8]

Lawrence Daily, a schoolteacher in Mississippi, got into a dispute with one family whose children enrolled at his school but never actually attended. Daily believed himself entitled to remuneration nonetheless, since the two girls were not prevented from attending due to illness or other unforeseen circumstances but instead chose to patronize another school in the area. He insisted that the decision to enroll the girls elsewhere could not possibly be based on his skills as a teacher, asserting, "I can venture to affirm (without vanity or boasting) that I am an acknowledged scholar which is generally known by all persons who are judges of Education within the Circle of my Acquaintance—and as to my Sobriety, attention to my school and moral behavior these are points that I never have been questioned upon." The teacher insisted on being paid the eight dollars due for tuition of the two girls, promising the family, "Rest assured I will have my pay and will not be fooled or trifled with."[9]

Given the challenges facing proprietors of private schools and academies, it may not be surprising that many such schools lasted only a few years. Some schools operated from a private home, while others rented existing schoolhouses. That meant that a schoolhouse might be vacant for years in between instructors. Yet the fluidity and impermanence of such institutions does not detract from their importance in educating children across the South. Where one school closed, another was often available to take its place, so that families with the financial means to support their children's educational endeavors were usually not without a school to patronize. In 1850, the U.S. Census reports 143 private schools in Louisiana, 166 in Alabama, 171 in Mississippi, and

34 in Florida, with a total of 21,501 students attending in all four states. Clearly, private schools played a vital role in educating children in the Gulf South.[10]

Many private school proprietors expended great efforts to hire competent and accomplished teachers for their schools. In 1855, Thomas Ellis received a request from a friend to come teach at the Pleasant Valley Academy, a school run in part by his uncle, noting that the proprietors would pay whatever Ellis demanded in order to ensure a competent teacher for the pupils.[11]

One Connecticut woman, Lucy Fisher, moved to Louisiana in 1834 at the suggestion of her brother, who explained that teachers were in great demand in the South. Her brother would not allow her to take her first job offer at an academy in New Orleans for fear of yellow fever, so she ended up in Baton Rouge. She began as a private tutor, eventually married, and opened a private girls school with her husband in the 1830s. The institution thrived, and she continued running it after her husband's death in 1843. Enrollment increased so that the house where she conducted classes was completely full. A grandfather of one of her students bought and paid for a new brick structure for her to use as long as she continued the school. Fisher's school succeeded in no small part because she went to considerable efforts to procure teachers of sufficient accomplishments to instruct her students. At one point when she struggled to find qualified teachers in the local community, she asked her sister to attempt to find suitable instructors in their native Connecticut who would be willing to relocate. The sister seems to have hired two young women without properly screening them in advance. Fisher anxiously awaited the new instructors, whose arrival coincided with the Christmas recital. The school was lavishly decorated for the occasion, which was attended by the city's social elite, including future president Zachary Taylor. When the young instructors arrived, Fisher was disappointed in their awkward, plain appearance, which stood in stark contrast to the splendor of the school's decorations and the festivities of the evening. Unfortunately for the new hires, one of whom was filling the position of music teacher, the crowd insisted the teachers showcase their skills. After attempting to excuse herself, the new music teacher was forced to play, revealing her mediocrity. According to Fisher, "she did not play as well as the youngest of our pupils." After months of anticipation, both employees proved incapable of filling the positions for which they had been hired. Despite all Fisher's efforts to "get the best teachers and have our seminary second to none in the State," the result was an embarrassment.[12]

Certain schools languished due to incompetent instructors, some of whom had less educational experience than the pupils they were hired to teach. The sobriety and moral aptitude of teachers concerned parents as much as their academic skill, and unfortunately many instructors, once hired, proved incapable of providing the desired instruction. Some parents went to great lengths to insure high quality instruction for the children. An 1828 contract for a schoolteacher reveals some of parents' expectations. In this instance, seven gentlemen collectively hired Mr. Thomas T. Hale to take charge of a schoolhouse standing on the land of one of the men. The contract lays out the subjects Hale should teach, including reading, writing, arithmetic, English grammar, and "most of the branches of polite literature usually taught in Grammar schools." Lessons would last from eight a.m. to five p.m., with the teacher promising "to be punctual in his attendance [to] the school, to govern with impartiality and strict justice, and to use his best exertions to promote the moral as well as literary interest of his pupils." The seven men each pledged a specific payment to Hale, ranging from $25 to $125, with the explicit stipulation that they "have equal privileges in the school and be at liberty to send their own children and as many or as few as they may choose and they who subscribe more than they can make with their own to have the liberty of sending others to make it up."[13]

Competent teachers often found eager pupils and grateful families who valued their instruction. Albert Batchelor continued to correspond with a former teacher for years after leaving his school, and Lucy Fisher maintained a correspondence with some of her students for decades. Many children grew close to their teachers and to the families they boarded with while attending school. One young woman preparing to leave school in Lexington, Kentucky, to return home to Natchez, Mississippi, explained that she would find it difficult to part with the family with whom she had been boarding. While teachers generally may have been underpaid and underappreciated during the antebellum period, many found welcoming families and doting students with whom they established lifelong friendships.[14]

One of the difficulties in procuring instruction for one's children was the cost. Many parents sacrificed so as to finance their children's education. One overseer in south Louisiana requested transfer to a different plantation owned by the same family in order to allow his children to attend school without having to board. Other southern families likewise rearranged their lives in order to allow their children to pursue their studies. An early inhabitant of Louisiana, John Palfrey, explained to a friend in 1810 that since his son devoted himself so diligently to his studies, "I will by any sacrifice I can make endeavor to carry him through College." Many families made similar sacrifices throughout the antebellum period.[15]

The Batchelor Family of Point Coupee Parish saw their fortunes decline as southern secession unfolded, but it did not stop the parents from attempting to keep their children in school. The mother, Martha L. Batchelor, who passed away in 1862, did everything she could to keep her children in school even after the war broke out. Oldest son Albert attended the Kentucky Military Institute and would leave once the war began to fight in the 2nd Louisiana Infantry Regiment. All the sons of service age fought for the Confederacy during the war, while the daughters continued to attend school throughout the conflict. As the mother explained, "if I can command the money they shall have an education if they get nothing else. Without an education they cannot command anything but with it they may command the highest position."[16]

The difficulty many families confronted in finding the means to pay tuition is one reason that the southern state governments attempted to assist in providing instruction for their residents. From the earliest years of statehood, the southern state governments registered a concern for helping to extend the benefits of schooling beyond those who could afford to pay for it themselves. The original state constitutions of most Gulf South states explicitly pledged support for education, and southern governors consistently spoke out in favor of doing more to support public schooling. Throughout the 1820s and 1830s, state legislatures tried to support the educational demands of their constituents by assisting already established private schools. Each state offered assistance by incorporating schools and academies, often exempting them from taxation and authorizing lotteries to raise funds and sometimes contributing a onetime appropriation from state coffers. Additionally, state governments took charge of the sixteenth-section lands allotted by the U.S. Congress for use to support schools. The income generated from these funds as well as additional resources were allocated to support schools as local officials chose. Sometimes the funds were used to build new schoolhouses and start new institutions, while at other times the state allocations supported private ventures already in operation. In 1835 the state of Louisiana allocated parish schools $50,000 while granting private institutions over $125,000 in state aid.[17]

Despite assistance allocated in order to build entirely new schools, states did not yet register an intention to provide schooling free of charge. In Louisiana, the legislature required any school receiving state aid to admit a number of indigent children who received free tuition and supplies. This stipulation allowed a clear distinction to emerge between paying students and "pauper" students who attended free of charge. Though legislators considered this requirement their most significant contribution to education, ensuring that poor children could enjoy the benefits of education, they greatly misjudged its impact on the population. Most parents refused to accept the label of *pauper* in order to send their children to school tuition free. In fact, the negative association of "free schools" with poverty would haunt public school systems in parts of the South throughout the antebellum period.[18]

While Louisiana's education initiatives during the 1810s and 1820s fell far short of the public free schools which many historians consider the benchmark in educational legislation, the system employed there offered many advantages. Leaving decisions up to local officials meant that people most familiar with the idiosyncrasies of each parish would be making decisions on how best to encourage education in their area. Allowing local officials to decide if their constituents would be better served by using state aid to support private schools rather than building new schools meant that many parishes were able to save money on the construction of schoolhouses. Likewise, the state did not require parishes to put into operation schools that would compete with existing educational institutions. Given the scarcity of teachers in many rural areas and students' irregular attendance, many parishes would have been unable to support an additional school had they been forced to provide it. The legislative stipulation demanding the admittance of students free of charge, although it generated some problems, was at least a token measure aimed at assisting Louisiana's neediest children.

The legislative records for the southern states are filled with statutes and commentaries pledging state support for schools, yet each state vested control of education in the local communities. There would be no statewide education official until later in the antebellum period, and true public schools would emerge much later. Throughout the 1820s and 1830s, there is a clear indication that southern legislators believed education, if not strictly a family affair, certainly remained a local concern.

The Panic of 1837 devastated education funds set aside by state governments. In Mississippi, for instance, the state's Literary Fund used to support schools was invested in the state bank. Rather than allotting cash payments to each county, the state distributed bank stock, appropriated based on population. Perhaps state officials hoped for a return on their investment that would allow greater support of schools. Instead, the bank failed in 1840, unable to withstand the economic downturn, and wiped out the state's school fund with it. A similar situation occurred in Alabama, where the education funds, also invested in the state bank, vanished when the bank collapsed in 1843. Some scholars have concluded that legislators were concerned with propping up the state banks rather than protecting the education funds. When bank failures wiped out the education funds, the people mourned for the schools, while lawmakers grieved for the banks.[19]

An interesting phenomenon highlights the limitations of southern lawmakers' willingness to support education initiatives. In 1844, southern politicians were debating accepting a distribution of the federal surplus to the states. Passed as part of the compromise ending the Nullification Crisis, Henry Clay had been promoting his scheme to distribute the federal surplus to the states in order to rid the federal government of the embarrassing wealth it had amassed as a result of the protective tariff. Democrats, especially southerners, who opposed the protective tariff balked at Clay's plan, wanting to use the embarrassment of riches in the U.S. Treasury in order to lobby more effectively for repeal of the tariff. But the idea of a large distribution of federal money proved irresistibly attractive to the states.[20]

Interestingly, education became tied up in this debate. In order to receive their portion of the federal surplus, states had to petition the federal government to request distribution of the money. In Alabama, the legislature twice voted down Whig measures to request the funds from Congress. In order to make this distribution more palatable to the Democratic majority in the state legislature, Whig lawmakers proposed using the money to establish a common school fund. But Democrats would not be so easily lured. State senator Benjamin Hudson reported for the select committee tasked with considering the proposal, announcing to his colleagues "the Legislature has twice refused to accept her share of the proceeds of the sales of public lands, upon the principle of distribution, because it is but another mode of sanctioning the protective tariff." He went on to explain, "the application of the fund to the support of common schools does not change the principle upon which it would have to be raised, if received at all. For these reasons in brief the committee concluded that it is inexpedient to pass the bill." The Whig effort did not succeed, and Alabama continued to refuse her portion of the federal surplus.[21]

The Democrats' opposition to the protective tariff is well documented, so their refusal to accept the federal distribution makes sense. In abstract terms, refusing the federal funds was justifiable. Emptying the federal treasury of the surplus would have stripped the Democrats of that tool for bludgeoning the opposition. Yet the Whig effort to use the disbursement to establish a common school fund cast the issue in different terms. The Whigs hoped that by tying the money directly to the educational welfare of the state, they would make refusal to request the dispersal more politically dangerous for the Democrats. Rather than just a vote against the protective tariff, their denial to accept the funds was now a vote against a common school system. It was a clever maneuver by the Whigs, who were linked more directly with public education initiatives than were the Democrats. But the party of Jackson would not be so easily dissuaded.

Throughout the 1830s, state government assistance to local schools caused only limited improvement. In the early 1840s, however, the ideas of Jacksonian democracy percolated throughout the Gulf South region, and residents began to demand more from their legislators. Privileges previously reserved for the elite came to be demanded as rights belonging to all. Education was one of the domains where common folk insisted access be broadened. The genesis for truly public schools came from the urban areas of the South. Cities enjoyed an obvious advantage in creating schools because concentrated populations offered a larger tax base and more clients within an accessible distance. The South's leading city, New Orleans, established a thriving free school system that stood as an example to the rest of the South. The Crescent City established free public schools in 1841 at the urging of two prominent citizens from the American Quarter of the city. Samuel J. Peters and Joshua Baldwin lobbied the state legislature, which responded with legislation allowing each municipality in New Orleans to levy taxes to support public schools in their area. Immediately, each of the three municipalities of the city, which functioned autonomously at the time, commenced preparations for instituting public schools. Many inhabitants exhibited hesitation if not outright hostility to the proposals. The city's large French Catholic population believed that schooling was the proper domain of the church, not the state, and feared the implications of secular schools. Catholic educators worried that public schools would erode their power in the community, while other private teachers did not want the state institutions siphoning away their customers. Additionally, wealthy citizens who could afford to pay tuition did not want to be taxed for the education of other people's children, and general public opinion opposed free "pauper" schools serving the entire community. According to municipal officials, "the community regarded the enterprise with distrust, if not entirely opposed to it." Despite local resistance, all three municipalities opened schools in their districts in 1841, and within one year they elicited praise from across the nation. As one set of scholars explain, "New England educators who normally scoffed at the educational backwardness of the South took notice of the New Orleans achievement."[22]

An examination of the rapidly increasing enrollment in the New Orleans public schools reveals the system's immediate success. In 1843, after only two years of operation, enrollment in the public schools of the Second Municipality increased from the original number of twenty-six students taught by three teachers to 1,574 students enrolled taught by thirty-three teachers. Likewise, attendance in the First and Third Municipalities increased rapidly. In 1845, the combined enrollment in the three municipalities reached 3,336 students taught by eighty teachers, and by 1850 the number of students climbed to 6,285. Officers of the Second Municipality bragged that a number of families moved within its borders strictly to gain access to its schools.[23]

On average, New Orleans public schools operated from 9:00 a.m. to 2:30 p.m., five days a week, ten months a year. Some primary schools dismissed pupils under the age of eight earlier in the day in order to allow teachers to focus on the more advanced students.[24] School administrators constantly boasted of the quality of instructors employed in their schools, noting their diligence, attentiveness, and faithfulness. The school board had their pick of teachers, since applications poured into their office year after year. The high salary offered in New Orleans schools no doubt played a role in attracting qualified applicants. In 1856, head instructors in New Orleans' boys grammar schools received $1,320, more than teachers in the same position received in Cincinnati or Philadelphia and only slightly less than they received in New York. School directors also prided themselves on the comparatively higher salaries enjoyed by female teachers in New Orleans. For instance, while Boston paid their male grammar school principal teachers $1,800, female principal teachers received only $450. In contrast, New Orleans paid female principal teachers $1,000, with men in the same position receiving $320 more. The lower salaries commanded by female teachers might be one reason Crescent City schools displayed a clear preference for the gentler sex. In 1854, schools in the Second Municipality employed fifty-one female teachers and fourteen males. According to the school board, they chose to hire mostly women "after mature deliberation," since women proved "better adapted to instruct young scholars, by their quicker perceptions; their instinctiveness fondness for, and tact in communicating knowledge; greater patience and more gentleness than the males."[25]

Not just content to provide primary, intermediate, and secondary schools, public school administrators in New Orleans wanted to extend the avenues of learning as far as possible and instituted numerous community programs that ingratiated larger and larger segments of the city's population to the public school system. The school system established a public library, which housed over twelve thousand volumes by 1861, as well as a lyceum series offered to the New Orleans community. In the 1850s, New Orleans opened a public normal school to train teachers, as well as night schools for pupils of both genders who worked during the day. While the operation of night schools may not seem like a significant contribution, such an undertaking reveals that those in charge of the New Orleans school system remained truly committed to educating the entire population, even those ordinarily beyond the reach of public schools.[26]

Unlike public schools in other parts of the South that resorted to charging tuition when state support proved insufficient, New Orleans schools remained free to all throughout the antebellum period, and they also provided books and stationery to their pupils. State appropriations fell far short of what was needed to run the schools, so the city council spent considerable sums to keep the system going, with generous assistance from private donations, and wealthy and poor alike patronized the city's public schools.[27]

Without question, New Orleans boasted the preeminent public school system in the Gulf South and one of the most notable in the nation. Surrounding areas looked to her example when they began to implement their own systems, and many towns adopted identical methods when establishing their first public schools. In the discussion leading up to the establishment of a free public school in Natchez, for example, the New Orleans school system was continually referenced, and when the Natchez Institute was established in 1846, the board adopted "the rules, regulations, and organization, of the New Orleans schools, almost entirely."[28]

The Natchez Institute, like public schools in New Orleans, had the support of the city's residents, who helped get the school off the ground. One of the leading merchants in Natchez, Alvarez Fisk, donated land and buildings capable of holding one thousand students on the condition that the property "be used solely and entirely for the accommodation of Free Schools forever." Fisk, like Samuel Peters in New Orleans, was a New England transplant who hoped to see public schools in the South resemble those he knew in the Northeast. The community supported public schools; Natchez newspapers of the day are filled with letters to the editors in support of establishing public schools in the city and responding to critics who worried about increased taxation, the only argument offered against such a system. One critic, Lucy Neal, worried that unmarried white men and free people of color might find the increased taxation oppressive, since they would not benefit from the operation of the public schools. Ms. Neal explained that she felt no sympathy for bachelors, who could only blame themselves that they had no children to send to school. But since black children were prohibited from attending school, she believed free black adults should be exempted from paying taxes to support the school. Despite concerns over taxation, the Natchez public school prospered so that by 1849 the school enrolled 555 students and 856 pupils in 1856.[29]

The attempt to create a public school in Mobile, Alabama, differed from the situation in Natchez and New Orleans. The Alabama legislature made provisions to support schools there as early as 1826, but like other southern states at the time, the funds went to assist private schools rather than to found wholly public institutions. In 1835, prominent citizens Henry Hitchcock and Silas Dinsmore arranged for private donations to help supplement state aid for the construction of a large public schoolhouse in the city. This structure, known as Barton Academy, still stands in Mobile today as a testament to the early support for education exhibited in that city. Unfortunately, despite the efforts made to finance its construction, the building left the school commissioners overdrawn in the amount of $12,000, leading them to charge tuition in order to retire this debt. A few years later, the school made provisions to admit poor children free of charge, but due to economic trouble following the Panic of 1837 and a smallpox epidemic that hit Mobile in 1839, the school commissioners closed the free departments that year. The city continued to spend much of its education funds to support private institutions throughout the 1840s.[30]

In 1852, the city witnessed a spirited debate over a proposal to sell Barton Academy in order to disburse the proceeds to the various private schools in the area. Residents thoughtfully considered the future of public schools in their city, choosing between selling the school and committing to support private institutions or maintaining Barton Academy and attempting to institute wholly public schools. After a spirited debate among the city's inhabitants, politicians, and business leaders, the public referendum held in August 1852 showed clear support for establishing public schools, with 224 voters approving the sale and 2,225 voting against it. After the election revealed such a clear desire among city dwellers to support a public school in Barton Academy, the newly elected school board set out to do just that. Less than three months later, four hundred students began class at the reorganized school. By February of the following year, 854 students attended, more than double the previous year's enrollment. Soon the school was divided into four departments. The lower departments, termed primary and intermediate, remained free while the upper departments, junior and senior high, charged tuition. The rates, however, were much reduced compared to those of private schools in the area, and free entrance was given to any students whose family could not afford to pay.[31]

Schools in the urban areas of the South were thriving by the approach of the Civil War, witnessing increased enrollments, receiving large numbers of teaching applicants, and offering more advanced courses. While cities enjoyed many advantages over the predominantly rural areas that made up the rest of the Gulf South, residents outside of the urban centers began to demand public schools in their areas during the 1840s and 1850s. The example of urban schools, along with the spread of Jacksonian democracy and the economic recovery following the Panic of 1837, combined to lead residents to insist that their elected officials make good on their promises to promote education.

In Louisiana, a new constitution adopted in 1845 demanded the legislature provide statewide public schools. Legislation to do so came in 1847, directed by a state superintendent of education appointed by the governor and locally elected parish superintendents. Conditions differed from parish to parish, with some areas instituting successful schools that served large numbers of children while other locales had trouble procuring accommodations, finding

teachers, and attracting students. Despite obstacles, the new system represented a dramatic improvement over the previous state-funded system. By
1849, more than sixteen thousand Louisiana children reported attending public schools, amounting to 56 percent of school-age children in those areas.[32]

Unfortunately, the progressive mood of Louisiana lawmakers shifted in
1852, as evidenced by a much more restrictive state constitution adopted that
year. Likewise, legislation aimed at cutting the size and cost of government
drastically reduced the pay and duties of the state education superintendent
and eliminated the position of parish superintendent altogether. The impact of
this legislation was disastrous, and outcry from local officials immediate. Unlike in other southern states where schools progressed in the decade leading up
to secession, in Louisiana public schools that had been thriving now faltered.[33]

At the same time that Louisiana's 1845 constitution demanded action on
public schools, Mississippians applied enough pressure to force both political parties to pledge education reform, resulting in new legislation in 1846.
Unfortunately, the legislation required the written consent of a majority of
the heads of household in each county in order for a local tax to be levied.
Additionally, the law allowed any county to exempt itself altogether if a majority of the heads of households issued a written protest before a certain date.
New legislation passed in 1848 governed different counties by different rules,
so that five separate school laws operated concurrently, each applying to a
portion of the state. School regulations became even more localized as the
antebellum period progressed. From 1859 to 1860, twenty-six different school
laws were passed which pertained to different counties. As one observer explained, "this legislation was local government run riot and it destroyed every
trace of a system." Despite the fractured system, educational opportunities for
young Mississippians improved throughout the years so that in 1860 the state
housed 1,116 schools served by 1,215 teachers and enrolling 30,970 students.

Alabama politicians spent much of the 1840s lamenting the disappointing
status of public education but failing to do anything substantive to help remedy the problems. A continual topic of debate in the state at this time revolved
around consolidating the various sixteenth-section funds held separately by
each township into one large state fund. Politicians could not agree on consolidation, so they sent the issue to the voters as a referendum in 1853. Out of
forty-five counties that voted on the proposition, only six registered a majority
of voters against consolidation; 793 townships voted in favor of consolidation,

with 227 voting against. However, because of the number of townships that failed to register any vote at all, the total in favor of consolidation amounted to less than a majority, thus defeating the proposal.[34]

The 1853 popular vote on consolidating the sixteenth-section funds of the various townships in Alabama reveals a split between wealthier areas of the state that voted against consolidating the funds and less affluent areas that tended to favor consolidation. The counties that voted against the proposition were wealthy and enjoyed large sixteenth-section funds, which they stood to lose to offset smaller funds in other areas. Not all wealthy areas opposed consolidation, but the areas that did oppose consolidating the school funds consisted of counties that enjoyed better than average wealth.[35]

Perhaps even more important than the trends visible in the 1853 vote is that the debate over consolidation garnered such interest and excitement among the state's inhabitants that the following year the legislature enacted provisions to establish a statewide public school system. The agitation on the question of consolidation helped to arouse public interest in education, forcing the legislature to act soon thereafter. According to J. Mills Thornton, "the issue was now sufficiently before the public so that ambitious politicians were beginning to seize upon it as a possible means to secure approval." There is a discernible correlation between public interest in education and action on the part of the state legislatures.[36]

Thanks in part to pressure from the Know Nothing Party in the 1853 elections, many Alabama legislators came into office pledged to support internal improvements. They appointed a Mobilian reformer, Alexander B. Meek, to head the committee on education. Meek proposed legislation to establish at least one free primary school in each township of the state; it passed both houses by large majorities. In 1856, additional legislation further assisted the school system in Alabama so that by the following year a reported 89,013 students attended 2,262 public schools across the state.[37]

Mississippi and Louisiana established statewide public school systems in 1846 and 1847, respectively, yet the legislation that followed the initial laws proved more detrimental than beneficial, retarding public school progress in both states. Alternately, Alabama lawmakers made provisions that improved the functioning of its school system after it was established. Legislators there heeded the advice of the state superintendent and instituted measures to improve school administration, funding, and access.

If residents in all three states desired greater access to education through public schools, why was Alabama the only state to continually improve its school system prior to the Civil War? One might expect that political partisanship played a role in determining each state's educational policy, since the national Whig party had pledged support for public education. In some instances, there is evidence of a split between Democrats and Whigs in the Gulf South when it came to state support for schools. Such a divide between the parties occurred, for instance, in the debates of the Louisiana constitutional convention of 1845. Likewise, when Alabama politicians sparred about accepting their share of the distribution of the federal surplus, the state senate split along party lines. But in other instances, the divide is not so clear. There are plenty of cases of loyal Jacksonian Democrats supporting increased state action on education. For example, Democratic Mississippi governor John J. Pettus argued in 1859, "the education of the youth should then be regarded as an object of the first magnitude, to be promoted by the untiring efforts of those who govern the State." Likewise, Alabama, which made the most positive educational progress in the last decade of the antebellum era, was largely dominated by the Democratic Party, although it did have a large Whig presence that succeeded in affecting some legislation. In Louisiana, there was a visible divide in 1845 with Whigs calling for more support to education. In 1852, when the state retrenched education spending with detrimental consequences, the legislature was controlled by Whigs. Such evidence reveals that one cannot simply attribute the educational progress of the southern states to the strength of a particular political party.[38]

The divergent trends in the three states can be more fully explained by looking at the governmental structures in each. In Louisiana and Mississippi, the governors exercised considerable power, including the privilege of appointing numerous state officials. Gov. Thomas B. Robertson of Louisiana went so far to argue in 1824, "the people have no right to say who is to govern them. The constitution places the power in my hands." In Alabama, by contrast, the governor enjoyed very little power. Instead, the office was merely a "salaried honor," which allowed him to address the legislature annually on issues he deemed important, but then he faded into the background for another twelve months. Not only did the legislature have all the power in the Cotton State, but those lawmakers were closer to the voters than in the other states. Alabama instituted white male suffrage in its first constitution in 1819, ensuring that a broader segment of the population had a say in electing officials, making lawmakers there more responsive to the masses than in other states with more restrictive suffrage requirements. These characteristics ensured that Alabama would prove most sensitive to the demands of the populace. Though tardy in its enactment of a state school system, the legislature continued to improve the system even as the sectional crisis diverted attention away from such domestic issues. In Louisiana and Mississippi, however, planter political dominance allowed officials to act with impunity against the public interest. Such disregard for the public certainly caused rumbling among the voters, but the planter control was such that few suffered politically for their behavior. One Louisiana resident reported in 1851 of the trouble in his parish stemming from the operation of the school system: "Parents think they are oppressed, that they have to pay their taxes and receive no benefit of any importance from it."[39]

The limits of private education led residents to demand that their state governments do more to improve access to education. This yearning among the masses is significant. Scholars have failed to recognize the number of schools and the amount of learning going on in the antebellum South, while also ignoring education's centrality in southern culture. The establishment of statewide public school systems came from public insistence that governments uphold the promises made in their state constitutions to foster education. Such agitation, along with the evidence that southern families up and down the socioeconomic ladder embraced avenues for learning when available, reveals that the previous historiographical consensus that there were few schools in the South because southerners did not value education demands revision. While politicians in the three states responded with differing levels of action, the impulse was the same among the people. Southerners embraced, valued, and demanded education.

The public school systems in all three states suffered from problems that would linger until after the Civil War, yet those troubles did not condemn public schools entirely. Local inhabitants worked to overcome obstacles facing their schools, including lack of direction from state agencies and vague and contradictory legislation. Even inadequate funding from the state did not defeat local schools. Residents struggled to keep classes in operation, whether by passing local taxes, soliciting private donations, or charging tuition to keep teachers employed. Such local initiative ensured that access to education would remain a public policy issue.

The trend of educational development in the Gulf South states of Louisiana, Mississippi, and Alabama was not a straight trajectory of progress over time. It was punctuated with experimentation and retrenchment, which hampered overall success. Nonetheless, learning remained central to the lives of young people of varying social classes. The importance of learning to all white southerners, not just the elite, undermines the assumption that wealthy planters led an ignorant mass of poor white trash into a war in defense of slavery. The southern middle class valued education, sought out various avenues to encourage learning, and even forced their state governments to provide public schools in some form. While statewide school systems did lag behind those of New England states, this fact does not indicate a disregard for the intellectual wellbeing of young southerners. When considering the achievements of southern education, one must jettison the historiographical bias that measures all academic progress in relation to the establishment of public schools in Massachusetts. When one considers the South in context, including its frontier-like setting, low population density, and the informal modes of learning available, it is obvious that education remained a central concern of southern society throughout the antebellum era. This fact helps to shed light on the people who inhabited the region in the nineteenth century and demands inclusion in the larger narrative of southern history. Furthermore, the educational progress of the South, punctuated as it was, reveals that the slaveholding elite were not dictating to an ignorant mass as they demanded secession. The white South, slaveholding and not, together committed themselves to secession and southern independence.

NOTES

1. Gerald Gutek writes in a 1991 study that "thus far formal education in the South has not been considered, for the simple reason that, except for the tutoring provided for the upper class children of plantation society, it was not readily available," in *An Historical Introduction to American Education,* 2nd ed. (Prospect Heights, IL: Waveland Press, 1991), 10. See also William J. Reese, *America's Public Schools: From the Common School to "No Child Left Behind"* (Baltimore: Johns Hopkins University Press, 2005), 43, 71. William J. Cooper Jr. and Thomas E. Terrill argue that "during the antebellum era no statewide public school system existed," in *The American South: A History,* 4th ed., 2 vols. (Lanham, MD: Rowman and Littlefield, 2009), 1:273.

2. Catherine Clinton, *The Plantation Mistress: Woman's World in the Old South* (New York: Pantheon, 1982), 50.

3. Celine Fremaux Garcia, *Celine: Remembering Louisiana, 1850–1871* (Athens: University of Georgia Press, 1987), 28–29.

4. Thomas C. W. Ellis Diary, January 1–2, 1856, Buck-Ellis Family Papers, Louisiana and Lower Mississippi Valley Collections, Hill Memorial Library, Louisiana State University, Baton Rouge (hereinafter cited as LLMVC).

5. Hagaman (Abraham) Memoir, Mississippi Department of Archives and History, Jackson, Mississippi (hereinafter cited as MDAH).

6. Joseph G. Tregle Jr., *Louisiana in the Age of Jackson: A Clash of Cultures and Personalities* (Baton Rouge: Louisiana State University Press, 1999), 44.

7. Martha L. Batchelor to Albert A. Batchelor, March 2, 1861, Albert A. Batchelor Papers, LLMVC.

8. William Lacey to Thomas Butler, June 25, 1847, Ellis-Farar Papers, LLMVC; Caroline Lee Hentz Diary, February 11, 1836, Hentz Family Papers, Southern Historical Collection, the Wilson Library, University of North Carolina at Chapel Hill (hereinafter cited as SHC).

9. Lawrence Daily to James Williams, November 11, 1803, Ker Family Papers, SHC.

10. *U.S. Census (Seventh Census), 1850*. For a discussion of the availability of private schools in the South, see, e.g., James W. Mobley, "The Academy Movement in Louisiana," *Louisiana Historical Quarterly* 30 (Jan.–Oct. 1947): 738–978; Oscar W. Hyatt, "The Development of Secondary Education in Alabama Prior to 1920" (EdD diss., George Peabody College for Teachers, 1933); Maggie Lea Causey, "A Study of Education in Alabama Prior to Statehood" (MA thesis, University of Alabama, 1938); Willis G. Clark, *History of Education in Alabama, 1702–1889* (Washington, DC: Government Printing Office, 1889); Edward Mayes, *History of Education in Mississippi* (Washington, DC: Government Printing Office, 1889); Julia H. Nguyen, "Molding the Minds of the South: Education in Natchez, 1817–1861" (MA thesis, Louisiana State University, 1995); Christie Anne Farnham, *The Education of the Southern Belle: Higher Education and Student Socialization in the Antebellum South* (New York: New York University Press, 1994).

11. Thomas Millsaps to Thomas Ellis, September 14, 1855, Buck-Ellis Family Papers, LLMVC.

12. Lucy Maria W. F. Fisher Memoirs, 14–15, LLMVC.

13. School Article for 1828, Clinton School Papers, LLMVC.

14. Albert A. Batchelor Papers, Mss. 919, 1293, LLMVC; Fisher Memoirs, 14–15, LLMVC; Mary Baker to Susan Metcalfe, July 23, 1818, Ker Family Papers, SHC. For another fond appraisal of one's teacher see also Isaac Henry Charles to J. E. Liddall, January 9, 1842, Isaac H. Charles Letters, LLMVC.

15. Richard Ellis to Thomas Butler, September 27, 1837, Ellis-Farar Papers, LLMVC; John Palfrey to Mark Pickard, December 29, 1810, Palfrey Family Papers, LLMVC.

16. Martha L. Batchelor to Albert A. Batchelor, December 11, 1860, Albert A. Batchelor Papers, LLMVC.

17. Alabama Constitution (1819), art. 3, sec. 5; Mississippi Constitution (1817), art. 6, sec. 16; Raleigh A. Suarez, "Chronicle of a Failure: Public Education in Antebellum Louisiana," *Louisiana History* 12 (1971): 115.

18. "An Act to extend and improve the system of Public Education in the State of Louisiana, approved February 16, 1821," Henry A. Bullard and Thomas Curry, *A New Digest of the Statute Laws of the State of Louisiana, From the Change of Government to the Year 1841, Inclusive* (New Orleans: E. Johns and Co., 1842), 358; *Louisiana Senate Journal*, 1st Sess., 1833, 4; *Louisiana Senate Journal*, 2nd Sess., 1833, 2; *Louisiana Senate Journal*, 2nd Sess., 1842, 4.

19. George Duke Humphrey, "Public Education for Whites in Mississippi, A Historical and Interpretive Study" (EdD diss., Ohio State University, 1939), 32–34; Earl Wayne Adams, "The History of Public School Finance in Mississippi" (EdD dissertation, University of Mississippi, 1980), 36–37; Forrest David Matthews, "The Politics of Education in the Deep South: Georgia and Alabama, 1830–1860" (PhD diss., Columbia University, 1965), 271; Stephen B. Weeks, History of Public School Education in Alabama (Washington, DC: United States Government Printing Office, U.S. Bureau of Education Bulletin, 1915, no. 12; reprint, Westport, CT: Negro University Press, 1971), 50. Humphrey argues that "a planter-controlled Legislature was selling Mississippi down the river, and in so doing squandering educational funds, and every other kind they could get their hands on." He goes on to surmise that the history of Mississippi's early banking system reveals that "the planter class, who for a long time dictated legislative policies, actually did much to retard the development of public education in the State by getting control and squandering the funds that had been intended for educational purposes" ("Public Education for Whites in Mississippi," 38–39).

20. Richard E. Ellis, *The Union at Risk: Jacksonian Democracy, States Rights, and the Nullification Crisis* (New York: Oxford University Press, 1987), 176.

21. *Alabama Senate Journal*, Twenty-Sixth Session, 1844–1845, 207.

22. *Louisiana Senate Journal*, First Session, 1841; Robert C. Reinders, "New England Influences on the Formation of Public Schools in New Orleans," *Journal of Southern History* 30 (1964): 183; *Second Annual Report, Council of Municipality Number Two* (New Orleans: printed at the office of the Commercial Bulletin, 1844), 25; Donald E. Devore and Joseph Logsdon, *Crescent City Schools: Public Education in New Orleans, 1841–1991* (Lafayette, LA: The Center for Louisiana Studies, University of Southwestern Louisiana, 1991), 22, 23.

23. *Second Annual Report of the Council of Municipality Number Two*, 15.

24. *Annual Report of the Board of Directors of the Public Schools of the First District of New Orleans, for the Year ending June 30, 1856*; Alma H. Peterson, "A Historical Survey of the Administration of Education in New Orleans, 1718–1851," (PhD diss., Louisiana State University, 1962), 244.

25. *[First] Annual Report of the Council of Municipality Number Two; Second Annual Report of the Council of Municipality Number Two; Annual Report of the Board of Directors of the Public Schools of the First District of New Orleans, for the Year ending June 30, 1856* (New Orleans: printed at the office of the *Creole*, 1856). For typical comments on the qualifications of teachers, see reports of the municipalities, included in "Report of the State Superintendent of Education," *Louisiana Legislative Documents*, 1854, 92–97; 1858, 96–102; 1859, 84–91; 1861, 41–49.

26. *Third Annual Report of the Council of Municipality Number Two*, 34; *Report of the Board of Directors of the Public Schools of the Second Municipality*, 1848; *[First] Annual Report of the Council of Municipality Number Two. . .*, 10; "Report of the State Superintendent of Education," *Louisiana Legislative Documents*, 1861, 42; *Second Annual Report of the Council of Municipality Number Two*,

17; "Report of the State Superintendent of Education," *Louisiana Legislative Documents,* 1854, 92–97; ibid., 1861, 47. See also "Report of the State Superintendent of Education," *Louisiana Legislative Documents,* 1857, 12; 1856, 10; 1858, 9; 1859, 84, 101.

27. *Report of the Board of Directors of the Public Schools of the Second Municipality,* 1848; Report of the Secretary of State on the Public Education of Louisiana," *Louisiana Legislative Documents,* 1843, vi; *Third Annual Report of the Council of Municipality Number Two,* 38; *Second Annual Report of the Council of Municipality Number Two,* 20, 34; "Annual Report of the Treasurer of the Parish of Orleans, Second District, to the State Superintendent," included in "Report of the State Superintendent of Education," *Louisiana Legislative Documents,* 1861, 44; Peterson, "A Historical Survey of the Administration of Education in New Orleans," 49, 98, 196; [*First*] *Annual Report of the Council of Municipality Number Two,* 6.

28. "Eleventh Annual Report of the Board of Visitors of the Natchez Institute: Made to the President and Selectmen of the City of Natchez" (Natchez, MS: printed at the *Courier* office, 1856), 11; *Mississippi Free Trader and Natchez Gazette,* February 18, 20, 1845.

29. *Mississippi Free Trader and Natchez Gazette,* February 11, 18, 20, 25, 27, 1845; *Fourth Annual Report of the Board of Visitors of the Natchez Institute: Also, the Report of the Board of Examiners. July 4th, 1849* (Natchez, MS: printed at the *Courier* book and job office, 1849), 6; "Eleventh Annual Report of the Board of Visitors of the Natchez Institute" (n.p., 1856), 5.

30. *Acts Passed at the Seventh Annual Session of the General Assembly of the State of Alabama, begun and held in the Town of Cahawba, on the Third Monday in November, 1825* (n.p., [1826?]), 35; Hyatt, "The Development of Secondary Education," 13; Harriet Amos Doss, *Cotton City: Urban Development in Antebellum Mobile* (University: University of Alabama Press, 1985), 181–84; Harriet B. Ellis, "Mobile Public School Beginnings and their Background" (MS thesis, Alabama Polytechnic Institute, 1930), 23–24; Nita Katharine Pyburn, "Mobile Public Schools before 1860," *Alabama Historical Review* 11, no. 3 (July 1958): 180–81.

31. William F. Perry, *Report of William F. Perry, Superintendent of Education of the State of Alabama, Made to the Governor, for the year 1857* (Montgomery, AL: N. B. Cloud, state printer, 1858), 57; Matthews, "The Politics of Education," 348–49; Clark, *History of Education in Alabama, 1702–1889,* 222–24.

32. Louisiana Constitution (1845), title VII, art. 133–39, 352–53; Richard Loucks, *An exposition of the laws of Louisiana relating to free public schools* (Baton Rouge, LA: printed at the office of the *Delta,* 1847), 1, 9–12; "Report of the State Superintendent of Education," *Louisiana Legislative Documents,* 1849, 2.

33. Suarez, "Chronicle of a Failure," 117–18.

34. Alabama Secretary of State, Election Files—state and national, 1823–ongoing, Alabama Department of Archives and History, Montgomery, Alabama (hereinafter cited as ADAH); *Alabama Senate Journal,* Fourth Biennial Session, 1853–54, 34–35; Forrest D. Matthews, "The Politics of Education in the Deep South: Georgia and Alabama, 1830–1860," (PhD diss., Columbia University, 1965), 345–46; J. Mills Thornton III, *Politics and Power in a Slave Society: Alabama, 1800–1860* (Baton Rouge: Louisiana State University Press, 1978), 300.

35. Alabama Secretary of State, Election Files—state and national, 1823—ongoing, ADAH; *U.S. Census (Seventh Census), 1850,* 414–33.

36. Thornton, *Politics and Power in a Slave Society,* 300.

37. Ibid., 324–27; *Alabama Senate Journal,* Fourth Biennial Session, 1853–54, 57, 306–9.

38. *Journal of the House of Representatives of the State of Mississippi,* Regular Session, 1859, 102 (quote); Sarah Hyde, "'Teach Us Incessantly': Lessons and Learning in the Antebellum Gulf South" (PhD diss., Louisiana State University, 2010), 220–24; Daniel Walker Howe, *The Political Culture of the American Whigs* (Chicago: University of Chicago Press, 1979), 36; Thornton, *Politics and Power in a Slave Society,* 38; Cooper and Terrill, *The American South,* 1:188, John M. Sacher, *A Perfect War of Politics: Parties, Politicians, and Democracy in Louisiana, 1824–1861* (Baton Rouge: Louisiana State University Press, 2007), 125, 142.

39. *Louisiana House Journal,* 7th Legislature, 1st Sess., 1824, 2–8; John B. Dawson to William Hamilton, April 6, 1825, in Hamilton Papers, LLMVC; Alabama Constitution (1819), art. 3, sec. 5, 7; Thornton, *Politics and Power in a Slave Society,* 12; Matthews, "The Politics of Education in the Deep South, 227–28; "Report of the Livingston Parish Superintendent of Education," in "Report of the State Superintendent of Education," *Louisiana Legislative Documents,* First Session, 1852, 27.

CHAPTER THREE

Preaching Disunion
Clergymen in the Louisiana Secession Crisis
Julia Huston Nguyen

On November 29, 1860, Benjamin Palmer addressed an overflow crowd at First Presbyterian Church in New Orleans. It was Thanksgiving, a holiday commonly celebrated with feasts and church services that praised God for his many blessings. That day, however, Palmer had a different purpose. Abraham Lincoln's election had taken place just a few weeks earlier and already radical southern rights advocates were pushing for secession. The church, which held as many as two thousand people, was crowded with listeners who had come to hear how Palmer would acknowledge the crisis and what counsel he would have for his flock. In his sermon, later published and circulated throughout the South, Palmer expounded on "the most fearful and perilous crisis which has occurred in our history as a nation," explaining why slavery was ordained by God and urging Louisianans to protect it by supporting secession. The sermon caused an immediate sensation, was reported on all over the country, and fanned the flames of secessionist enthusiasm.[1]

During the secession crisis of 1860–61, southerners from all walks of life worried, speculated, and argued about national events and the best course of action. Ministers were no different in their concern for the future, and their pulpits sometimes provided a forum in which to express those concerns. In sermons preached from the time of Lincoln's election to the outbreak of fighting, ministers had the opportunity to express their thoughts on the nation's crisis, ask God for guidance and blessings, and attempt to persuade southerners of the best course of action. Palmer's sermon has received considerable attention from historians, but he was just one of several clergymen who addressed the secession crisis. Examination of his actions along with those of other ministers can reveal the breadth of ministerial support for secession and the differences that existed. The activities of ministers in the weeks leading up to secession as well as during the spring months that followed provide insight into support for secession and the role of churches during the crisis.

Preaching on political topics did not occur without controversy. In the first decades of the nineteenth century, many Americans found any involvement of clergymen in politics to be inappropriate. At the same time, however, as Richard Carwardine demonstrates for the Methodist church, evangelical concern for moral improvement meant that political issues increasingly became intertwined with religious expression, especially in northern churches where evangelicalism placed emphasis on reforming society. Carwardine argues that while few ministers would openly preach support for a political party, they frequently "helped set an agenda for moral purpose in public affairs," discussing current issues including temperance and slavery. As some northern evangelical Protestants began to take an antislavery stance and sectional differences intensified, southern ministers went on the defensive. Southerners lashed out at northern clergymen for taking up causes like abolition, accusing them of bringing politics into the pulpit, where it had no place. Theodore Clapp, a Massachusetts-born Presbyterian-turned-Unitarian who spent thirty-five years preaching in New Orleans, stated in his 1858 autobiography that "hundreds of ministers in the Northern States have been engaged, the past summer, in preaching politics," which he believed "should be left to the exclusive management of statesmen and professed politicians." In 1860, William Leacock criticized the "weak, or designing, or infidel preachers" who had stirred up abolition sentiment in the northern states. This assertion that northern ministers were overstepping their bounds by preaching about political matters—especially slavery—was cited by many southerners as further proof that their rights and way of life were under attack.[2]

Despite their criticism of northern ministers for preaching about politics, however, some southern ministers also addressed political issues, especially slavery, in their sermons. Religion was a crucial element in arguments supporting slavery, as southerners pointed to biblical descriptions of slavery as proof that the institution was ordained by God. Clapp criticized northern clergymen in his autobiography, but twenty years earlier he had preached a sermon, later published, in which he undertook a defense of slavery on scriptural grounds. He pointed to Abraham, Moses, and other biblical patriarchs who owned slaves as justification for the practice and refuted the arguments of northern ministers such as fellow Unitarian William Ellery Channing before telling slaves that "the most enlightened philanthropists, with unlimited resources, could not place you in a situation more favorable to your present and everlasting welfare, than that which you now occupy." Clapp, like many other southern ministers, argued that his sermon was acceptable because he was defending southern institutions against criticism by northern observers. Some ministers also justified preaching on political topics when those topics touched on moral or religious values. Not surprisingly, a defense of slavery on biblical grounds frequently fulfilled this criterion.[3]

As a result of increasing evangelical activism in many northern churches and determined silence or outspoken defense on the part of southern preachers, differing opinions about slavery caused serious trauma in antebellum churches, and denominational conventions were often roiled by the issue. In 1844, the Methodist Episcopal Church, one of the largest Protestant denominations in the country, fractured when the General Convention voted to suspend a Georgia bishop who owned slaves. This act was the culmination of growing antislavery sentiment among northern evangelical ministers, and the southern Methodist churches could not countenance open censure of slaveholding. The following year, southern Baptists left the national body and formed their own convention over the question of whether slaveholders could serve as missionaries. And, although revivalism and governance were the primary causes of the 1837 split of the Presbyterian Church, the Old School branch included a large majority of southern churches, while the New School was comparatively northern in makeup. In 1857, the southern synods withdrew from the New School branch over slavery. As historians C. C. Goen and Mitchell Snay note, leaders of the South's three largest churches had placed preserving slavery above national denominational unity. With this precedent, then, it was relatively easy for them to place preserving slavery above national political unity in 1861.[4]

These three denominations constituted the vast majority of southern Protestants. Thus, by the time the secession crisis erupted, most southern Protestants worshiped in a setting where clerical support for slavery was taken for granted. Ministers in these sectional churches might call for more humane treatment of slaves or criticize the slaveholders who failed to expose their slaves to Christianity, but they did not, as a rule, preach that slavery should come to an end. As Edward Crowther argues, religion and proslavery arguments fused to form a code of "sacred honor" in the antebellum South. For those few churches that retained a national membership, like the Protestant Episcopal Church and the Old School Presbyterians, silence on political issues, especially those related to slavery or its expansion, was both desirable in terms of their understanding of how a minister should properly behave and necessary in order to keep the denominations together.[5]

With the election of Abraham Lincoln, the sectional question could not be ignored. During the winter and spring of 1860 and 1861, many churches and their leaders found that it was almost impossible to remain aloof from the struggle over slavery and sectionalism. Men—and women—argued, lobbied, and schemed, hoping to sway the outcome, especially of the elections for convention delegates who would decide each state's course of action. Debates over these matters animated ministers no less than others. Even some who had previously remained silent on political issues felt compelled to weigh in on the great struggle for the future of the nation. They began to preach about current events, and their sermons and prayers became part of the cacophony of voices that accompanied the southern states on their march toward secession and war. Louisiana's ministers would garner especially intense attention during these unsettled months.

Thanksgiving offered an early opportunity to address current events. Although Louisiana had only celebrated it in an official way since the mid-1840s, by 1860 it was an established holiday. It was generally observed on the last Thursday in November, which that year fell on the twenty-ninth, and church attendance was a traditional part of Thanksgiving observance. This year, it would take on special significance, especially in New Orleans. It is difficult to know if the people who gathered knew what to expect when they walked into churches that day, but some must have expected that the topic that had filled newspapers, letters, public meetings, and private conversations for weeks must also leak into the churches.

At Christ Episcopal Church, the oldest Protestant church in Louisiana and the preferred church for many of New Orleans's commercial and political elite, rector William T. Leacock delivered a sermon that began by reminding his congregation of the holiday's purpose: to give thanks to God for the blessings he had bestowed in the previous year, even when "God's dispensations are not always self-evident mercies." In his estimation, the current crisis was one such mercy. The United States, Leacock noted, existed in a state of prosperity and relative peace. "The agitation of the slavery question" was the only cloud on the horizon, but Leacock aimed to show how even in this, "God has made a blessing to us." The South was blessed, Leacock argued, because the sectional crisis currently unfolding had made southerners, who had previously "trembled at the bare mention of the subject," confident and ready to meet abolitionists "not only on Constitutional grounds, but on reason, on religion, on expediency, and dare them to their face to dislodge us from our position." Lincoln's election had also, Leacock asserted, opened the eyes of southerners, who "thought, a few months ago, that the Abolitionists were few" to their numbers and power in the North. Thus "awakened . . . in full time to check their destructive career," southerners must be thankful. Their society was in danger, and they were now alert and ready to mount a defense. In making this defense possible, Leacock saw the hand of God.[6]

The unchecked malice of abolitionists toward the South had also, Leacock continued, "hastened the period of adopting such measures as are best calculated for our interest." What these measures might be, Leacock left to his congregation "for your own hearts to answer." Leacock did not believe that he should prescribe a course of action but should merely "say what I believe to be the hand of God, in what has been done—that the recognition of that hand might add fervor to our thanksgiving and praise." In the tradition of antebellum distrust of ministers' political speech, Leacock was careful not to overstep by pushing explicitly for action. Just a few weeks earlier in the immediate aftermath of the election, he reminded them, he had "counseled you, from this place, to avoid all precipitate action; but at the same time to take determined action—such action only as you felt you could take with the conscious support of reason and religion." According to Leacock, his advice remained the same now, but by now "I give it as my firm and unhesitating belief, that nothing is now left us but secession." Abolitionists had perverted northern politics until "our enemies are not on the Constitution," and the South must "administer among ourselves the Constitution which our fathers have left us." Here, Leacock made an argument that would have been familiar and compelling to his congregation, maintaining that the South was the true heir of the nation's founding legacy. He also demonstrated an evolution in his own thought that he clearly hoped his listeners would undergo as well. Leacock was walking a fine line. He claimed that he was not advising his listeners but merely explaining what he personally thought was the right and godly course of action. Leacock almost certainly recognized the power of moral suasion that ministers held over their congregants. Without giving "advice," Leacock was, in fact, telling his parishioners what to do. The rush of events over just a few weeks had made any other course of action, to him, impossible. Leacock closed with the rhetorical device so often used by southerners when defending slavery: "I am willing, at the call of my honor and my liberty, to die a freeman; but I'll never, no, never live a slave; and the alternative now presented by our enemies is secession or slavery."[7]

Benjamin Palmer also preached on secession at New Orleans's First Presbyterian Church that Thanksgiving Day. Already a noted clergyman, Palmer was a founder of the *Southern Presbyterian Review* and had been at First Presbyterian since 1856. During the first part of his career in South Carolina and during his years in New Orleans, he had gained a reputation as a theologically conservative clergyman in the Old School tradition who believed that churches should remain true to strict Calvinist theology. He was also a powerful preacher. In just four years, he had built the church's membership from 350 to more than 500; as many as two thousand people came to hear his Sunday sermons, which were frequently reprinted in New Orleans newspapers.[8]

On this occasion, Palmer chose texts from Psalm 94—"Shall the throne of iniquity have fellowship with thee, which frameth mischief by a law?"—and from Obadiah: "All the men of thy confederacy have brought thee even to the border; the men that were at peace with thee have deceived thee, and prevailed against thee; they that ate thy bread have laid a wound under thee; there is none understanding in him." These were hardly unambiguous texts for his listeners, and they set the tone for what was to be a fiery defense of slavery and secession.[9]

At the outset, Palmer hastened to assure his listeners that until the current crisis, "interested as I might be in the progress of events, I have never obtruded, either publicly or privately, my opinions upon any of you; nor can a single man arise and say that, by word or sign, have I ever sought to warp his sentiments or control his judgment upon any political subject whatsoever." Even during the fevered presidential campaign just past, he reminded the congregation, "the seal of a rigid and religious silence has not been broken." Now, however, events had overtaken the normal observance of Thanksgiving, and Palmer felt he had no choice but to address those events from the pulpit. Thus, he placed his sermon in the context of traditional distrust of political preaching. In normal times, he, too, distrusted the intrusion of ministers into political matters, but these were not normal times for Palmer and his congregation. This justification was a way of giving his words legitimacy, as he dismissed the traditional criticism that listeners might make. Underscoring the rarity of his political speech was also a way to render the sermon even more powerful.[10]

Now, Palmer had decided that he could not keep silent, as "whoever may have influence to shape public opinion, at such a time must lend it, or prove faithless to a trust as solemn as any to be accounted for at the bar of God." Palmer's compulsion to speak came in part from his sense of the ministry's place in shaping public opinion. It also stemmed from recognition that the slavery question was "a question of morals and religion," and as such fell within his purview. The issue had already split the Baptist and Methodist churches and now threatened to do the same to the nation. This was as serious a crisis as the nation had ever faced, Palmer thought, and he believed that his duty to God and country demanded action.[11]

After laying out his justification for preaching on a political question, the remainder of Palmer's sermon explained what he discerned to be the South's duty in the present crisis, a duty demanded by both patriotism and religion. At the center of this argument, Palmer placed the "trust providentially committed to us" to "*conserve and to perpetuate the institution of domestic slavery as now existing.*" Drawing on the proslavery defense that had developed during the antebellum period, he devoted much of his sermon to explaining why the South's true duty lay in the vigorous defense of the institution. Slavery, he asserted, must be preserved because it underpinned southern society; because slaveholders took care of their slaves and civilized them; because much of the commercial prosperity of the North, England, and other parts of the world depended on slave-produced agricultural goods; and, finally, because "the Abolition spirit is undeniably atheistic." As Palmer maintained, "to the South the highest position is assigned, of defending, before all nations, the cause of all religion and of all truth." This her residents would do by defending the institution of slavery, sanctioned in the Bible and assigned by God to the region.[12]

Against this picture of southerners as brave defenders of their God and their way of life, Palmer placed "a system of aggression" instigated by northern abolitionists over the previous thirty years. And now, Lincoln's election with no southern votes showed "that from henceforth this is to be a government of section over section." He argued forcefully against the position of those who counseled caution. Abolitionists in the North had perverted democracy and could be trusted only to abuse the power they had acquired for their avowed purpose of ending slavery. Palmer, like many other secessionists, claimed the heritage of the American Revolution, proclaiming, "I throw off the yoke of this union as readily as did our ancestors the yoke of King George III." Like the colonists of the 1770s, southerners had no choice but to act now that the crisis was at hand, forced upon them by tyranny and demagoguery.[13]

What action must they take? Palmer called on the people of the southern states to form conventions, where delegates "in solemn counsel assembled" must make the decision to leave the union "and initiate measures for framing a new and homogeneous confederacy." He hoped that conservatives in the North would, recognizing the gravity of such a step, "arise and crush the Abolition hydra" or that the United States would let the South go in peace. Either outcome would allow the South to defend an institution of slavery "open to expansion, subject to no limitations, save those imposed by God and nature." By doing so, Palmer argued, the South would save the North, and indeed the world, from the destruction of commerce and the race war that abolition of slavery must eventually cause. Here, he invoked the specter of the Haitian Revolution. The significance of this would not have been lost on listeners in any of the slaveholding states, but it was especially powerful in Louisiana, where as many as ten thousand people fleeing Haiti had settled in the early nineteenth century.[14]

Palmer closed with yet another justification for his incursion into political topics. Convinced "that the salvation of the whole country is depending upon the action of the South," he felt compelled to speak in a way that would "deepen the sentiment of resistance in the Southern mind." He ended on a relatively optimistic note. "Bright and happy days are yet before us," he predicted, if only the South could stay the course, and he called down the blessing of God on the South "in this her day of battle!" Like Leacock, Palmer was convinced that God would bless the South if her citizens took the right course of action.[15]

Preachers like Leacock and Palmer, no less than any other intellectually engaged people in 1860, recognized what was at stake in the secession crisis, and they attempted to answer similar questions: What would be the fate of southern states and the institution of slavery in a Lincoln-governed United States? Should states exercise their oft-claimed right to leave the Union? And, crucially for men of the cloth, was secession God's plan for the South? On the same day that Leacock and Palmer answered this last question in the affirmative in front of their New Orleans congregations, John Gierlow, the rector of St. James Episcopal Church in Baton Rouge came to a different conclusion. He gave his Thanksgiving sermon the title, "An appeal for peace," and he counseled supporting the Union if at all possible. Gierlow began by reminding his congregation that Thanksgiving was a national holiday, the celebration of which "can never fail to waken associations that move the heart to national sympathy." As Palmer did, Gierlow acknowledged that the pulpit was not the proper place for political discourse. On an occasion, however, when people thanked God for his mercy and favors, "it behooves us to ascertain whether the state of the national heart will warrant such a favor." He also made a case for the outspokenness of ministers during the present crisis because "when danger is threatening the peace of the nation, it becomes the ambassadors of peace to open their mouths in the name of the Lord."[16]

Gierlow, a native of Denmark, considered himself an American, but one "fully identified with the South." Like so many southerners during this period, including Palmer and Leacock, he invoked the American Revolution, though he saw the founding legacy as something that must be preserved within the Union. Looking back to the nation's founding, he noted that the United States had embarked on a great experiment of self-government, which had been—thus far—successful. In the present tumultuous situation, he believed that "the spirit of war breathes out her baneful voice among us and threatens the demolition of the proudest nation." At the founding, Americans fought a war confident that they did so with God's guidance and blessing. Could Americans do the same in 1860? Gierlow thought not.[17]

Part of what Gierlow hoped to avoid was the horror of war, "a score of battlefields, white with the bones of brothers." He foresaw great tragedy if the southern states did not alter their course toward secession. Both Palmer and Leacock had alluded to the possibility of war in their sermons, and Leacock acknowledged that "the consequences of such a course . . . are perilous" and expressed willingness "at the call of my honor and my liberty, to die a freeman." Only Gierlow, however, emphasized the brutal, fratricidal nature of what must happen if southern states seceded and the U.S. government tried to stop them. He then turned to the Bible, reminding his listeners that King Solomon had mediated between two women who claimed the same child. The woman who would not allow the child to be split in two was its true mother. "This incident," Gierlow noted, "would not be inappropriate as an Allegory, applied to the present contention of the people." Here, he clearly placed his own sympathy—and God's favor—on the side of those who hoped to keep the Union intact.[18]

Gierlow also framed a constitutional argument, asserting that one state—or a section made up of several states—could not leave the Union without the consent of the other states. He noted that the United States had reached a level of stability and prosperity that seemed certain to continue growing if left alone. To do otherwise, he deemed "folly," and he found it difficult to imagine any benefit of secession that would not be even greater if the South stayed within the Union. One of the most important of these benefits was that so much of North America, stretching from ocean to ocean, was ruled by one nation, free from the divisions that might lead to war. "The sun," he asserted, "probably shines on no space so vast, where internal peace is so secure." By the same token, the way that citizens worked for the good of all sections was another advantage that flowed from the national union. Gierlow went on to criticize as selfish "the man who looks only to his personal comfort, and the convenience of those whom he may call his own." Southerners who desired secession were acting in just such a manner.[19]

Even more dangerously, they threatened to reduce a proud nation to ruin, so that what institutions remained would reflect its former glory "as modern Italy represents the grandeur of the Roman Empire." Italy in 1860, struggling to bring together several small states still warring with each other and beset by poverty, was an example few of Gierlow's listeners would have wished to emulate. All this would happen, he warned, because men put profit and influence ahead of their principles. If they could only cling to those principles transmitted to them by faith in God, then "our republic will flourish while time shall last." Gierlow finished by exhorting his congregation, "prepared on the basis of Christian love, to support the Union that makes us a nation on its true principles of wide benevolence, as an instrument of immense good intended for the human race." He also assured them that his sole intention was to promote peace among the states, and, knowing that many of his congregants disagreed vehemently with his position, he asked them to "bear with my freedom of speech." He said that he lacked the power truly to convey the beauty and power that the Gospel had revealed to his soul, but by choosing peace, he hoped that they would come nearer to God. Gierlow never mentioned slavery, nor did he dwell on northern activism against slavery. Unlike Palmer and Leacock, who placed the blame on northern abolitionists, politicians, and ministers, Gierlow recognized that southerners were pushing secession and that they could pull back from the brink. He placed that responsibility squarely on the shoulders of his listeners.[20]

The response to these Thanksgiving sentiments was immediate. The judgment of those in New Orleans, according to one newspaper account, was that Palmer's sermon, "strongly in favor of secession," was "eloquent" and "thrilling." The same account noted that Leacock's "hearers were greatly moved by his discourse." News of the sermons, especially Palmer's, spread quickly. The publishers of the *True Delta,* outspoken secessionists, printed the text in their weekly edition. By one account, they sold more than thirty thousand copies, which then spread throughout the South. William Wadley of Vicksburg visited New Orleans for business in early December. He picked up a copy of the *Weekly True Delta* with Palmer's sermon, which he took home and circulated among his family and friends. He also predicted that the sermon would eventually be published in pamphlet form, which would guarantee wider dissemination. His teenaged daughter Sarah hoped so, because "Dr. Palmer is a talented minister, well known throughout these states, and his sermon . . . will influence many." The *True Delta* was merely the first. As the *Nashville Union and American* noted when it published the full text in early December, Palmer's discourse had been "extensively published both North and South." Notice of the sermon was spread by telegraphic service and appeared in newspapers in several states, from the *Cincinnati Daily Press* to the *National Republican* in Washington, D.C., to the *New York Daily Tribune* and the *Salt Lake City Mountaineer.* Palmer's words helped fuel the frenzy, as did those of other ministers, and they spread from person to person across Louisiana. Thomas Pollock sent a copy of Palmer's discourse and one by William Leacock of Christ Church, New Orleans, to his mother and recommended that she share them with friends.[21]

Many of those in Louisiana who read the sermon printed in New Orleans papers were impressed with Palmer's forthright defense of slavery and secession. Theodore Johnston of Grosse Tete found in it "evidence of profound thought, whilst in its beauty of style, construction of sentences, and in its richness and beauty of language, it is almost unparalleled." Johnston addressed head-on the potential for criticism of Palmer's subject, noting, "it may be remarked by some that the discussion of this question is out of place in the pulpit. I think differently. This question is not a political question, but one in fact of *life* and *death*." Johnston praised the sermon's "clarion notes of alarm," which would, he predicted, "be heard and felt throughout the land—and in response, is there a Southern heart that will not throb with tumultuous, irrepressible emotion?" He thought that it was appropriate that Palmer speak on secession because sermons "reach the ears and convictions of those who could not, *except thro' some such channel, be made to hear and believe*," and he called for even more such sermons to beat back the tide of abolitionist sentiments he argued were issuing forth from northern pulpits.[22]

Newspapers were just the first step in the viral publication of secessionist sermons. The *True Delta* issued a pamphlet edition of Palmer's address before the year was out. Additional versions were printed in Louisiana, Alabama, and New York, among other locations, and according to historian Jon Wakelyn, as many as ninety thousand copies of the sermon were eventually circulated. Early in 1861, a pamphlet containing Palmer and Leacock's sermons was issued with the title *The Rights of the South Defended in the Pulpits*, and both were included, along with sermons from several other northern and southern clergymen, in *Spirit of the Pulpit with Reference to the Present Crisis*. Interested persons throughout the South and beyond could, within just a few weeks, read what the *Richmond Daily Dispatch* called their "remarkable" defense of slavery and Palmer's call for the South to resist the forces of abolition that he believed threatened not just the South but the entire nation. Already a noted divine in the 1850s, he would become especially celebrated. He left New Orleans shortly before Federal occupation and spent the remaining war years as a Confederate chaplain, hailed as a hero of the Confederate cause. After the war, he returned to his post at First Presbyterian, where he became a leading contributor to the burgeoning Lost Cause mythology.[23]

In this way, the fire-eating words of Palmer and—to a lesser extent—Leacock spread throughout the South. While it is impossible to know exactly how much influence they had on southerners in Louisiana, South Carolina, or any other state, their sermons joined a chorus of men who agitated and pushed for secession as their countrymen tried to decide the best response to Lincoln's election. As one New Orleanian observed, respected clergymen's eloquent sermons, supporting slavery's place in the southern states and arguing that those states now had no viable option but secession, gave weight to the position of men pushing for an immediate dissolution of the Union. Fire-eaters cheered to garner support for Leacock, Palmer, and ministers in other churches who expressed similar sentiments. Despite lingering suspicion of ministers' political activity—Palmer, after all, opened his Thanksgiving sermon by reminding his listeners that he had always avoided political questions and vowing that only the gravity of the crisis moved him to broach the topic—they were generally respected for their learning and rhetorical skills and were looked to as moral guides. Secessionist preachers, especially Palmer, were influential and persuasive voices in the chaotic months following the presidential election, and they helped push Louisiana toward disunion.[24]

Although Palmer and others were celebrated for their sermons during the winter of 1860–61, not all Louisianans approved of such activism in the churches. The *Baton Rouge Gazette and Comet*, on the same day that it published "by request" John Gierlow's "appeal to peace," issued a statement condemning the political content of recent Thanksgiving sermons, stating that "one of the ugliest features in the distorted physiognomy of the times, is the introduction of local and party politics into the pulpit." With a dig at northern preachers who advocated abolition, the writer went on to lament, "the hope was indulged that in this section of the Union the clergy would have the spiritual strength to withstand the torrent of what is called public opinion, but mortal as they are, and subject to all the passions and emotions of their flocks, they have fallen in with the tide." The author did not mention any ministers by name, but with Leacock and Palmer already receiving widespread attention for their sermons, readers would naturally have thought of them.[25]

The *Gazette and Comet* saw considerable danger in their actions, noting, "if the pulpit has any influence to bring into the area of politics, it should be of peace." The writer, like many others in Louisiana, placed much of the blame for the current crisis on northern agitators who "would abolish not only the law, but the gospel of the law, to establish an equality that cannot and will not exist in the nature of things," but he also saw danger in the prospect of disunion, adding "it is much easier to destroy than it is to construct." Louisiana did not need clergymen to inflame matters further. Instead, they needed wise leaders, "sober men," who would help them calmly assess the current situation and determine the best way to move forward. Men of God should not stir up their listeners, especially when political actions were likely to lead to war. Secession was, as many in Louisiana recognized, a serious step that could have serious, even disastrous, consequences for that state and the rest of the South.

To the *Gazette and Comet*, encouraging such a step, especially from the pulpit, which should be a font of deliberate wisdom, seemed reckless.[26]

Some private citizens also found pro-secession sermons distasteful. Reluctantly, Unionist Dora Richards went with a relative to hear Palmer's Thanksgiving sermon. Although "the church was crowded to suffocation" with people who favored his sentiments, Richards enjoyed neither the experience nor the words. The service "over at last," she was thankful that such an experience need not be repeated because her own Episcopal church had a "fixed liturgy" that limited the rector's time for expressing political beliefs. Later that day, when asked if Palmer had convinced her of slavery's justness and the need for secession, Richards retorted, "I was so busy thinking how completely it proved too that Brigham Young is right about polygamy that it quite weakened the force of the argument for me." Others who read the address had a similar reaction. In Livingston Parish, W. H. Pearce condemned the Thanksgiving sermons of both Palmer and Leacock and thought that "the influence of such men when they become Partizans . . . must be potent for evil." Pearce and others like him believed that ministers should remain aloof from politics, especially during the secession crisis. As John Ellis remarked to his mother, he missed Palmer's Thanksgiving discourse, "& am glad of it." Ellis supported states' rights and eventually served in the Confederate army, but he was uncomfortable with the strong disunion statements issuing from the pulpit. In early January 1861, the *New York Times* published a letter from a New Orleans merchant who witnessed the extreme enthusiasm of his fellow citizens for Palmer's sermon with bewilderment and fear. He saw Palmer's popularity as part of an atmosphere where "the class who rule by noise" agitated loudly for secession, "and none others are yet heard."[27]

Leacock and Palmer remained the figures on whom the debate over ministers' political speech was focused. Gierlow, whose Thanksgiving sermon was probably least attuned to prevailing opinion as expressed in newspapers and other public venues, received much less publicity. There are several plausible reasons. Events in New Orleans, a major port city of more than 150,000, were more likely to garner notice than events in Baton Rouge, which, despite being the state capital, was a relatively insignificant town of just over five thousand. Likewise, the New Orleans churches, First Presbyterian and Christ Church, were much larger than St. James in Baton Rouge. Palmer was already a celebrated figure whose sermons, even before the secession crisis, were frequently printed in local newspapers. Finally, he and Leacock preached dramatic sermons that both supported the arguments of vocal secessionists and confirmed the fears of observers in other parts of the country. Gierlow's address, on the other hand, rambled among several points and went against the grain by calling for peace. Few ministers in Louisiana tried to express dissenting views in their sermons, and those who did could expect opposition. Gierlow admitted as much when he asked his congregation to "bear with my freedom of speech." Beyond this "appeal to peace," little evidence exists for sermons preached against immediate secession.[28]

At the same time, however, many in Louisiana were opposed to immediate secession and hoped either for combined action by southern states or to stay in the Union. In New Orleans, for example, many of the city's more than 65,000 foreign-born residents opposed secession, as did a proportion of those who were born in non-slaveholding states. It is perhaps not insignificant that Gierlow was himself an immigrant who would in 1861 resign his position in Baton Rouge and move to Maine. Unionist Dora Richards, born in the Caribbean to an English father, grew increasingly uncomfortable as the secessionist fervor of her family and friends grew. By January of 1861, Richards reported that many Unionists, even those who were not Episcopalians, attended Trinity Episcopal Church because the structure of the service meant "the pastor has not so much chance" to preach in favor of secession. Bishop Leonidas Polk, who supported secession, was rector of Trinity, but even he could not easily subvert the *Book of Common Prayer*'s structure. At Episcopal and Catholic churches, the sermon or homily was shorter and played a less prominent role than in Baptist, Methodist, or other evangelical churches, where preaching was the primary activity.[29]

Those Louisianans who had commercial ties to other states and regions also frequently opposed secession because they recognized that their interests would be much better served if the Union remained intact. For example, Haller Nutt, who owned plantations in Louisiana and Mississippi and had trade relationships throughout the United States, hoped that cooperationist men would be elected to the upcoming convention that would decide Louisiana's fate because "the commercial interests of New Orleans are too important to take hasty steps without due reflection." Many in that city agreed. In early 1861, the *New York Times* printed a letter from a New Orleans merchant who opposed secession but saw "the immense popularity of Dr. PALMER's Thanksgiving sermon" as proof that "fire-eaters are in the ascendant still, and nothing but dissolution will do, nor can I see anything to indicate any ray of hope for the maintenance of the Union." In his view, Palmer's sermon was in line with the sentiments that he heard expressed in public and in private. He noted that trade had slowed and that "quiet, sensible people see anarchy and oligarchy approaching, and look forward with fear." Even among this population, however, a range of opinions existed, and those opinions could change as time passed.[30]

Voting patterns in the 1860 presidential election and the 1861 election for the secession convention reflect the complexity of political sentiment in the state. Louisiana's electoral votes went to John C. Breckinridge, who received 44.9 percent of the popular vote, while 40 percent went to John Bell of the Constitutional Union Party and 15.1 percent went to Stephen Douglas. Most of the support for Bell and Douglas came from New Orleans and its surrounding parishes. Those who voted for Bell and Douglas could be considered at least suspicious of the idea of immediate secession. By the time Louisianans voted for delegates for the secession convention on January 7, just two months after the presidential election, the situation had worsened for those who opposed secession. Almost 53 percent of the vote and at least 80 of 130 available seats went to secessionists, who advocated leaving the Union immediately. Secessionists were more vocal and more organized than Cooperationists, a grouping that encompassed a variety of opinions about the best course of action, ranging from staying in the Union to seceding in concert with the other southern states. Secessionists had prominent clergymen like Palmer on their side, proclaiming the rightness of disunion from the pulpit. Moreover, by early January 1861, South Carolina and several more states looked likely to do the same, setting a precedent and making a course of action that just a few months earlier had been almost unthinkable now seem inevitable. As John Sacher has noted, Louisiana's Unionism was always conditional. When the state's citizens believed that the problems of staying in the Union outweighed the effects of secession, they voted for disunion. Palmer, Leacock, and others who preached in favor of secession played a significant role in helping Louisianans come to that belief.[31]

As they had done during times of crisis in previous decades, civic leaders declared days of fasting and prayer throughout late 1860 and early 1861. President James Buchanan set January 4, 1861, as one such day. Following this request, the Episcopal bishops of Mississippi and Louisiana issued prayers to

be used in their denomination's churches. Bishop Polk's prayer first acknowledged that national and individual sins had provoked God's wrath and begged
for His mercy before asking, "if it please thee, compose and heal the divisions
which disturb us." By this point, however, just three days before the election
of a secession convention, few in Louisiana, including Polk, believed that the
divisions could be healed. The prayer went on to ask "that the spirit of wisdom
and moderation may preside over our council, that the just rights of all may be
maintained and accorded." There is little evidence that the fast day provoked
the same kind of fiery sermons that had been preached on Thanksgiving Day
five weeks earlier, likely because so many believed that the outcome of the
election and the actions of the convention were foregone conclusions.[32]

At the secession convention, clergy continued to offer their support for
the enterprise, as they did for other official business. Rev. W. E. M. Linfield,
a Methodist minister, opened the proceedings with a prayer on January 23.
When secession was proclaimed, Linfield again offered a prayer, and the state
flag was blessed, "according to the rights and forms of the Roman Catholic
Church," by Father Darius Hubert. With that important step taken, the convention then had to turn to such matters as amending the state constitution
to reflect the current circumstances and appointing commissioners to meet
with representatives from other southern states, and it remained active until
March 26. Each session was opened with a prayer from one of the state's ministers, including Presbyterians Benjamin Palmer and T. R Markham, Catholics
Napoléon-Joseph Perché and J. Moynihan, and Episcopalians C. S. Hedges and
Charles Goodrich, among others.[33]

Once accomplished, Louisiana's secession necessitated changes to worship
services, especially in Episcopal churches. Unlike the Baptists, Methodists,
and Presbyterians, the Protestant Episcopal Church in the United States remained intact in early 1861. In Episcopal churches in every part of the nation,
prayers for the president and Congress were a standard part of the liturgy.
Once Louisiana left the Union, Bishop Polk was faced with the question of
how to proceed. He sprang quickly into action. In a pastoral letter issued just
after Louisiana seceded, he provided new prayers for the governor and legislature of the state to replace those for U.S. officials. Polk admitted that he
lacked authority under the constitution and canons of the national church to
alter the liturgy in this way, but he believed that "the duty we owed to the Law
of Christ Himself" justified the step. More was needed, however. As members

of the Committee on the State of the Church noted, the denomination was a national body. Now, several southern states had left the United States, which left their Episcopal dioceses in an uncomfortable limbo. Bishop Polk declared that, in Louisiana "an Independent Diocesan existence" prevailed. Other bishops, most notably Thomas Atkinson of North Carolina, were uncomfortable with this declaration, and all agreed that the status of the churches must be regularized. As the southern states banded together into a confederacy in the spring of 1861, southern Episcopal dioceses did the same. Polk led the way. On March 23, he and Stephen Elliott of Georgia, as the senior bishops among those whose states had seceded at that point, sent a letter to their brother bishops arguing that political events "forced upon us by a stern necessity" meant that they must now reconsider their relationship to the U.S. Episcopal Church. They invited each diocese to send delegates to a July convention in Montgomery, Alabama, where the Episcopal Church in the Confederate States would be formed.[34]

The other national religious organization left in 1861 did not face the same problems. The Catholic Church was an international institution, so the disintegration of national bonds did not affect the relationship of individual dioceses or archdioceses to the larger denomination. Moreover, Catholic doctrine did not oppose slavery, which meant that southern bishops could uphold the institutions of the states in which they lived with clear consciences. During the antebellum period, American Catholic bishops had rarely spoken on political matters, and most continued this course during the secession crisis. In Louisiana, the death of archbishop Antoine Blanc in the summer of 1860 left a void that was not filled until Pius IX appointed Jean-Marie Odin, the French-born bishop of Texas, in February 1861. Odin was consecrated in New Orleans in May 1861 and was an ardent secessionist, supporting his priests as they blessed departing regiments and prayed for the fledgling nation.[35]

In the spring and early summer of 1861, military units began to leave for the front, and many churches held special dedication services, during which the minister blessed the regimental standard and preached a sermon in honor of the soldiers and their cause. In May, Dora Richards reported that regiments filled "the prominent churches" in New Orleans for these ceremonies, and she attended a service at Christ Episcopal Church where William Leacock blessed the Washington Artillery before its departure. The artillery's flags were placed along the chancel rail, and Leacock gave an address reminding the soldiers of their position as Louisiana's finest, assuring them, "our prayers will ascend for your safety and return." Similar scenes occurred in houses of worship across the state. Kate Sully, for example, witnessed the blessing of a local company's flag at the Catholic Church in Mandeville, and the event made a profound impact upon her. In northern Louisiana, several members of the Stone family attended the ceremony for the Madison Parish Militia and reported a large crowd present. As sermons in favor of secession had done, these services gave the blessing of the clergy to southern efforts to achieve independence.[36]

Louisiana ministers did not act in isolation, of course. Although Palmer was perhaps the most visible of the politically active ministers, clergymen in other states, North and South, preached on the secession crisis as well, and all of their voices combined to add to the political ferment of the time. When Sarah Ker Butler of Terrebonne Parish read Thomas Atkinson's January 1861 fast day sermon, she noted that "it embodies the feeling, which has made it impossible (to me) to feel enthusiasm on *our* side." Atkinson, Episcopal bishop of North Carolina, was a rare southern clergyman who opposed secession. His sermon asked southerners to consider the horrors of civil war rather than charging recklessly toward secession, a sentiment that resonated with Butler. She believed that "we should demand & defend our *rights*, but it seems *awful* to see *Brethren* arrayed against one another." Atkinson would continue to preach against the tide through the spring of 1861 until North Carolina seceded."[37]

Atkinson, like Gierlow, was an exception. As in Louisiana, most ministers in other southern states were strongly in favor of secession. In Vicksburg, William Lord, rector of Christ Episcopal Church, delivered a sermon on December 10 that became part of the rising chorus calling for secession. Preaching on a text from Isaiah, he "pronounced woe upon those who setting up their own judgement and their own code of morals instead of religion, and the scriptures, condemn that which has been sanctioned both by the bible, and by ancient usage." Although he spoke "so delicately that he did not once speak the word slavery, or secession, . . . yet everyone knew what he was speaking of," according to parishioner Sarah Wadley. She and her family had admired Palmer's Thanksgiving address and were pleased to hear their own minister preaching in the same vein. Pro-secession sermons were preached all over the South by leading divines such as James Henley Thornwell and by little known clergymen at small churches.[38]

Religious expression became no less important during the war years.

Churches were places where victories were celebrated and losses mourned. In areas controlled by Union troops, sermons and prayers became political speech that could exacerbate existing conflicts between occupiers and occupied. After Federal forces took New Orleans and the surrounding area, for example, Episcopal ministers continued to include prayers for Jefferson Davis and the Confederate government in the liturgy, which drew the attention of Benjamin Butler, Union commander of New Orleans. Eventually, Butler arrested seven Episcopal ministers and sent three of them, including William Leacock of Christ Church, to a military prison in New York. Union army chaplains replaced the rebellious ministers. Although most Episcopal churches continued to function, the issue still simmered as late as March 1864, when Charles Hilton, an Episcopal minister residing in New Orleans, lamented, "I am not permitted to preach in my own Church unless I use the prayer for the President of the United States. What is this but compulsion?" Hilton refused to obey, and later that month the Federal commander banished him into Confederate-held territory. Northerners, many of them Union chaplains, were placed in the pulpits of several Baptist, Methodist, and Presbyterian churches as well.[39]

Additionally, both the United States and the Confederacy appointed fast and thanksgiving days at periodic intervals, which offered time for civilians to gather in church to support their cause through preaching and prayer. Once the Union army arrived in south Louisiana, commanders demanded that churches abandon Confederate holidays and take up those of the United States. Not surprisingly, some ministers in occupied areas like New Orleans and Baton Rouge refused to do so. This type of resistance to Federal officials was a way for clergymen to show their continued support for the Confederacy even though they no longer lived or preached within its borders and could express that support only through prayers.[40]

In these frenzied months of 1860 and 1861 when southerners debated and feared for their future, sermons and religious services played an important role in the process. Churches are institutions that support community norms and give them the sanctity of God's approval. By extension, ministers were seen as moral guides whose sermons showed men and women how they must live. Sermons in favor of secession lent credibility to those who argued in favor of an immediate dissolution of the Union. At the same time, religious services provided an outlet for anxiety over events that most could not control. When ministers preached in favor of secession, arguing that God was on the side of the South, the message was comforting to those who considered dissolution of the Union the right course of action. Clergymen, even the persuasive Palmer, did not lead southerners out of the Union, but they helped create an atmosphere in which secession seemed morally and politically acceptable. With God on their side, how could secessionists lose?

NOTES

1. Benjamin Palmer, *Thanksgiving Sermon, Delivered at the First Presbyterian Church, New Orleans* (New York: George F. Nesbitt & Co., 1861), 4. For a description of the event, see George C. Rable, *God's Almost Chosen Peoples: A Religious History of the American Civil War* (Chapel Hill: University of North Carolina Press, 2010), 35–36.

2. Richard Carwardine, "Methodists, Politics and the Coming of the American Civil War," *Church History* 69, no. 3 (Sept. 2000): 583–86; Theodore Clapp, *Autobiographical Sketches and Recollections during a Thirty-Five Years' Residence in New Orleans* (Boston: Phillips, Sampson, & Company, 1858), 362–63; W. T. Leacock, "Thanksgiving Sermon, Preached in Christ's Church, New Orleans, on Thanksgiving Day," in *Spirit of the Pulpit with Reference to the Present Crisis,* supplement to *The Rebellion Record,* ed. Frank Moore (New York: G. P. Putnam, 1861), 53. For discussion of southern views on political sermons, see Mitchell Snay, *Gospel of Disunion: Religion and Separatism in the Antebellum South* (Cambridge: Cambridge University Press, 1993), 142–43; Bertram Wyatt-Brown, "Church, Honor, and Secession," in *Religion and the American Civil War,* ed. Randall M. Miller, Harry S. Stout, and Charles Reagan Wilson (New York: Oxford University Press, 1998), 96–98.

3. Theodore Clapp, *Slavery: A Sermon Delivered in the First Congregational Church in New Orleans* (New Orleans: Office of the True American, 1838), 66 (quotation). For Clapp's views on slavery, see Patrick Reilly, "Parson Clapp of New Orleans: Antebellum Social Critic, Religious Radical, and Member of the Establishment" *Louisiana History* 16, no. 2 (Spring 1975): 183–84. See also Carwardine, "Methodists, Politics, and the Coming of the American Civil War," 583–84; Edward Crowther, "Holy Honor: Sacred and Secular in the Old South," *Journal of Southern History* 58, no. 4 (November 1992): 634–35; Snay, *Gospel of Disunion,* 142–43.

4. Carwardine, "Methodists, Politics, and the Coming of the American Civil War," 598–99; C. C. Goen, *Broken Churches, Broken Nation: Denominations Schisms and the Coming of the American Civil War* (Macon, GA: Mercer University Press, 1985), 66–67; Snay, *Gospel of Disunion,* 115–38.

5. Crowther, "Holy Honor," 620. According to Benjamin Palmer's biographer, Old School Presbyterians remained intact until 1861 by agreeing that political pronouncements lay outside a minister's purview. There were also relatively few southern churches in the Old School branch. Christopher M. Duncan, "Benjamin Morgan Palmer: Southern Presbyterian Divine" (PhD diss., Auburn University, 2008), 123. See also Goen, *Broken Churches,* 134–35; Rable, *God's Almost Chosen Peoples,* 37, 59–60.

6. Leacock, "Thanksgiving Sermon," 51–53.

7. Ibid., 53–54.

8. Duncan, "Benjamin Morgan Palmer," 4, 68–69, 105–6, 130.

9. Palmer, *Thanksgiving Sermon*, 3. See Snay, *Gospel of Disunion*, 156–57. Snay also provides a close explication of Palmer's sermon (175–80).

10. Palmer, *Thanksgiving Sermon*, 4–5.

11. Ibid., 6.

12. Ibid., 8–12. See Snay, *Gospel of Disunion*, 177–78.

13. Palmer, *Thanksgiving Sermon*, 13–16. See Snay, *Gospel of Disunion*, 178; John Patrick Daly, *When Slavery Was Called Freedom: Evangelicalism, Proslavery, and the Causes of the Civil War* (Lexington: University Press of Kentucky, 2002), 141.

14. Palmer, *Thanksgiving Sermon*, 17–19. See also Snay, *Gospel of Disunion*, 178–79; Matthew Clavin, *Toussaint Louverture and the American Civil War: The Promise and Peril of a Second Haitian Revolution* (Philadelphia: University of Pennsylvania Press, 2009), 62–63.

15. Palmer, *Thanksgiving Sermon*, 19–20.

16. John Gierlow, "An Appeal to Peace," *Baton Rouge Daily Gazette and Comet*, December 4, 1860.

17. Ibid.

18. Ibid.; Leacock, "Thanksgiving Sermon," 54.

19. Gierlow, "An Appeal to Peace."

20. Ibid. Not surprisingly, most southern ministers preferred, like Leacock and Palmer, to place blame for the crisis on the North. See Snay, *Gospel of Disunion*, 148.

21. "From Louisiana," *Nashville Union and American*, December 4, 1860; Sarah Wadley Diary, December 4, 1860, Documenting the American South, University of North Carolina at Chapel Hill, http://docsouth.unc.edu; Benjamin Palmer, "The Question of the Day: Thanksgiving Sermon," *Nashville Union and American*, December 12, 1860; "Fire-Eating Preachers in the South," *Cincinnati Daily Press*, December 10, 1860; "Latest from the South," *Washington National Republican*, December 3, 1860; "Louisiana," *New York Daily Tribune*, December 1, 1860; "Eastern News," *Salt Lake City Mountaineer*, January 5, 1861; Thomas Pollock to his mother, n.d., Abram David Pollock Papers, Southern Historical Collection, University of North Carolina. See also Rable, *God's Almost Chosen Peoples*, 36.

22. "Letter from Theodore Johnston," *Plaquemine Gazette and Sentinel*, December 8, 1860.

23. "Interesting Sermons," *Richmond Daily Dispatch*, January 22, 1861. For publishing estimates, see Jon Wakelyn, introduction to *Southern Pamphlets on Secession, November 1860–April 1861* (Chapel Hill: University of North Carolina Press, 1996), xv. For Palmer's wartime and postwar career, see Duncan, "Benjamin Morgan Palmer," 142–53.

24. "Sentiment of Louisiana: Extract of a private letter from a Merchant of New-Orleans to a Gentleman in New-York," *New York Times*, January 7, 1861. John Sacher gives Palmer considerable credit for helping persuade Louisianans about secession in *A Perfect War of Politics: Parties, Politicians, and Democracy in Louisiana, 1824–1861* (Baton Rouge: Louisiana State University Press, 2007), 291, 296.

25. "Thanksgiving Sermons," *Baton Rouge Daily Gazette and Comet*, December 4, 1860.

26. Ibid.

27. Dora Richards Miller Civil War Diary, May 27, 1862, Special Collections, Howard-Tilton Memorial Library, Tulane University, New Orleans, Louisiana (hereinafter cited as TU); Sarah Ker Butler to Margaret Butler, April 16, 1861, Margaret Butler Correspondence, Louisiana and Lower Mississippi Valley Collections, Hill Memorial Library, Louisiana State University, Baton Rouge (hereinafter cited as LLMVC); W. H. Pearce to John W. Gurley, December 3, 1860, John W. Gurley Papers, LLMVC; E. John Ellis to Emily Ellis, November 31, 1860, E. John and Thomas C. W. Ellis and Family Papers, LLMVC; "Sentiment of Louisiana."

28. Historical Census Browser, University of Virginia, Geospatial and Statistical Data Center, http://mapserver.lib.virginia.edu/collections/stats/histcensus/index.html; Gierlow, "An Appeal to Peace." As George Rable notes, the most determined and loudest voices received the most attention, and those voices were calling for immediate secession. Rable, *God's Almost Chosen Peoples,* 39. For discussion of Unionist sermons, primarily in the upper South, see Snay, *Gospel of Disunion,* 200–201.

29. Historical Census Browser, University of Virginia, Geospatial and Statistical Data Center; George Burgess, "Annual Address," *Journal of the Forty-Fourth Annual Convention of the Protestant Episcopal Church in the Diocese of Maine* (July 8, 1863): 18; Dora Richards Miller Civil War Diary, December 1860, January 28, 1861, TU.

30. Haller Nutt to Alonzo Snyder, December 16, 1860, Alonzo Snyder Papers, LLMVC; "Sentiment of Louisiana." See Sacher, *Perfect War of Politics,* 293.

31. For discussion of secession in Louisiana, see Sacher, *Perfect War of Politics,* 287–91, 294–97, 299–301.

32. Leonidas Polk, "Pastoral Letter of January 30, 1861," in *Extracts from the Journal of the Twenty-Third Annual Convention of the Protestant Episcopal Church in the Diocese of Louisiana* (New Orleans: Bulletin Book and Job Office, 1861), 9, Documenting the American South.

33. *Official Journal of the Proceedings of the Convention of the State of Louisiana* (New Orleans: J. O. Nixon, 1861), 3, 18, 19, 24, 30, 33, 34, 36, 39, 42, 45, 47, 51, 68. See also Sacher, *Perfect War of Politics,* 297.

34. Leonidas Polk, "Address," in *Extracts from the Twenty-Third Annual Convention,* 4 (first quote); Leonidas Polk, "Pastoral Letter of January 30, 1861," 9 (second quote); "Report of the Committee on the State of the Church," in *Extracts from the Twenty-Third Annual Convention,* 16; "Circular of the Rt. Rev., the Bishops of Louisiana and Georgia, 23 March 1861," in *Proceedings of a Meeting of Bishops, Clergymen, and Laymen, of the Protestant Episcopal Church in the Confederate States, at Montgomery, Alabama, On the 3d, 4th, 5th, &6th of July, 1861* (Montgomery: Barrett, Wimbish & Co., 1861), 3–4. See Jon L. Wakelyn, "The Contributions of the Southern Episcopal Church to Confederate Unity and Morale," in *Confederates Against the Confederacy: Essays on Leadership and Loyalty* (Westport: Praeger, 2002), 81–83.

35. Rable, *God's Almost Chosen Peoples,* 59–61; Randall M. Miller, "Catholics in a Protestant World: The Old South Example," in *Varieties of Southern Religious Experience,* ed. Samuel S. Hill (Baton Rouge: Louisiana State University Press, 1988), 122–23, 126–29; James M. Woods, *A History of the Catholic Church in the American South, 1513–1900* (Gainesville: University Press of Florida, 2011), 286.

36. Dora Richards Miller Civil War Diary, May 27, 1862, TU; William Miller Owen, *In Camp*

and *In Battle with the Washington Artillery of New Orleans* (1885; Baton Rouge: Louisiana State University Press, 1999), 8–9; Kate Sully to Mary Jane Robertson, June 28, 1861, Mary Jane Robertson Papers, LLMVC; John Q. Anderson, ed., *Brokenburn: The Journal of Kate Stone, 1861–1868* (Baton Rouge: Louisiana State University Press, 1995), 25–26. See also Jefferson Davis Bragg, *Louisiana in the Confederacy* (Baton Rouge: Louisiana State University Press, 1997), 59; Rable, *God's Almost Chosen Peoples*, 69–72; Daly, *When Slavery Was Called Freedom*, 142–45. Gardiner Shattuck, *A Shield and Hiding Place: The Religious Life of the Civil War Armies* (Macon: Mercer University Press, 1987), 35–36, specifically examines the ceremony for the Washington Artillery.

37. Sarah Ker Butler to Margaret Butler, April 16, 1861, Margaret Butler Correspondence, LLMVC; Thomas Atkinson, *Christian Duty in the Present Time of Trouble* (Wilmington, NC: Fulton and Price Steam Powered Press Printers, 1861), Documenting the American South. See Wakelyn, *Southern Pamphlets*, 391; Snay, *Gospel of Disunion*, 200–201.

38. Sarah Wadley Diary, December 10, 1860. The twenty-one sermons collected in *Spirit of the Pulpit*, e.g., included discourses by James Henley Thornwell and Robert Dabney, as well as the Thanksgiving sermons by Palmer and Leacock. See also Snay, *Gospel of Disunion*, 152–53, 155–56, 200–201.

39. Benjamin F. Butler to E. M. Stanton, October 25, 1862, in Jessie Ames Marshall, ed., *Private and Official Correspondence of Gen. Benjamin F. Butler During the Period of the Civil War*, 5 vols. (Norwood, MA: Plimpton Press, 1917), 2:407–8; W. C. Corsan, *Two Months in the Confederate States: An Englishman's Travels Through the South*, ed. Benjamin H. Trask (1863; Baton Rouge: Louisiana State University Press, 1996), 21–22; Kate Mason Roland and Agnes Croxall, eds., *The Journal of Julia LeGrand, 1862-1863* (Richmond: Everett Waddley, 1911), 53; Charles L. Harrod Account, October 31, 1862, Christ Church, New Orleans, and General Butler Collection, TU; Diary of Charles Hilton, March 17, 1865, TU; *Shreveport Semi-Weekly News*, "Report on the Presbyterian and Baptist Churches," November 15, 1864. See also Rable, *God's Almost Chosen Peoples*, 322–23, 325–26.

40. For celebration of Confederate fast and thanksgiving days, see, e.g., Hephzibah Church Books, June 13, 1861, and July 1861, LLMVC; Anderson, *Brokenburn*, 24–25, 44–45, 106; *Shreveport Semi-Weekly News*, December 13, 1864, and February 28, 1865. For Federal fast days, see Broadsides, April 27 and November 24, 1863, Baton Rouge Civil War Broadsides, LLMVC; Diary of Rev. Charles Hilton, January 24, 1865, TU. For defiance of Federal fast days, see Calvin S. Hendrick to J. M. Rugall, May 19, 1862, Hendrick Letter, LLMVC; Benjamin F. Butler, General Orders No. 27, Marshall, *Private and Official Correspondence*, 1:477. See also Rable, *God's Almost Chosen Peoples*, 73–74; Snay, *Gospel of Disunion*, 160–66.

PART II

THE DIVERSE CHALLENGES OF WAR

CHAPTER FOUR

Confederate Dilemmas

The Strange Case of Clement L. Vallandigham

George C. Rable

O n January 21, 1861, the *Charleston Mercury* reported from Washington that even northern Democrats had "drifted from the States Rights doctrines of the fathers" and had declared that "they owed no allegiance to their States, but to the Federal Government, immediately and alone."[1] The source of this information was Ohio congressman Clement Laird Vallandigham, a man who had seemingly remained true to the old faith. Secessionists and later Confederates would grow to appreciate Vallandigham, whose political career had begun at a county Democratic party convention when he was barely out of his teens. Well might the *Mercury* have applauded this Buckeye, who had been a consistent states' rights man and had shown nothing but contempt for abolitionists.[2] Yet his political career could most charitably be described as checkered. He had lost his first four runs for public office. On a fifth try (and his third contest for Congress), he had been defeated again, though by only nineteen votes, and after contesting the election was seated by a Democratic-controlled House of Representatives.

Perhaps because of his family's Virginia roots and his wife's ties to Kentucky, he soon developed cordial relations with southern House colleagues. He claimed to abhor the institution of slavery yet considered it a local concern and like many of his southern friends dismissed abolitionists as wild-eyed "Jacobins." Reelected in 1858—this time without the help of disputed returns—Vallandigham sided with Stephen A. Douglas in his fight with James Buchanan over the Kansas troubles but nevertheless voted with southern Democrats on some key measures, including the possible annexation of Cuba. When Republican editors later denounced the Ohioan as the slaveholders' lackey, it could only have improved his standing in the South. By 1860, however, Vallandigham refused to go along with southern Democrats' demands for some guarantee of protection for slavery in the national territories, campaigned for presidential candidate Stephen A. Douglas, and headed the National Democratic Campaign Committee. With secession threats flying should Republican Abraham Lincoln win the presidency, Vallandigham stated privately and publicly that he would not "vote one dollar of money whereby one drop of American blood should be shed in a civil war."[3] In December 1860, he even traveled to Richmond, Virginia, to make a heartfelt plea for sectional compromise and later denounced federal "coercion" of any state in unmeasured language.

As congressional discussion of compromise proposals began, Vallandigham weighed in with a wildly impractical and complicated scheme to divide the country into four sections for purposes of electing the president and vice president by "concurrent voice" (à la John C. Calhoun). This thirteenth amendment to the U.S. Constitution would then be followed by a fourteenth amendment allowing a state to secede under certain conditions and a fifteenth amendment essentially establishing the principle of popular sovereignty in all national territories. On February 20, 1861, Vallandigham addressed the House at considerable length, calling for peace but once again rejecting efforts to coerce a state back into the Union.[4] After the Confederates fired on Fort Sumter, Vallandigham condemned Lincoln's response but hoped that somehow the war fever would eventually break in both sections. Many Ohioans were outraged over such talk, and the Confederate press carried an account of a mob assaulting Vallandigham and destroying his house—a false report soon corrected.[5]

Besides turning into a political lightning rod, Vallandigham had become the spokesman for the most uncompromising antiwar Democrats. A public letter denouncing Lincoln's "audacious usurpation of power" and even suggesting that the new president "deserves impeachment" naturally created a sensation in the northern states.[6] At the same time, Vallandigham was attracting notice in the newly established Confederate capital, Richmond.[7] On the evening of July 4, he attended a Democratic caucus and stood alone against war and for compromise; soon rumors appeared in the southern press that he had loudly declared a preference for peace over preservation of the Union.[8]

From this point on, Confederates paid increasing attention to the Ohio congressman. The southern press reprinted his speeches and closely followed his actions in Congress; Republican denunciations of Vallandigham as a secessionist and traitor undoubtedly added to his renown below the Mason Dixon line. His more strident remarks made him stand out among northern politicians who appeared united against the southern rebellion and likely made some Confederates see Vallandigham as an ally if not a champion of their cause. A long speech in the House on July 10, 1861, offers a case in point. Vallandigham traced the war back to aggressive antislavery politicians who had failed to respect southern property rights. Aside from blaming Republicans for the war, he criticized the Lincoln administration's policies as dangerous and unconstitutional usurpations.[9] Many Confederates could not have said it better themselves, and in any case they could read the full text of the speech in their newspapers. And read it they did. At a family dinner in Charleston, young Emma Holmes read aloud from this "splendid speech," quoting with approval Vallandigham's constitutional exegesis but also appreciating his "scorn & sarcasm" against "Old Abe." In her diary, she added an encomium seldom accorded a Yankee by a South Carolinian: "all honor is due to one of the few honest men left at the North." Near Manassas, Virginia, an Alabama soldier who was unwell lay in his tent one Sunday morning poring over Vallandigham's address in his hometown newspaper. He admired the attack on the Lincoln administration, as did many southern editors who spread the speech across their front pages.[10]

It did not take long for Confederates, eager to seize on any divisions among their enemies, to begin exalting Vallandigham as a heroic figure. Perhaps his ideological rigidity and commitment to "principle" also won their applause, even as it reflected a mindset akin to that of the most ardent disunionists. Summing up the views of many Confederates, a Mississippi editor praised him as a "noble champion of Constitutional freedom." Others thought him worthy of comparison with the great figures of Greek and Roman antiquity. Proslavery ideologue George Fitzhugh noted Vallandigham's Huguenot ancestry and found him a perfect foil to the northern descendants of the bigoted Puritans. More often, Confederates preferred to see themselves as the legitimate heirs of the American founding fathers and maintained that subjugation by the cowardly Yankees was unthinkable, so they naturally appreciated Vallandigham's quoting William Pitt's (Lord Chatham) famous remark of 1777: "My lords, you cannot conquer America." Some editors therefore trumpeted Vallandigham as the Chatham of the current war.[11]

Even this early, however, thinking about their newfound defender threw Confederates into confusion, revealing their uncertain appraisals of northern opinion. Was Vallandigham's a lone voice crying out in a wilderness of howling Yankee barbarians and demagogues? That was one common assessment.

But at the same time, Confederate newspapers searched for, reported on, and often exaggerated the degree of northern support for Vallandigham and other peace Democrats.[12]

Much of this reflected rosy assessments of Confederate prospects. Early victories, especially Manassas, bred confidence if not overconfidence that the new southern nation was not only holding its own against Union forces but was about to assume its rightful place in the world. Confederate hopes for European intervention (the kind of intervention that had tipped the scales in the Revolutionary War) and an early end to the fighting suddenly rose when U.S. Navy captain Charles Wilkes stopped the British mail steamer *Trent* and seized Confederate commissioners James M. Mason and John Slidell. But Lincoln and secretary of state William H. Seward defused the crisis by releasing the diplomats while also claiming that the traditional American position on the rights of neutral vessels had been recognized by the British. Many Confederates viewed the outcome of the *Trent* crisis as an abject surrender by a spineless Lincoln administration. The *Athens Southern Banner* sounded dismissively contemptuous, claiming that the Yankees had proven themselves to be a "nation of cowards or a nation of fools." Not to be outshone when it came to blackguarding the enemy, a well-educated Georgia enlisted man thought it would be necessary to "call on the Hottentots & wild Africans to produce an instance of equal cowardice & self-stultification."[13]

At the outset of the diplomatic crisis, Vallandigham had predicted just such an outcome. "We have heard the first growl of the British lion," he remarked as events unfolded. "Now let us see who will cower." He expressed no doubt on that score, pointing with some relish to the "blustering and cowardly statesmanship" of the House Republicans and forecasting that Mason and Slidell would be quickly "surrendered," a well-chosen word that summed up his view of the pusillanimous Lincoln administration. After the president released the Confederate commissioners, Vallandigham defended himself in tense exchanges on the House floor as he continued to strike a belligerent stance toward the British. For their part, Republicans threw around words such as "disloyal," "rebel," and "traitor," and there was some talk of expelling Vallandigham from the House. Yet his most strident comments only reaffirmed what many Confederates already believed about the *Trent* affair and more generally about Yankee character, and they only added to southern esteem for Vallandigham.[14]

Again the reactions and analysis were scattershot and inconsistent. One

Georgia editor rejoiced over Vallandigham's remark that once Mason and Slidell boarded a British navy ship bound for England, they would be in effect "envoys and ambassadors of a recognized independent State." But others suggested that what the Ohioan really hoped was that several northern and western states would negotiate a separate peace with the Confederacy. The always-independent North Carolina editor William W. Holden even raised the possibility of "reunion"—a dangerous word to fling about in the Confederacy but one he uttered without flinching. Holden's editorial rival in Raleigh preferred to praise Vallandigham's "manliness and independence," along with his fearless defiance of the "Lincoln despotism"—even at the risk of being thrown into a northern "Bastille." He was now in Confederate parlance the "noble" Vallandigham who had dared speak the truth about the northern administration.[15]

Whatever the incongruities involved, Confederates kept heaping praise on their favorite northern congressman. He was after all a western man—not a "true Yankee"—though in wartime rhetoric that distinction often vanished. Indeed, in his remarks on the *Trent* matter, Vallandigham had shown how Lincoln and his advisors themselves displayed an often contradictory character, at once bullying and cowardly. At the same time, Confederates struggled to figure out the significance of Vallandigham's brave stand in the Yankee Congress. He was still an exception to the "vulgar, unprincipled, and conscienceless demagogues" in that body, sniffed the *Richmond Dispatch*. "Not as many righteous men can be found in Washington as were required to save Sodom from destruction." A Nashville editor conceded that Vallandigham's manner was "too hasty and passionate" but claimed that "for dauntless bravery, keen management and independent spirit, he stands before the whole of them." And perhaps he would not remain a lone figure for long. Making the wish the proverbial father to the thought, the *Vicksburg Whig*, duly noting the great fury in the North aroused by Vallandigham's speeches, still predicted the "incarceration of so courageous and prominent a gentleman might stir up the whole Northwest against the Administration and result in the overthrow of Seward [and] Lincoln."[16]

In forecasting Vallandigham's arrest, the editor obviously proved prophetic, but on the matter of assessing Vallandigham's real influence among their enemies, Confederates had much greater difficulty. In May 1862, after the U.S. Congress had adopted a measure abolishing slavery in the District of Columbia, North Carolina plantation mistress Catherine Edmondston noted how over the past several months Vallandigham had made a "splendid effort to arouse Congress to reason" but had "failed." She could only admire his political courage: "He is the only Northern man I ever desire to see during the whole remnant of my natural life & I would go far to see & thank him!"[17] Yet she admitted that so far his had been a lone-wolf brand of courage, and that cut to the very heart of the problem. For the time being, Edmondston and other Confederate commentators ignored Vallandigham's new political mantra: "The Constitution as it is, the Union as it was." Attention focused on military campaigns and the fall elections. The Republican majority in the Ohio legislature had redrawn the congressional district lines to remove one strongly Democratic county from Vallandigham's district and add a Republican one, so even in what would prove a good year for Democrats, his chances for reelection were poor. Although he had made a name for himself and the war's mounting casualties and apparent stalemate in the eastern theater, along with controversies over emancipation and the suspension of habeas corpus, greatly boosted his party, Republican charges of disloyalty hurt and helped send Vallandigham down to defeat.

During the summer and fall, the Confederate press paid little attention to their recently anointed paladin. A few sketchy reports told of Vallandigham stumping in Ohio and drawing large crowds or expressed hope that his example might spark a political uprising against the Lincoln administration in the old Northwest. His eventual defeat could largely be explained away by Republican gerrymandering, but Democratic gains across the North certainly heartened Confederates. At the same time, the man who for several months had been praised by southern editors as a courageous defender of states' rights and constitutional liberty was now simply a lame-duck congressman.[18]

Defeated but not forgotten—especially as Confederates interpreted recent events at the polls and on the battlefields as sure signs of northern war weariness. Vallandigham addressed a large meeting in New York City the day before the disastrous battle of Fredericksburg and called for peace based on some unspecified compromise. As the lame-duck congressional session began in early December, he warned Republicans against any attempt to destroy a state or set up a dictatorship but suggested that peace could only be made on the basis of reunion.[19]

Would Confederates accept peace on such terms? Did Vallandigham believe they would? And equally important, how did Confederates interpret the sentiments of their erstwhile northern ally? If he was, in fact, an ally at all. While a thoughtful Louisiana sergeant believed that Vallandigham was genuinely for peace, he also worried that a growing number of southerners might willingly come back into the Union. This soldier hardly considered that an acceptable settlement but feared that others did; worse yet, some likely favored "reconstruction," a word that had by this time become anathema to loyal Confederates.[20]

On January 14, 1863, in a set speech in the House, Vallandigham finally spelled out at greater length his ideas for reunion and peace.[21] He began by repeating a familiar indictment of the Republicans as a sectional party that had rejected all reasonable compromise and had thereby brought on the war. Under the ill-conceived policies of the Lincoln administration, liberty had become the war's major casualty; thus far, a weak Congress had kowtowed to executive usurpation. Echoing Confederate descriptions of the Lincoln administration's intentions and using strikingly similar language, he could imagine a war of "subjugation" and "conquest," while a war for "union" seemed like a contradiction and an impossibility. Indeed, despite considerable expenditure of money and men, the rebellion had not been defeated and the Union had not been restored. Confederates could well have cheered at this point, yet a more difficult issue arose. "But ought this war to continue?" Vallandigham asked. "I answer, no—not a day, not an hour. What then? Shall we separate? Again I answer, no, no, no! What then?" And with that question came the rub.

Before answering it, he returned to a historical analysis of the war's lessons that would have pleased Confederate politicians and editors. First of all, it had been abolition not slavery that had caused disunion. Vallandigham contemptuously rejected any claptrap about "the aggressions of the slave power," a "miserable spectre, that unreal mockery, has been exorcised and expelled by debt and taxation and blood." Indeed, if southerners—and most notably the Democratic party—still ruled in Washington, the country would be much better off. He had equally little use for talk about "the sin and barbarism of African slavery." There was "more of barbarism and sin, a thousand times, in the continuance of this war, the dissolution of the Union, the breaking up of this Government, and the enslavement of the white race, by debt and taxes and arbitrary power." Denying any "irrepressible conflict" between freedom and slavery or between North and South, he ridiculed the notion that emancipation could come through the sword or through proclamations.

Despite having once condemned slavery as an evil, he readily threw in some proslavery boilerplate: "African slavery has been, and is, eminently conservative. It makes the absolute political equality of the white race every-where practicable. It dispenses with the English order of nobility, and leaves every white man, North and South, owning slaves or owning none, the equal of every other white man. It has reconciled universal suffrage, throughout the free States, with the stability of government." Therefore, the source of the strife must lie elsewhere. Vallandigham reconfigured sectionalism by pointing to the "long standing mutual jealousies of New England and the South" that "will always be the chief obstacle in the way of full and absolute reunion." Turning to familiar literary and political themes that resonated in Confederate propaganda, he pointed to the "old conflict of the Cavalier and the Roundhead, the Liberalist and the Puritan; or, rather, it is a conflict, upon new issues, of the ideas and elements represented by those names. It is a war of the Yankee and the Southron." The Ohioan appeared to be speaking the lan-guage of Confederate nationalism. "I am inexorably hostile to Puritan domi-nation in religion or morals or literature or politics," though he still hoped for a conservative reaction even in Yankee New England. Arguing that there were no grounds for contention between the West and the South, he offered a dire warning. "And if you of the East who have found this war against the South, and for the negro, gratifying to your hate or profitable to your purse, will continue it till a separation be forced between the slaveholding and your non-slaveholding States," they risked "eternal divorce between the West and the East." Slyly noting that all secessionists had really wanted was "Security against Abolitionism within the Union: protection from the 'irrepressible con-flict,' and the domination of the absolute numerical majority . . . a change, of public opinion, and consequently of political parties in the North and West, so that their local institutions and domestic peace should no longer be en-dangered," Vallandigham held that they might soon receive the desired reas-surance. This would occur because the northern people were "fast becoming satisfied that the price of the Union is the utter suppression of Abolitionism or anti-slavery as a political element, and the complete subordination of the spirit of fanaticism and intermeddling which gave it birth." Surely, they now stood ready for a return to the status quo antebellum.

But how and under what circumstances would all these matters be settled? That remained the central question even as Vallandigham offered a compli-cated answer that no doubt greatly alarmed many loyal northerners even as it may well have misled hopeful Confederates. On one level, the solution was simple: "Stop fighting. Make an armistice—no formal treaty. Withdraw your Army from the seceded States." Soon trade and communication would be restored. The next steps would quickly follow: "Migrate. Intermarry. Let slavery alone. Hold elections at the appointed times. Let us choose a new President in sixty-four. And when the gospel of peace shall have descended again from Heaven into their hearts, and the gospel of abolition and of hate been expelled, let your clergy and the churches meet again in Christian intercourse, North and South. Let the secret orders and voluntary associations everywhere reunite as brethren once more."[22]

He anticipated objections, especially from the Union side, but in doing so he may well have planted seeds of further misunderstanding in the Confederacy. Northern critics naturally accused him of favoring diplomatic "recognition of the Confederacy." He responded by drawing some subtle if not sophistical distinctions whose meaning could readily have eluded friend and foe alike. The correct policy was not "formal recognition," Vallandigham conceded, but he instead proposed "informal, practical recognition." Whatever that meant—and it certainly sounded impractical and absurd—in his view such an approach reflected current realties. Were not the two sides exchanging prisoners and observing "the laws, forms, and courtesies of war," in themselves "acts of recognition" and "does any man doubt, to-day, that there is a Confederate Government at Richmond, and that it is a 'belligerent'?" Going one step further, Vallandigham not only accepted but welcomed the prospect of "foreign mediation."

Already the war had shown that "the South is not weak, dependent, unenterprising, or corrupted by slavery, luxury, and idleness; but powerful, earnest, warlike, enduring, self-supporting, full of energy, and inexhaustible in resources." No wonder he faced charges of being a Confederate apologist, and he even parroted a standard wartime version of the proslavery polemic. Not only had the war revealed the moral and intellectual bankruptcy of abolitionism, it had further reinforced the power of white supremacy as rich and poor alike joined the Confederate ranks. "African slavery, instead of being a source of weakness to the South," Vallandigham pointedly observed,

is one of her main elements of strength . . . We have learned, also, that the non-slaveholding white men of the South, millions in number, are immovably attached to the institution, and are its chief support;

and Abolitionists have found out, to their infinite surprise and disgust, that the slave is not "panting for freedom," nor pining in silent, but, revengeful grief over cruelty and oppression inflicted upon him, but happy, contented, attached deeply to his master, and unwilling—at least not eager—to accept the precious boon of freedom, which they have proffered him . . . African slavery as an institution, will come out of this conflict fifty-fold stronger than when the war began.

The most ardent Confederates had predicted the war would prove the world wrong on the subject of African slavery, and here Vallandigham came perilously close to embracing their proslavery millennialism.[23]

Presumably Vallandigham spoke for many other disillusioned Yankees, but however that might be, Confederates followed signs of war weariness and divisions in the northern states with obvious delight and mounting interest. Newspapers reported political troubles in Indiana and Illinois, speeches by leading "Copperheads" in New York City, and peace talk more generally, though Confederates were much better at gathering such information than assessing it. There was speculation about resistance to the Lincoln administration or even a secession of the western states. Of course, many Yankees remained hell-bent on subjugating the southern states, a Georgia editor warned, adding that even Vallandigham and other supposed northern friends offered little but empty talk of conciliation. Part of their problem, claimed the *Richmond Dispatch,* was a simple failure to understand the nature of the conflict. Vallandigham talked of a "civil war," but in fact it was a "sectional war," a contest between "two people who are as distinct as the Russians and the Danes, or the Saxons and the Dutch." The editor sought to inform Vallandigham and anyone else who might not realize it that this was an unbridgeable chasm: "The great wonder is not that the two sections have fallen asunder at last but that they held together so long. It would be almost as rational to form the whole continent of Europe into a single State, and then expect it to continue such."[24]

That Vallandigham had not conceded the impossibility of reunion was troubling, but many Confederates chose to emphasize those aspects of his speech that most closely aligned with their beliefs, assumptions, and hopes. And they indulged in no little amount of wishful thinking. Vallandigham was now described as the leader of the Democratic Party (conveniently forgetting all those Democrats who still supported the war and were appalled by his recent speech). One editor even quoted a rabidly Republican sheet to prove that the northern Democrats had fallen under the Ohioan's sway. In this case, perhaps a Yankee newspaper could be taken at its word—that is, as long as one ignored the possibility that Republicans might be describing Vallandigham as the leader of the opposition to emphasize Democratic disloyalty. Even a fairly sophisticated Virginia cavalry officer who regretted Vallandigham's "blind adherence to the thought that peace will be the signal for the return of the seceded States to their allegiance" still believed that "his influences will tell greatly upon the future course of the North, and his speech will assist in hastening the revolution which is just beginning in Abraham's home."[25]

Other voices sounded equally sanguine. Vallandigham had declared the war hopeless, welcome news given the high price that Confederates had already paid in their struggle for independence. His words on that subject were widely quoted in the southern press, and his proposed withdrawal of Union forces from the southern states naturally won plaudits. Perhaps the northern people were at last waking up to their perilous situation. An editorial in the *Atlanta Southern Confederacy* found quite believable northern suspicions that Vallandigham was plotting to lead some kind of uprising against the Lincoln administration—one extending far beyond any talk of a "Northwest Confederacy." Even the *Charleston Mercury,* while duly noting that there had been much that was "absurd and impractical" in Vallandigham's speech, applauded his recommendations for a ceasefire and troop withdrawal. In his usual bombastic style, editor Robert Barnwell Rhett Jr. excitedly commented: "Vallandigham unfurls the white flag in the very halls of the Yankee Congress." Even though the Ohioan had only suggested European "mediation" in the conflict, a Virginia newspaper mentioned the rumor that he might favor European "intervention." And what better way to warm southern hearts than to quote John C. Calhoun, as Vallandigham had done at least three times in his recent speech? To a Mississippi editor, this simply showed the man's "genius" and "matured statesmanship."[26]

Maybe Vallandigham was indeed a southerner at heart, and the speech had touted his southern family connections. Unlike most northerners, he understood the origins of the war and southern grievances against what Confederates termed the "universal Yankee nation." A Louisiana private predicted that Vallandigham's great speech would "be read by future generations

as the most patriotic effort made to save a people from destroying themselves."
Expecting even more immediate results, a clerk in the Army of Tennessee saw
Vallandigham's "flaming speech" on the House floor as "a terrible blow to the
radicals [Republicans] and they acknowledge it themselves." On both counts,
this statement was largely fantasy, but one could hardly blame Confederates
after nearly two years of war for grasping at any apparent signs of weakness in
the enemy camp. News of a burgeoning northern peace movement, presumably with Vallandigham at the forefront, brightened hopes that the fighting
might soon end.[27]

Only a month after delivering his address in Congress, Vallandigham spoke
to an overflow gathering of New Jersey Democrats in Newark. This time, his
remarks were brief, but they were also pointed. After alluding to the government's "arbitrary arrests," he praised the brave men now derided as "butter-
nuts" and "copperheads" and even cited the oft-quoted scripture: "blessed
are the peace-makers." Yet politicians such as secretary of state William H.
Seward and his New York political henchman Thurlow Weed sought to keep
the war going so they could eventually "blot out the South." The only realistic
alternative to such a disastrous policy was an "immediate armistice" and a
reconstruction of the Union brokered by the people of the Northwest and the
people of the South.[28]

Here were more signs of hope to hearten Confederate partisans, who could
then dream about a bright future of peace and prosperity. Why not admit the
disaffected northwestern states into the Confederacy? That question, posed by
an Alabama editor, conveniently ignored the early debates in the Montgomery
convention over whether free states might be allowed into the new southern
confederation. And even now such an idea generated no little amount of controversy as Confederates pondered the latest reports and rumors of northern
disaffection and sought to parse Vallandigham's remarks in New Jersey.[29]

Confederates increasingly had to sort out what all the news from the North
meant and how to respond. Perhaps the revolution in Yankeeland was much
more serious than anyone could have at first imagined. Maybe Vallandigham
was no longer a lone voice of reason; northern Democrats might indeed be
rallying around his standard and public opinion that appeared to favor an early
end to the war. Not so fast, some editors advised. The *Richmond Enquirer*—
widely considered the semiofficial organ of Jefferson Davis's administration—
warned that trust in northern peace efforts in general and Vallandigham in

particular might prove every bit as delusive as faith in King Cotton or hopes for French intervention. Fortunately, the army would not be tantalized by such a chimera, and the sure cure in any event would be more Confederate victories to shatter Yankee armies and Yankee illusions. A Mobile editor was far more blunt, dismissing Vallandigham's speech in the House as "a splendid display of balderdash . . . a mixture of sense and nonsense, frenzy and folly, madness and reason." His "hallucination" about reunion after all the suffering southerners had endured was "ludicrous and laughable." What had he offered Confederates beside an "insult?"[30]

The sticking point remained, as always, the question of reunion. "We don't want to deceive Vallandigham, or the Northwest, or the Yankees of Massachusetts even," the *Atlanta Southern Confederacy* editorialized. "We went them to know that reconstruction is an utter impossibility, and that we cannot entertain any proposition or make any arrangement looking to that as a result." That Vallandigham had expressed many sentiments that meshed with Confederate views on the war hardly seemed to matter. Yet alongside this uncompromising editorial there appeared a letter from "Brutus," who advised that the "reactionary sentiment at the North West as headed by the noble Vallandigham should not be lightly treated by the press, and the people of the South." Vallandigham had gone about as far as he could in sympathizing with the Confederacy, and even his stance as a "reconstructionist" was likely more strategic than sincere. His real intention appeared to be the creation of a western confederacy.[31] Such contrary views appearing the same day in the same newspaper epitomized Confederate difficulties in gauging their enemies' intentions, much less coming up with a tactical response.

And if Vallandigham was in fact playing a clever political game, perhaps Confederates could afford to do likewise. Fire-eater Edmund Ruffin, whom nobody could accuse of being a peace man or reconstructionist, carefully recorded in his diary a summary of Vallandigham's views and saw no reason to worry or despair. Let the Ohioan and his fellow peace Democrats cling to some farfetched notion that reunion was still possible; that "illusion" would cost true southerners nothing. Indeed, Ruffin sounded like a Confederate version of Vallandigham: "I am willing to make peace almost without conditions, & leave it to the future, & our then established strength and abundant means for war, to assert and maintain any rights ignored or passed over at first. But if peace is made, & the boundaries of the recognized C.S. merely include the slave-holding states which by their free & formal votes choose to make parts of the C.S., though many of our just & important rights of property may be unsatisfied." A widely reprinted editorial in the *Richmond Whig* largely agreed with Ruffin. Vallandigham had called for reunion and perhaps not just out of a desire for political cover at home; he was likely a sincere reconstructionist, but that "should not excite surprise, and still less resentment in the Southern mind." He deserved much credit for having stood up to the abolitionists and to his own government. "Let us first take the beam out of our own eyes before we grow restive and pettish, because of the mote in the eye of Mr. Vallandigham," the editor advised. He deplored "the somewhat churlish greeting which his well meant overtures have been [*sic*] received in Richmond." This may have been a shot aimed at Davis and secretary of state Judah Benjamin, since the *Whig* often criticized the Confederate administration, and the editor concluded by praising Vallandigham as a stalwart defender of liberty in a land where that "fire . . . has long since died out."[32]

Whether the fire of liberty had died out in the North would soon be tested, and Vallandigham would play an even more prominent role in the unfolding drama. A growing peace movement, rumors of treasonable activity, and simple partisan bickering had produced increasing alarm in Washington and elsewhere. Vallandigham's cries for liberty and unmeasured denunciations of the Lincoln administration soon put political patience and respect for free speech to a severe test. His rhetorical offensive continued in determined attacks on measures ranging from the National Banking Act to conscription. Whether or not Vallandigham's strident talk meant that he was courting martyrdom, as his biographer has argued, he would soon have the opportunity that he supposedly craved.[33]

In mid-April, the newly appointed commander of the Department of the Ohio, Gen. Ambrose E. Burnside, issued a sweeping order declaring that "all persons found within our lines who commit acts for the benefit of the enemies of our country" could be tried for treason and sentenced to death. In a passage aimed at prominent Copperheads such as Vallandigham, he added, "The habit of declaring sympathy for the enemy will not be allowed in this department," and warned that persons committing such acts could "be sent beyond our lines into the lines of their friends."[34] With his political stock apparently falling among Ohio Democrats as he sought the party's gubernatorial nomination, this was the very opening Vallandigham needed. He could become once again the stalwart defender of liberty, and if he were arrested, so much the better: martyrdom might well be the ticket for reviving his flagging political career. Not surprisingly, Vallandigham's newspaper organ in Dayton, Ohio, lashed out at Burnside and warned against a growing threat of military despotism.[35]

After hearing that Vallandigham would address a Democratic rally in Mount Vernon on May 1, 1863, Burnside dispatched two captains with instructions to take notes. Vallandigham did not disappoint. In a two-hour oration, he blasted the Lincoln administration for arbitrary arrests and executive usurpation; he accused the party in power of having no interest in restoring the Union but instead seeking to erect a "despotism." Soon the government would begin enforcing conscription, and citizens must defend their liberties, using the power of the "ballot box" to depose "King Lincoln.[36]

Near the beginning of the speech, Vallandigham had pointedly asked why he needed permission from General Burnside to address a public meeting, and Burnside in effect answered by ordering his arrest. A squad arrived at Vallandigham's Dayton home in the middle of the night and took him into custody. A trial by military commission predictably found him guilty of violating Burnside's order by expressing sympathy for the rebels and spouting disloyal sentiments. The sentence: "close confinement" for the war's duration.[37]

Rioting in Dayton by Vallandigham supporters who set fire to a Republican newspaper office perhaps marked a turning point in northern opinion, or so some Confederates hoped. Southern newspapers reprinted highly partisan and overblown accounts of the arrest and aftermath from the northern Copperhead press. Richmond editors found historical analogies for the Lincoln despotism in Austria, Italy, and even China, though their fevered imaginations did not produce any useful or revealing comparisons. Vallandigham had become a great martyr to liberty and received even more praise from southerners eagerly anticipating the next outrage from the northern states. Maybe this time the Yankee administration had gone too far, and Confederates awaited news of a northern uprising. The wildly optimistic could almost imagine revolutionary mobs gathering in the major cities and even in Washington.[38]

Such speculation hardly squared with the typical assessments of Yankee character that permeated Confederate propaganda, and so naturally it met with considerable skepticism. Ruffin wrote of an impotent northern opposition but still wondered whether "democrats & malcontents of Ohio & the North-West" might actually resist. On second (or perhaps third) thought, he decided they would more likely "submit" to this latest outrage "like the crouching & cowardly slaves of an Asiatic despot." Where were all those northern conservatives who would supposedly die defending liberty? One editor even took the opportunity to disparage the Whiggish supporters of the Constitutional Union party who had proved absolutely feckless—though his editorial barbs were aimed more at southern political rivals than anyone else. And of course in the wake of the Army of Northern Virginia's recent victory at the battle of Chancellorsville, there appeared to be no reason to worry about, much less rely on, northern protests. "We perceive clearly that we will have to fight to the bitter end," a usually cautious South Carolina editor concluded. "It is folly to expect help from that quarter."[39]

Overconfidence may have blinded Confederates to opportunities as well as perils. Their opinions remained inconsistent and confused. Could Confederates take advantage of divisions in the enemy camp, divisions that could yield political and diplomatic dividends? Vallandigham's arrest surely proved that the Union government greatly feared his influence. After all, he presumably spoke for many northern Democrats, and the Chancellorsville defeat would further enflame and empower northern opponents of the Lincoln administration. Vallandigham had openly declared that the southern states could never be subjugated, and he had proven to be a great "thorn in the flesh" to a despotic government. He therefore needed to be crushed, but the incongruous image of crushing a thorn pointed to some larger problems in Confederate thinking.[40]

How to gauge Vallandigham's actual position on the war and his real influence in the northern states was only part of the difficulty, and Confederates would soon have to do more than react to the arrest and trial. For the time being, they could follow the legal proceedings with great interest, while still differing in their expectations and still searching for ways to exploit the Yankees' political troubles. Any signs of a determined northern reaction against the Lincoln administration garnered attention. Reports of strong resolutions adopted at a public meeting in Indianapolis, citizens shouting for Jefferson Davis, and several men arrested sounded promising. A protest meeting in New York City brought out a surprisingly large crowd. Congressman James Brooks accused the Lincoln administration of attempting to "subjugate" the northern states as well as the southern states—a charge that only reconfirmed what the most ardent Confederates already believed about northern war aims. Surely Vallandigham's arrest and trial would only strengthen the northern peace faction, assuming that words would finally be translated into deeds. The issue had come down to a contest of strength between the abolitionists and the Democrats, a South Carolina editor maintained. "They [the Democrats] can dodge the question of resistance no longer without disgrace and dishonor. We predict they will cave in and cowardly yield their necks to the oppressors."[41]

Reports of defiance alongside predictions of capitulation sounded contradictory but in fact reflected not only uncertainty but also serious barriers to understanding. Confederates had every opportunity to read the words of northern Copperheads, whose speeches received full and often front-page newspaper coverage. Readers might logically conclude that Vallandigham and others spoke for a large swathe of northern opinion because the newspapers seldom published any extended excerpts from addresses by Republicans or war Democrats. Yet, at the same time, editors disparaged the wisdom and the courage of their erstwhile northern friends. Even those Democrats who had spoken most eloquently at that New York indignation meeting also trumpeted their own patriotism and devotion to the Constitution; their words about dire threats to northern liberty rang hollow when they still somehow supported the war. There was even an occasional admission that all the "Copperheads" whom Confederates loved to quote might not speak for the Democratic Party leadership. Vallandigham had been arrested, quickly tried, and on last report taken to Cincinnati and would soon be imprisoned. It had all been done, as one Georgia editor noted, "without bloodshed" and with no reaction beyond the passage of some empty "resolutions." Catherine Edmondston predicted that these supposed northern defenders of liberty would "brag, bluster, and submit," and she marveled at such a people who would "give up the dearest rights of freemen without a struggle." They deserved to have Lincoln as their dictator. His administration could thus act with impunity because, as Edmund Ruffin assessed the situation, the president and his minons could estimate "the value of the threatened resistance . . . at nothing."[42]

Northern conservatives' failure of nerve made all the peace talk ring hollow, and in any event, the Democrats seemed to be a quite inept and spineless opposition. They appeared no match for Lincoln, who deftly avoided turning Vallandigham into a martyr by commuting his sentence to transportation "beyond our military lines" into the Confederacy. Southerners followed every twist and turn of this bizarre case. Burnside had certainly exceeded any legitimate authority in his order and his arrest of Vallandigham, one Richmond editor pointed out, and then Lincoln had violated the Constitution just as glaringly by overturning the military commission's sentence. Presumably, all this would simply compound the administration's troubles, but again it came down to a question of whether the northern opposition showed any real backbone.[43]

"Thus the famous baboon [Lincoln] gets rid of the only man who has the courage to denounce his usurpation of power and the unholy war which is being waged against us," Louisiana sergeant Edwin H. Fay wrote in digesting the latest news. There would undoubtedly be more meetings and protests, which perhaps would end up hurting Lincoln. Some Confederates dismissed the president's critics as ineffective one day but then the next decided all the noise and oratory might amount to something after all. Perhaps old Abe had outsmarted himself. The military commission might have imposed the death penalty and Lincoln might have approved that sentence, so perhaps he could not really act with impunity and would have to pay some political price. The northern people might force the president to truly declare the kind of oppressive government he sought to create. And the Confederate government too would have something to say about this ploy of sending Vallandigham into exile.[44] In any case, the "mights" and "coulds" and "maybes" kept piling up, awaiting Vallandigham's arrival in Dixie.

On May 19, Vallandigham was escorted onto the Union gunboat *Exchange* docked at Cincinnati. Writing to Manton Marble, editor of the *New York World*, he expressed hope for a "united Democratic party" and still expected to "foil and counteract" Lincoln's stratagem. Ohio Democrats would soon make him their gubernatorial nominee. Vallandigham evidently did not spend much time thinking about how he would approach his Confederate hosts, simply declaring to New York governor Horatio Seymour that "South or North, I am the same Union man." He composed a brief address, "To the Democracy of Ohio," vowing to stand firm in his principles even as he was being forced into exile by "an arbitrary and tyrannic power." On May 22, the *Exchange* steamed to Louisville, and from there he was taken under guard to Murfreesboro, Tennessee, where he met with Gen. William S. Rosecrans. The general, who loved talking politics and theology late into the night, engaged the prisoner in a four-hour conversation on the subject of loyalty.[45]

Once this confab had ended, at nearly two a.m. according to one newspaper reporter, a Union colonel and two companies of cavalry formed the escort. The always voluble Vallandigham chatted away with the colonel about the war and constitutional liberty. After stopping for a rest at dawn, the party passed through the last Union pickets. They enjoyed a farmhouse breakfast prepared by a Mrs. Alexander, who was pleased about hosting a distinguished guest and remarked that she had "been reading only last night of your wonderful doings!" There was a bit of difficulty with the Confederate pickets, but after some delay Vallandigham read a prepared statement about entering the Confederates lines as a citizen of the United States "by force and against my will." It still took some time to straighten everything out, but finally Vallandigham was driven to Gen. Braxton Bragg's headquarters in Shelbyville.[46]

All the awkwardness and punctilio reflected Vallandigham's uncertain status as well as the difficulties that his arrival presented to Confederates. This was a most delicate situation, and Bragg would have to seek guidance from Richmond. Vallandigham retired for the night, intending to wake up refreshed for what promised to be an interesting if possibly difficult meeting. He stayed in a house near the general's headquarters and was surprised that he could walk around freely the next morning, but that scarcely signified an open-arms welcome. Bragg hardly knew how to proceed. After stiffly congratulating Vallandigham "on your arrival in our land of liberty where freedom of speech and of conscience is secured to all," Bragg quickly turned to the question of the Ohioan's status. "As a private citizen, exiled by a foreign Government with which we are at war," Bragg pointed out, there would have to be some "restraints" on his movements. He issued Vallandigham a pass that was good only "within this department." In a letter to his wife that was soon published in a Dayton newspaper (but never apparently made it into the Confederate press), Vallandigham described how he had been received "very kindly," adding that his position on a restoration of the Union "is well known here" and his hopes for a "future settlement" had if anything been "strengthened."[47]

A report first appearing in a Chattanooga paper and then widely reprinted described Vallandigham's arrival in Shelbyville. This account emphasized the complications and discomfiture of the situation but depicted the exile as "cheerful" and able to "breathe free on escaping from the Lincoln despotism." Vallandigham reportedly "desires to avoid all public demonstration, and only asks that he may find a quiet refuge in our midst, until such time as the voice of his people, relieved from despotic influence, shall call him again to their midst." He seemed a pleasant enough man who recognized the "embarrassment of his position." For once, Vallandigham apparently was cautious and clearly sensed the unease his sudden arrival had caused. Despite not feeling very well, the noted Confederate chaplain Charles Todd Quintard could not pass up the opportunity of dining with General Bragg's famous guest. He found Vallandigham "extremely easy and polite," quite "fluent and entertaining in conversation," and, as newspapers had reported, "very desirous of avoiding all public demonstration."[48]

Realizing that Lincoln had placed them in a most difficult position, Jefferson Davis and his advisers no doubt agreed that Vallandigham should keep a low profile. Vallandigham had long been praised for standing up to the Black Republicans, yet he loudly proclaimed his loyalty to the old Union. That hardly endeared him to the Confederate government, and neither the president nor his cabinet apparently saw any political or diplomatic opportunity here. On May 30, secretary of war James A. Seddon instructed Bragg to have Vallandigham state his position: "If he claims to be a loyal citizen of the United States he must be held in charge or on parole as an alien enemy. He may be allowed on parole to proceed to Wilmington [North Carolina] and there report to General [William Henry Chase] Whiting." Bragg immediately asked Vallandigham to surrender his pass and respond in writing. "I came to your lines upon compulsion and against my consent as a citizen of Ohio and of the United States in exile, banished from my country for no other offense than love of constitutional liberty, my political opinions and resolute, undaunted opposition to the principles and policy of the party and administration in power in the United States," Vallandigham replied. Lincoln would not permit his return home, so he hoped to be treated as a paroled prisoner and allowed to leave the Confederacy. He intended to live in Canada and presumably conduct his gubernatorial campaign in absentia. Bragg immediately reported the gist of this statement to Richmond but suggested that someone in authority interview Vallandigham.[49]

Press reports often failed to recognize the tensions and cross-purposes here, generally ignoring Vallandigham's need to avoid even the appearance of siding with the Confederates. Given his political ambitions, he could hardly afford to lend further credence to Republican charges of disloyalty. Instead of wrestling with such questions, the newspapers emphasized Vallandigham's good spirits and gracious attitude. One dispatch assured readers that the

Ohioan was in "excellent" health and "not depressed." He would soon leave Shelbyville to spend a few days in Virginia, or at least that was the rumor. With some exaggeration but also considerable truth, a Mobile editor summed up the intense public interest: ""His name is a surfeit to us; it is in every newspaper and in everybody's mouth through the whole land; even the church-bells this morning seems as if they were saying nothing else than Val-land-dig-ham."[50]

Everybody seemed to have an opinion about how he should be received. "It is a vexed question," the editor of the *Macon Telegraph* admitted. On the one hand, "Lincoln should not be allowed to make the South a place of banishment for political offenses against his despotism." Vallandigham was in a sense an "alien enemy" who, regardless of his staunch opposition to Lincoln administration policies, had voted men and supplies for the Union army. Yet while claiming that in many respects Vallandigham was no better than Burnside, the editor admitted that there were "various considerations why as a matter of policy, as well as humanity, the door should not be closed against Vallandigham." At the same time, the conditions for his remaining in the Confederacy were quite rigid. He would presumably have to renounce loyalty to the United States, though as an Atlanta editor feared, "he has too much love for the Union."[51]

That was precisely the problem. To many Confederates, Vallandigham's continued faith in reunion overshadowed his record as an unrelenting opponent of the Lincoln administration. An Alabamian even suggested that Vallandigham be required to take an oath of allegiance and enlist in the Confederate army. On pragmatic grounds, his presence in the Confederacy could only help Lincoln and hurt his chances in the Ohio gubernatorial election, Edmund Ruffin insisted. Yet Ruffin also misread the situation because he could not believe that Lincoln had come up with such a clever ploy on his own; it must have been the brainchild of those dark eminences who pulled all the strings in the administration. To the always acerbic Richmond editor John M. Daniel, Vallandigham was simply "an enemy." Some suggested that the Ohioan be imprisoned in Richmond until the Federals agreed to an exchange. Others worried about some great popular demonstration in favor of Vallandigham, and though Confederate fortunes were riding high, there were signs of war weariness and a growing reluctance to make sacrifices. Even so, the pipe dream of a northern uprising never quite died. Although he was a "reconstructionist," a Georgian advised, the best policy would be to "receive Mr. Vallandigham as a gentleman entitled to the highest respect for his bold stand against the enormities of the Yankee rulers, and not as one claiming our fellowship or political affiliation."[52] Such diverse comments, assessments, and suggestions revealed ideological rigidity, along with understandable perplexity, and considerable dollops of wishful thinking.

As the press debated and the politicians remained largely silent, Bragg prepared to send Vallandigham on his way. Aside from a daily walk, he had largely stayed out of sight, though newspaper reporters offered detailed and favorable descriptions of his appearance and manner. On June 2, with Vallandigham about to leave Shelbyville, Confederate soldiers made a "friendly demonstration" as the Ohioan passed through their camps on the way to the train station. Their officers "promptly suppressed" this show of support, which could have proved embarrassing all around. One of Bragg's staff officers, along with Confederate congressman John Dewitt Atkins, conducted Vallandigham to Chattanooga. Atkins was a friend who had served with Vallandigham in the antebellum Congress; that he was also a frequent critic of Jefferson Davis may or may not have been significant. In Chattanooga, a crowd gathered at the depot, eager to catch a glimpse of the man who had often been praised in the Confederate press. Kentucky Confederate congressman Edward M. Bruce conducted Vallandigham to the Crutchfield House, where he held court in the lobby. A correspondent for an Atlanta newspaper described the reception as "respectful" but assured readers that there was "no manifestation of cordiality, or any expressions of sympathy." The usually perceptive nurse Kate Cumming, who was then working in a Chattanooga hospital, implausibly claimed that people took little notice of Vallandigham because "he is not a southerner" and "clings to the delusion that the Union can again be restored." Yet—and with Confederates and Vallandigham there always seemed to be a "yet"—she admired his "independence of character in defying Lincoln and his minions." Her conclusion was at once contradictory and optimistic: "Would that we had many more like him in the North, then our hopes of peace would be bright indeed. Many think if we can only hold out a little longer, that the peace party there will rise in its might, and demand of the black republicans to desist from this unholy strife."[53]

Whether Vallandigham would lead such an uprising remained to be seen, but he left Chattanooga on June 3 bound for Virginia and a meeting with Colonel Robert Ould, the commissioner in charge of prisoner exchanges. By order of Jefferson Davis, Vallandigham would be treated as an "alien enemy" and kept "under guard," but other Confederates assumed a more hospitable attitude. In Lynchburg, Vallandigham received a number of visitors. He apparently talked quite freely, gossiping about General Rosecrans (supposedly drunk during their late-night talkfest), Seward (allegedly involved in cotton smuggling), and Lincoln (a man of low and degrading character). A professor of Greek at Hampden-Sydney College (and old friend of Vallandigham) understood the Confederate government's dilemma but assumed the Ohioan might stay in the South and offered his home as a place to stay. Not surprisingly, there is no record of a reply by Secretary of War Seddon to this inquiry.[54]

Instead, Seddon sent Colonel Ould to meet with Vallandigham in Lynchburg. Denying any "desire or purpose of this Government to treat this victim of unjust and arbitrary power with other than lenity and consideration," the secretary of war reiterated Davis's point about Vallandigham being an "alien enemy." He could obviously not remain in the Confederacy, and therefore Ould should arrange his transportation "under arrest" to Wilmington. From there, he could depart for a "neutral port." In a long conversation with Ould, Vallandigham said if the Confederates could only hold out for the year, the "people of the North would sweep the Lincoln dynasty out of political existence." He offered one other telling piece of advice: a strong warning against another Confederate invasion of the North—a move guaranteed to unite the northern people and help Lincoln "crush all opposition." There were rumors of an earlier cabinet discussion, but whether Davis's advisers weighed Vallandigham's counsel is not known, and the administration kept a tight lid on their deliberations.[55]

Braxton Bragg later reported that Vallandigham was "sincerely for peace" but then added that the president was undoubtedly right in "withholding the expression of such sentiments, at least in part, until the public mind is ready to receive them." Ironically, the generals showed more imagination than the politicians when it came to thinking about Vallandigham and northern politics. Gen. P. G. T. Beauregard thought he saw a grand opportunity. He recommended to a congressional confidant that Bragg be reinforced for an offensive to destroy Rosecrans' army and advance into Kentucky. He expected the "friends of Vallandigham" would "rise up" to support Bragg with volunteers from Indiana, Illinois, and Missouri. Eventually, the entire northwest might secede from the Union and enter into an alliance with the Confederacy. To Beauregard, the main point was obvious: "Battles without diplomacy will never end this war."[56]

One can easily dismiss this scheme as a typical product of Beauregard's inventive but utterly impractical brain. Yet a much more prudent commander agreed that Confederates might well be missing an opportunity. Robert E. Lee candidly acknowledged the inferiority of Confederate resources in both men and materiel, and like Beauregard he thought the Confederacy should "neglect no honorable means of dividing and weakening our enemies." He recommended giving "all the encouragement we can, consistently with truth, to the rising peace party of the North." Going further than many Confederates, he saw no reason to make any great distinction between northerners who "declare for peace unconditionally" and those "who advocate it as a means for restoring the Union." Too many southern editors and other leaders, Lee believed, had insisted on drawing such distinctions with strident and uncompromising statements, thereby weakening and undermining northern conservatives. After speaking with Vallandigham near Petersburg, Alabama, senator Clement C. Clay Jr. concluded that the Ohioan was "at heart for peace, even at the expense of disunion and the independence of the Confederacy." In their conversation, Vallandigham had reiterated his earlier warning against another invasion of the North and added that retaliation against the white officers in African American regiments would not help either.[57]

In the end, none of this discussion or these suggestions seemed to matter. Lee was already preparing to head north again with the Army of Northern Virginia. Many Confederates had almost unlimited confidence in Lee and his army, and even after Gettysburg saw little need for considering any kind of negotiated peace. Despite having had to move his newspaper to Atlanta, a refugee Memphis editor spoke for many others: "A few more of Gen. Lee's late arguments [i.e., military victories] will convince them [the northern people] that even Mr. Vallandigham did not propose what would have satisfied the South at the time, and certainly will not now." There was at this point no extensive debate on political or diplomatic strategy. Press accounts spoke vaguely of a cordial correspondence between Vallandigham and Jefferson Davis. Reports of Vallandigham's arrival in Petersburg told of many people showing him "every mark of respect and sympathy." None of this suggested any serious weighing of options. North Carolina editor William W. Holden, who would soon become a leader of the peace faction, could not resist a politically pointed comment: "It would have been much better for the country and for the cause of human liberty, if the fire eaters of the South had heeded and acted on the advice which Mr. Vallandigham gave them at Charleston and Baltimore, in 1860."[58]

In the end, however, "Let him go to Canada" appeared to be the near universal sentiment among leading Confederates. "Policy demands that he leave us," Catherine Edmonston had scribbled in her diary even before Jefferson Davis had made that determination. Yet she could not help but speculate that if Vallandigham acted with "prudence and discretion" that "this arbitrary act of Lincoln" would eventually make the Ohioan president of the United States. She then added, "but little do I care who fills that seat." Such apparent indifference may also have reflected a dangerous overconfidence as well as a serious misreading of northern opinion. Some editorials recommended that Vallandigham might simply be sent back North where he could do battle with Lincoln.[59]

Vallandigham, New Yorker Fernando Wood, and other Copperheads were nothing but reconstructionists, a South Carolina editor sneered. "We have got no use for such men." In fact, dissecting Vallandigham's inconsistencies and weaknesses took up a good many columns in southern newspapers. Like other Confederates, a Mississippian writing under the name of "Publius" compared Vallandigham to the Earl of Chatham, though he quickly noted that the brave but "deluded" Vallandigham must finally realize that reunion was impossible.[60]

Here again, Confederates could not quite decide what to think. Vallandigham was a reconstructionist and should quickly leave the Confederacy, but at the same time the newspapers kept publicizing northern protests and peace meetings. This all reflected a persistent hope that at last the northern Democrats would stand firm and, as one North Carolinian put it, "rise and throw off Lincoln's hated yoke." Lengthy reports of resolutions and speeches condemning Vallandigham's arrest and expulsion presented a somewhat jarring contrast with editorials in the same papers declaring that the Ohioan and his political allies had nothing to offer.[61] Confederates who followed northern politics wondered whether all the sound and fury signified anything. Was it nothing but "bluster?" one North Carolina editor asked. The answer was "yes" because he fully expected that the Yankees would in the end tamely submit to most any outrage. Ohioans had displayed courage on the battlefield, Edmund Ruffin admitted; at home, however, they showed an incredible amount of "base cowardice."[62]

Ruffin believed that Lincoln could now proceed with all the imperiousness of a Russian tsar or Turkish sultan. Burnside had done the administration's dirty work, and then Lincoln and Seward had come up with the devilish trick of dumping Vallandigham on the Confederates. Although Confederate ordnance chief Josiah Gorgas believed the "device is too shallow," whether

Lincoln's alleged scheme would be effective remained to be seen. When congressman Erastus Corning sent Lincoln a set of resolutions from a Democratic meeting in Albany, New York, protesting the suppression of free speech and arbitrary arrests in the aftermath of the Vallandigham affair, Lincoln had just the opening he needed. After defending the suspension of habeas corpus, he claimed that Vallandigham had been arrested not because he had exercised his right of free speech in attacking the government but because he was "laboring, with some effect, to prevent the raising of troops, to encourage desertions from the army, and to leave the rebellion without an adequate military force to suppress it." Rather than relying on a less than persuasive defense of Burnside's actions, Lincoln appealed to loyalty, patriotism, and no little emotion in a masterful passage: "Must I shoot a simple-minded soldier boy who deserts, while I must not touch a hair of a wiley agitator who induces him to desert? This is none the less injurious when effected by getting a father, or brother, or friend into a public meeting, and there working upon his feelings till he is persuaded to write the soldier boy that he is fighting in a bad cause, for a wicked administration of a contemptible government, too weak to arrest and punish him if he shall desert. I think that, in such a case, to silence the agitator and save the boy is not only constitutional, but withal a great mercy." Some Confederates surely recognized such a statement's effectiveness, but Ruffin believed that the Lincoln administration's failure to arrest more Democrats for making even more violently antiwar speeches amounted to a confession of weakness.[63]

Once Vallandigham had left Wilmington bound for Canada via Nassau, some Confederates breathed a sigh of relief. Those who had from the day of his arrival insisted on an early departure felt vindicated. A North Carolina editor had heard more than enough and hoped everyone would "stop blowing and talking about Mr. Vallandigham." A Georgian was simply "glad that Vallandigham has gone." But then he added a statement that perhaps revealed more than was intended: "his presence in the Confederacy was a source of perplexity to the Government, and general uneasiness to the people."[64] That perplexity and uneasiness reflected not only frustration with Lincoln and his northern critics but also perhaps a fear that some diplomatic opportunity had slipped away.

Attention quickly shifted to Vallandigham the candidate. Confederates enjoyed reading about denunciations of Lincoln the tyrant during the Ohio Democratic convention that nominated the political exile for governor, and the southern press followed the Buckeye State's gubernatorial campaign with marked interest. Confederates especially appreciated Vallandigham's address to Ohio Democrats issued from Niagara Falls, Canada. He sounded many of the right notes: "It is in vain to invite the States and people of the South to return to a Union without a Constitution, and dishonored and polluted by repeated and most aggravated exertions of tyrannic power; it is base in yourselves, and treasonable to your posterity, to surrender these liberties and rights to the creatures whom your own breath created and can destroy." Vallandigham went on to berate Lincoln as a dictator and Burnside as a mere puppet. Ignoring the impact of Gettysburg and the Union capture of Vicksburg, he described and greatly exaggerated Confederate strength and determination: "Travelling a thousand miles and more through nearly one-half of the Confederate States, and sojourning for a time at widely different points, I met not one man, woman or child who was not resolved to perish rather than yield to the pressure of arms, even in the most desperate extremity . . . They are better prepared now every way to make good their inexorable purpose than at any period since the beginning of the struggle." Despite carping over Vallandigham's continued faith in reunion, the Confederate press widely publicized this remarkable document.[65]

If they did not exactly misunderstand Vallandigham, many misunderstood the state of northern politics. Some Confederates concluded that his gubernatorial nomination revealed the depths of Yankee discontent and even thought they could foresee the collapse of the Union war effort. However much Vallandigham and others might long for reunion, they would soon have to acknowledge the hopelessness of that goal. "If Vallandigham is elected governor . . ." was a tantalizing proposition that produced a great deal of optimistic speculation. According to a North Carolina editor, this would "expose the United States to one of the severest trials it has ever encountered." Might Lincoln order Vallandigham's arrest again? Would civil war then break out in the North? There would be peace in six months, remarked a war-weary Confederate soldier in Mississippi who preferred seeing Lee defeated in the field to Vallandigham beaten at the polls. The election of Vallandigham would certainly spell the end of Lincoln, a hopeful surgeon added. General Sterling Price's bedraggled men eagerly anticipated the Ohio contest because a favorable result would send his Missourians heading home.[66]

Whether Vallandigham would emerge triumphant remained to be seen. In late August, a sober-minded North Carolina soldier wrote to his equally cautious father that it would take at least one more big Confederate military victory for Vallandigham to win the election. Throughout the year, reports in the southern press remained upbeat. In mid-September the *Richmond Examiner*—which had hardly welcomed Vallandigham's presence in the southern states—expected him to rack up a fifteen-thousand-vote majority in Ohio. Another source predicted thirty thousand. Inevitably, a Virginia soldier believed a false report that Vallandigham had actually won.[67]

Disappointed Confederates could scream fraud, a routine postelection charge in this era, but they could hardly get around the fact that Vallandigham had been crushed by over 100,000 votes. For many, however, the returns merely confirmed their distrust of northern Democrats. Imprisoned on Johnson's Island in Lake Erie, John Dooley bitterly observed: "We have done wrong, are still doing wrong to place any dependence in any of those Copperheads, who do not send us *arms and money*. Arms and money are what we want and are the sole instruments by which our independence will be effected: give us these, gentlemen-democrats, and keep your kind wishes and knowing looks to yourselves." Speaking to an Illinois soldier, a Mississippi woman dismissed Copperheads as nothing but "cowards and traitors" who would do no one any good and surely could never be trusted. Others compared expectations of Vallandigham's triumph to the chimera of foreign intervention—two equally delusive phantoms. In the end, Vallandigham's defeat should convince Confederates, an Alabama editor maintained, "that there is no help for us except in our strong arms and stout hearts."[68]

Not everyone agreed, and when it came to Vallandigham, hope did spring eternal for overly sanguine Confederates. When the exile slipped back to Ohio in June 1864, they eagerly awaited a decisive confrontation with the Lincoln administration. Perhaps an emboldened democracy would even nominate Vallandigham for president. What would Lincoln do this time? Surely any attempt to arrest Vallandigham would ignite a civil war, and should the president passively accept his return, that could only be a sign of weakness and even fear. Maybe this time the Copperheads would actually resist their despotic government, and, of course, Confederates were once again cheered by signs of discontent in the northwest.[69] The Democrats' nomination of George B. McClellan on a peace platform befuddled many northerners yet hardly impressed Confederates. When Lincoln easily won reelection, Vallandigham seemed quickly forgotten, even as diehard Confederates still looked for some deus ex machina to rescue their dying cause.

The whole Vallandigham saga had revealed much about the contradictory character of Confederate expectations. In late May 1863, just as Vallandigham was being sent south, an editorial in a Mobile newspaper suggested that the Ohioan and his Copperhead comrades were presenting the Confederates a great opportunity to divide and conquer, a policy that if pursued correctly could lead to the overthrow of Lincoln's government. Whether such an opportunity ever existed is debatable, but in any event, Confederate leaders showed little inclination to consider it. Hustling Vallandigham off to Canada was about as effective as a Mississippi woman's attempt to "demoralize" Union troops by loudly asking if they would not like to see Vallandigham.[70] Part of the problem was that the nascent southern nation had a divided mind. Confederates welcomed and exaggerated reports of disaffection in the North but were not ready to offer peace Democrats any concessions. Newspapers misled people by printing so many Copperhead speeches that one could reasonably believe the Yankees were seething with discontent.[71] At the same time, especially with Confederate prospects seemingly so bright in the spring of 1863, there seemed little need for diplomacy, much less negotiation. This proved to be a fatal miscalculation when the tide quickly turned at Gettysburg and Vicksburg. Ironically, by overstating both northern divisions and Confederate strengths, it became easier to carry on an ever more bloody and costly war without adjustments in military or political strategy. Even after the war, Confederates could not agree on whether they had admired, pitied, or scorned Vallandigham.[72] In fact, they had done all these things, showing an all too human ability to see in him exactly what they wanted to see. The story of Vallandigham and the Confederates is part of a larger narrative that might be profitably pursued in a study entitled something like "Reading and Misreading the Yankees in the Confederate South."

NOTES

1. *Charleston Mercury,* January 21, 1861.

2. The standard biography remains Frank L. Klement, *The Limits of Dissent: Clement L. Vallandigham and the Civil War* (Lexington: University Press of Kentucky, 1970). I have relied heavily on this work for details of Vallandigham's wartime activities.

3. Ibid., 45.

4. Congressional Globe, 36th Cong., 2nd Sess., February 7, 20, 1861, 794–95, Appendix, 235–43. Entitled "The Great American Revolution of 1861," this lengthy address also appeared in pamphlet form. Clement L. Vallandigham, *Speech of Hon. C. L. Vallandigham, of Ohio, Delivered in the House of Representatives, February 20, 1861* (Washington, DC: Henry Polkinhorn, 1861). Ironically, at this point the Confederates were launching their own "revolution," even though they used the term cautiously. George C. Rable, "Rebels and Patriots in the Confederate 'Revolution,'" in William J. Cooper Jr. and John M. McCardell, eds., *In the Cause of Liberty: How the Civil War Redefined American Ideals* (Baton Rouge: Louisiana State University 2009), 63–86.

5. *Richmond Daily Dispatch*, April 20, 27, 1861.

6. Joel Silbey has observed that Vallandigham was one of those Democrats who refused to succumb to the "no-partyism" calls during the war's first year and appeared eager to resume the usual partisan warfare. Joel H. Silbey, *A Respectable Minority: The Democratic Party in the Civil War Era, 1860–1868* (New York: W. W. Norton, 1977), 48. Of course, by the spring and summer of 1862, the Democratic opposition as a whole would become much more rancorous.

7. James L. Vallandigham, *A Life of Clement L. Vallandigham* (Baltimore: Turnbull Brothers, 1872), 162; *Richmond Daily Dispatch*, May 3, 11, June 13, 1861.

8. *Memphis Daily Appeal*, July 12, 1861; *Raleigh Weekly Standard,* July 17, 1861. His opposition to the recently passed Morrill Tariff also received praise. *Memphis Daily Appeal*, July 12, 1861.

9. Congressional Globe, 37th Cong, 1st Sess., July 10, 1861, 56–60.

10. Emma Holmes, *Diary of Miss Emma Holmes, 1861–1866,* ed. John F. Marszalek (Baton Rouge: Louisiana State University Press, 1979), 68–69; G. Ward Hubbs, ed., *Voices from Company D: Diaries by the Greensboro Guards, Fifth Alabama Regiment, Army of Northern Virginia* (Athens: University of Georgia Press, 2003), 34; *Richmond Daily Dispatch*, July 27, 1861; *New Orleans Daily Picayune,* July 27, 1861; *Milledgeville Southern Federal Union,* August 13, 1861.

11. *Jackson Weekly Mississippian*, September 4, 1861; *Richmond Daily Dispatch,* July 24, September 11, 1861; George Fitzhugh, "The Huguenots of the South," *DeBow's Review* 30 (May and June 1861): 517.

12. *Shreveport Daily News*, August 22, 1861; *Richmond Daily Dispatch*, August 24, 1861.

13. *Athens (GA) Southern Banner*, January 8, 1862; Samuel A. Burney, *A Southern Soldier's Letters Home: The Civil War Letters of Samuel A. Burney, Cobb's Georgia Legion, Army of Northern Virginia*, ed. Nat S. Turner III (Macon, GA: Mercer University Press, 2002), 98.

14. Congressional Globe, 37th Cong., 2nd Sess., December 16, 17, 1861, 101, 120, 208–11; Klement, *Limits of Dissent,* 92–96. For initial Confederate criticism after Vallandigham had defended the seizure of Mason and Slidell, see *Richmond Daily Dispatch*, December 27, 1861.

15. *Athens (GA) Southern Banner*, January 15, 1862; Congressional Globe, 37th Cong., 2nd Sess., January 7, 1862, 208; *Raleigh (NC) Weekly Standard*, January 21, 1862; *Raleigh (NC) Weekly Register,* January 22, 1862; *Charleston Tri-Weekly Courier,* January 16, 1862; *Huntsville (AL) Democrat,* January 22, 1862. I am most grateful to Chris McIlwain for generously sharing his voluminous collection of articles from Alabama newspapers.

16. *Charleston Tri-Weekly Courier,* January 16, 1862; *Richmond Daily Dispatch,* January 31, 1862; *Nashville Banner,* n.d., in *Galveston (TX) Tri-Weekly News,* February 8, 1862; *Vicksburg (MS) Whig,* January 29, 1862.

17. Catherine Ann Devereux Edmondston, *"Journal of a Secesh Lady": The Diary of Catherine Ann Devereux Edmondston, 1860–1866*, ed. Beth G. Crabtree and James W. Patton (Raleigh, NC: Division of Archives and History, 1979), 168.

18. *Athens (TN) Post*, August 8, 29, November 7, 1862; *Athens (GA) Southern Banner*, August 6, 29, 1862; *Galveston (TX) Tri-Weekly News*, October 8, 1862; *Richmond Daily Dispatch*, October 16, 1862.

19. Vallandigham, *Life*, 221–23.

20. Edwin H. Fay, *"This Infernal War": The Confederate Letters of Sgt. Edwin H. Fay*, ed. Bell Irvin Wiley (Austin: University of Texas Press, 1958), 185.

21. Congressional Globe, 37th Cong., 3rd. Sess., January 14, 1863, Appendix, 52–60.

22. For an argument that Vallandigham and other Copperheads consistently misread Confederate opinion, see Jennifer L. Weber, *Copperheads: The Rise and Fall of Lincoln's Opponents in the North* (New York: Oxford University Press, 2006), 99–100. Of course, it is just as true that Confederates often misread northern critics of the war.

23. On these ideas, see Jack P. Maddex Jr., "Proslavery Millennialism: Social Eschatology in Antebellum Southern Calvinism," *American Quarterly* 31 (Spring 1979): 46–62.

24. *Clark County (AL) Journal*, January 20, February 5, 1863; *Selma (AL) Daily Reporter*, February 7, 12, 1863; *Macon Georgia Weekly Telegraph*, January 23, 1863; *Richmond Daily Dispatch*, February 7, 1863.

25. *Memphis Daily Appeal* (Jackson, MS), February 9, 1863; John Preston Sheffey, *Soldier of Southwestern Virginia: The Civil War Letters of Captain John Preston Sheffey*, ed. James I. Robertson Jr. (Baton Rouge: Louisiana State University Press, 2004), 142.

26. *Camden (SC) Confederate*, February 6, 1863; *Weekly Raleigh (NC) Register*, February 10, 1863; *Richmond Daily Dispatch*, January 24, February 3, 7, 1863; *Atlanta Southern Confederacy*, February 14, 1863; *Charleston Mercury*, January 27, 1863; *Abingdon Virginian*, January 16, 1863; *Jackson (MS) Daily Southern Crisis*, February 7, 1863. Confederate newspapers printed lengthy excerpts from Vallandigham's speech, and a pamphlet version was published in Vicksburg. *Mobile (AL) Advertiser and Register*, February 15, 1863; *Greensboro Alabama Beacon*, February 20, 1863; *Jackson (MS) Daily Southern Crisis*, February 17, 1863; Clement L. Vallandigham, *Vallandigham's Speech. Its Reception in Congress* (Vicksburg, MS: H. C. Clarke, 1863).

27. *Richmond Enquirer*, March 30, 1863; *Richmond Daily Dispatch*, February 27, 1863; William Henry King, *No Pardons to Ask, nor Apologies to Make: The Journal of William Henry King, Gray's 28th Louisiana Regiment*, ed. Gary D. Joiner, Marilyn S. Joiner, and Clifton D. Cardin (Knoxville University of Tennessee Press, 2006), 86; Robert Patrick, *Reluctant Rebel: The Secret Diary of Robert Patrick, 1861–1865*, ed. F. Jay Taylor (Baton Rouge: Louisiana State University Press, 1959), 89–90; *Mobile (AL) Advertiser and Register*, February 12, 1863.

28. *New York Times*, February 15, 1863.

29. *Selma (AL) Daily Reporter*, February 25, 1863; *Clark County (AL) Journal*, March 5, 1863; *Richmond Daily Dispatch*, February 20, 1863; *Athens (GA) Southern Watchman*, February 25, 1863; *Savannah (GA) Daily Morning News*, February 23, 1863; *Fayetteville (NC) Observer*, February 25, 1863.

30. *Richmond Daily Dispatch*, March 7, 20, 1863; *Athens (GA) Southern Banner*, March 11, 1863;

Richmond Enquirer, March 27, 1863; *Mobile Tribune,* n.d. in *Richmond Daily Dispatch,* March 16, 1863. A thoughtful Ohio officer stationed in Louisiana concluded: "The secesh are too honorable to have anything to do with the northern Copperheads. In all the rebel papers I see they speak of the Vallandighamers with derision." George K. Pardee, *My Dear Carrie: The Civil War Letters of George K. Pardee and Family,* ed. Robert H. Jones (Akron, OH: Summit County Historical Society Press, 1994), 85.

31. *Atlanta Southern Confederacy,* March 13, 1863.

32. Edmund Ruffin, *The Diary of Edmund Ruffin,* 3 vols., ed. William K. Scarborough (Baton Rouge: Louisiana State University Press, 1972–89), 2:616; *Richmond Whig,* April 3, 1863; *Memphis Daily Appeal* (Jackson, MS), April 8, 1863.

33. Klement describes Vallandigham's words and actions leading up to his arrest in a chapter entitled "Seeking Martyrdom." *Limits of Dissent,* 139–55.

34. *War of the Rebellion: A Compilation of the Official Records of the Union and Confederate Armies,* 128 vols. (Washington, DC: Government Printing Office, 1880–1901), ser. 1, vol. 23, pt. 2, 237 (hereinafter cited as *OR*).

35. Klement, *Limits of Dissent,* 138–52; *Dayton (OH) Daily Empire,* May 1, 1863.

36. Vallandigham, *Life,* 248–53; *OR,* ser. 2, 5:636, 640–41.

37. Klement, *Limits of Dissent,* 156–68; *OR,* ser. 2, 5:555, 646.

38. Holmes, *Diary of Miss Emma Holmes,* 256; *Athens (GA) Southern Banner,* May 13, 1863; Frank L. Klement, "Clement L. Vallandigham's Exile in the Confederacy," *Journal of Southern History* 31 (May 1965): 150; *Atlanta Southern Confederacy,* May 15, 1863; *Richmond Daily Sentinel,* May 18, 1863; *Richmond Daily Dispatch,* May 12, 1863.

39. Ruffin, *Diary of Edmund Ruffin,* 2:648–50; *Savannah (GA) Daily Morning News,* May 13, 1863; *Richmond Whig,* May 12, 1863; *Charleston Courier* (Tri-Weekly), May 16, 1863.

40. *Richmond Daily Dispatch,* May 12, 18, 1863; *Atlanta Southern Confederacy,* May 15, 1863.

41. *Fayetteville (NC) Observer,* May 21, 1863; *Atlanta Southern Confederacy,* May 28, 1863; Holmes, *Diary of Miss Emma Holmes,* 263; *Athens (GA) Southern Banner,* May 20, 27, 1863; *Camden (SC) Confederate,* May 22, 1863. For a good account of various northern protests, see Klement, *Limits of Dissent,* 178–83.

42. *Richmond Daily Dispatch,* May 23, 25, 1863; *Abingdon Virginian,* May 29, 1863; *Athens (GA) Southern Banner,* May 20, 1863; Edmondston, *"Journal of a Secesh Lady,"* 394, 398; Ruffin, *Diary of Edmund Ruffin,* 2:664

43. *Fayetteville (NC) Observer,* May 28, 1863; Edward A. Pollard, *The Lost Cause: A New Southern History of the War* (New York: E. B. Treat, 1867), 472–74; *OR,* ser. 2, 5:657; *Macon (GA) Daily Telegraph,* May 23, 1863; *Galveston (TX) Tri-Weekly News,* June 2, 1863; *Richmond Daily Dispatch,* May 26, 1863 For a detailed account of how Lincoln dealt with Vallandigham's arrest, see Michael Burlingame, *Abraham Lincoln: A Life,* 2 vols. (Baltimore: Johns Hopkins University Press, 2008), 2:503–10.

44. *Richmond Daily Dispatch,* May 20, 1863; Fay, *"This Infernal War,"* 266; Arch Fredric Blakey, Ann Smith Lainhart, and Winston Bryant Stephens Jr., *Rose Cottage Chronicles: Civil War Letters of the Bryant-Stephens Families of North Florida* (Gainesville: University of Florida Press, 1998), 230–31.

45. Klement, *Limits of Dissent,* 190–95; Vallandigham, *Life,* 296–99; Clement L. Vallandigham to Horatio Seymour, May 21, 1863, Vallandigham Letters, Ohio Historical Society, Columbus.

46. *OR,* ser. 2, 5:705–6; Klement, *Limits of Dissent,* 195–201; Vallandigham, *Life,* 299–300. Accounts taken from several northern newspapers appeared in *Richmond Daily Dispatch,* May 30, 1863; *Savannah (GA) Daily Morning News,* June 2, 1863.

47. Vallandigham, *Life,* 300–301; *OR,* ser. 2, 5:958; Klement, *Limits of Dissent,* 202–3.

48. *Chattanooga Daily Rebel,* n.d. in *Savannah Daily Morning News,* May 30, 1863; Charles Todd Quintard, *Doctor Quintard, Chaplain C.S.A. and Second Bishop of Tennessee: The Memoir and Civil War Diary of Charles Todd Quintard,* ed. Sam Davis Elliott (Baton Rouge: Louisiana State University Press, 2003), 67–68.

49. *OR,* ser. 2, 5:963–65.

50. *Weekly Raleigh (NC) Register,* June 3, 1863; *Richmond Daily Dispatch,* June 1, 1863; *Abingdon Virginian,* June 5, 1863; *Mobile (AL) Advertiser and Register,* June 14, 1863.

51. *Macon (GA) Daily Telegraph,* May 28, 1863; *Richmond Whig,* May 29, 1863; *Staunton (VA) Spectator,* June 2, 1863; *Atlanta Southern Confederacy,* May 19, 1863.

52. *Huntsville (AL) Confederate,* May 24, 1863; Ruffin, *Diary of Edmund Ruffin,* 2:662; Klement, "Vallandigham's Exile in the Confederacy," 151, 155; *Milledgeville (GA) Southern Recorder,* May 26, 1863; *Richmond Daily Dispatch,* May 20, 1863; *Columbus (GA) Enquirer,* May 20, 1863, in *Atlanta Southern Confederacy,* May 21, 1863. Vallandigham was also advised to remain quiet while in the Confederacy. *Atlanta Southern Confederacy,* June 2, 1863; *Camden (SC) Confederate,* June 5, 1863.

53. *Chattanooga Daily Rebel,* June 3, 1863; Klement, *Limits of Dissent,* 207–8; Vallandigham, *Life,* 301; *Richmond Whig,* June 2, 1863; *Atlanta Intelligencer,* n.d., in *Savannah (GA) Daily Morning News,* June 8, 1863; Kate Cumming, *Kate: The Journal of a Confederate Nurse,* ed. Richard Barksdale Harwell (Baton Rouge: Louisiana State University Press, 1959), 108.

54. Klement, *Limits of Dissent,* 208–9; *OR,* ser. 2, 5:965–66; Susan Leigh Blackford, compiler, *Memoirs of Life In and Out of the Army in Virginia during the War Between the States,* 2 vols. (Lynchburg, VA: J. P. Bell, 1894), 2:52–53.

55. *OR,* ser. 2, 5:968–69; John B. Jones, *A Rebel War Clerk's Diary at the Confederate States Capital,* 2 vols. (Philadelphia: J. B. Lippincott, 1866), 1:353, 357–58; Robert Garlick Hill Kean, *Inside the Confederate Government: The Diary of Robert Garlick Hill Kean,* ed. Edward Younger (New York: Oxford University Press, 1957), 65; Mary Chesnut, *Mary Chesnut's Civil War,* ed. by C. Vann Woodward (New Haven: Yale University Press, 1981), 450–51. Mark Neely has pointed out that Davis failed to mention Vallandigham in any public way. By this time, the Confederate government had made some arbitrary arrests of its own, and so Davis could no longer assume the high moral ground on habeas corpus or other civil liberties questions. Mark E. Neely Jr., *Southern Rights: Political Prisoners and the Myth of Confederate Constitutionalism* (Charlottesville: University Press of Virginia, 1999), 165.

56. Jefferson Davis, *The Papers of Jefferson Davis,* ed. Lynda Lasswell Crist, Mary Seaton Dix, and Kenneth H. Williams, 13 vols. to date (Baton Rouge: Louisiana State University Press, 1971–), 9:253; *OR,* ser. 1, 14:955.

57. Robert E. Lee, *The Wartime Papers of R. E. Lee,* ed. Clifford Dowdey and Louis H. Manarin

(New York: Bramhill House, 1961), 507–9; John Witherspoon DuBose, *The Life and Times of William Lowndes Yancey* (New York: Peter Smith, 1942 [1892]), 751.

58. *Memphis Daily Appeal* (Atlanta), n.d. in *Mobile (AL) Evening Telegraph,* July 14, 1863; *Charleston Mercury,* June 17, 1863; *Athens (GA) Southern Watchman,* June 10, 1863; *Edgefield (SC) Advertiser,* June 17, 1863; *Raleigh (NC) Weekly Standard,* June 17, 1863.

59. *Richmond Enquirer,* n.d. and *Richmond Sentinel,* n.d. in *Chattanooga Daily Rebel,* June 2, 1863; Kean, *Inside the Confederate Government,* 69; *Atlanta Southern Confederacy,* June 8, 1863; Edmondston, "*Journal of a Secesh Lady,*" 399; *Richmond Daily Dispatch,* May 30, 1863; *Mobile (AL) Advertiser and Register,* June 9, 1863; *Clark County (AL) Journal,* June 4, 1863.

60. *Edgefield (SC) Advertiser,* May 27, 1863; *Weekly Raleigh (NC) Register,* May 27, 1863; *Natchez (MS) Daily Courier,* June 18, 1863.

61. *Athens (GA) Southern Watchman,* June 3, 1863; *Weekly Raleigh (NC) Register,* June 3, 1863; *Athens (GA) Southern Banner,* July 1, 1863; *Galveston (TX) Tri-Weekly News,* June 9, July 1, 1863; *Richmond Daily Dispatch,* June 4, 1863; *Atlanta Southern Confederacy,* June 11, 1863.

62. *Fayetteville (NC) Observer,* June 1, 1863; Ruffin, *Diary of Edmund Ruffin,* 3:2.

63. Ruffin, *Diary of Edmund Ruffin,* 3:2, 34; *Weekly Raleigh (NC) Register,* May 27, 1863; *Atlanta Southern Confederacy,* June 2, 25, 1863; Josiah Gorgas, *The Journals of Josiah Gorgas, 1857–1878,* ed. Sarah Woolfolk Wiggins (Tuscaloosa: University of Alabama Press, 1995), 68; Abraham Lincoln, *The Collected Works of Abraham Lincoln,* 9 vols., ed. Roy P. Basler (New Brunswick, NJ: Rutgers University Press, 1954), 6:266–67.

64. *Atlanta Southern Confederacy,* June 8, 1863; *Wilmington (NC) Journal,* n.d. in *Camden (SC) Confederate,* June 26, 1863; *Augusta (GA) Daily Chronicle,* June 16, 1863.

65. *Richmond Daily Dispatch,* June 15, July 24, 1863; *Staunton (VA) Spectator,* July 7, 1863; *Galveston (TX) Tri-Weekly News,* July 20, 1863; Vallandigham, *Life,* 319, 321; *Milledgeville (GA) Southern Recorder,* August 4, 1863; *Chattanooga Daily Rebel,* July 28, 1863; *Raleigh (NC) Weekly Standard,* July 29, 1863; *Staunton (VA) Spectator,* July 28, 1863.

66. *Lynchburg Virginian,* n.d. in *Staunton (VA) Spectator,* June 23, 1863; *Fayetteville (NC) Observer,* August 13, 1863; Fay, "*This Infernal War,*" 342; William M. McPheeters, *I Acted from Principle: The Civil War Diary of Dr. William M. McPheeters, Confederate Surgeon in the Trans-Mississippi,* ed. Cynthia DeHaven Pitcock and Bill J. Gurley (Fayetteville: University of Arkansas Press, 2002), 72–73; *OR,* ser. 1, vol. 22, pt. 2, 661.

67. William Alexander Graham, *Papers of William Alexander Graham,* ed. Max R. Williams et al., 8 vols. to date (Raleigh: North Carolina Office of Archives and History, 1957–), 5:521; *Memphis Daily Appeal* (Jackson, MS), February 5, 1863; *Chattanooga Daily Rebel,* June 3, 1863; *Richmond Sentinel,* n.d. in *Milledgeville (GA) Confederate Union,* July 7, 1863; *Richmond Examiner,* n.d. in *Athens (GA) Southern Banner,* September 16, 1863; *Richmond Daily Sentinel,* September 15, 1863; Sheffey, *Soldier of Southwestern Virginia,* 193.

68. *Richmond Daily Dispatch,* November 16, 1863; John Dooley, *John Dooley's Civil War: An Irish American's Journey in the First Virginia Infantry Regiment,* ed. Robert Emmett Curran (Knoxville: University of Tennessee Press, 2012), 212; Asa Newton Paschal and Samuel Thomas Paschal, *From Beardstown to Andersonville: The Civil War Letters of Asa Newton Paschal and Samuel Thomas Paschal,* ed. Joseph Edward Fulton. (Bowie, MD: Heritage Books, 1998), 35; *Talladega (AL) Democratic Watchtower,* November 4, 1863; *Selma (AL) Daily Reporter,* October 24, 1863.

69. *Athens (GA) Southern Watchman,* June 29, 1864; *Columbia Daily South Carolinian,* June 28, 1864; James C. Bates, *A Texas Cavalry Officer's Civil War: The Diary and Letters of James C. Bates,* ed. Richard Lowe (Baton Rouge: Louisiana State University, 1999), 303–4; *Richmond Daily Sentinel,* June 25, 1864; *Richmond Examiner,* n.d., in *Milledgeville (GA) Confederate Union,* July 26, 1864; Edmund DeWitt Patterson, *Yankee Rebel: The Civil War Journal of Edmund DeWitt Patterson,* ed. John G. Barrett (Knoxville: University of Tennessee Press, 2004), 172–73. See also *Rebellion in the North!! Extraordinary Disclosures! Vallandigham's Plan to Overthrow the Government! The Peace Party Plot!* [Richmond: n.p., 1864].

70. *Mobile (AL) Advertiser and Register,* May 31, 1863; Emilie Riley McKinley, *From the Pen of a She-Rebel: The Civil War Diary of Emilie Riley McKinley,* ed. Gordon A. Cotton (Columbia: University of South Carolina Press, 2001), 31–32. Even earlier, Richmond editors had exchanged barbs over whether to pursue a "divide and conquer" strategy toward the northwestern states. *Richmond Whig,* March 27, 1863.

71. For an excellent analysis of what might be termed "sectional misrepresentation" during the early years of Reconstruction, see Michael Perman, *Reunion without Compromise: The South and Reconstruction, 1865–1868* (Cambridge: Cambridge University Press, 1973), 144–81.

72. Benjamin C. Truman, "An Evening with a Copperhead," *Confederate Veteran* 17 (November 1909): 563; M. W. Sims, "Vallandigham—Spirit of Vindication," *Confederate Veteran* 18 (February 1910): 74.

CHAPTER FIVE

Rich Man's Fight

Wealth, Privilege, and Military Service in Confederate Mississippi

Paul F. Paskoff

Few characterizations of the Confederacy's conduct of the Civil War have been as provocative as that which describes the conflict as "a rich man's war but a poor man's fight." The epithet reflected popular resentment over a series of conscription laws that permitted the hiring of substitutes, the purchase of exemptions from service, and the exemption of men, including planters, who held twenty or more slaves. (Beginning in 1864, the law applied to those who held at least fifteen slaves.)[1] The bitterness of the sentiment presumably undermined the Confederate war effort by breaking down internal cohesion and contributing to a loss of the will to fight and of planters' political power. Most recent historical scholarship on the subject supports this view and the assertion that many of the wealthiest white male southerners of military age avoided military service, thereby shifting the burdens and dangers of such service to less affluent men.[2]

Although there has never been any substantial evidence offered to support this assertion, it has nevertheless acquired the status of fact through frequent repetition and successive, serial citation. It has done so, moreover, despite a slowly growing body of work that has called its validity into question.[3] For good reason, much of this recent work is quantitative in character. Ultimately, any reliable determination of the truth of the "rich man's war, poor man's fight" characterization of the Confederate war should rest on a solid foundation of quantitative evidence and analysis because the assertion, itself, is inherently quantitative in nature.

A determination that the wealthiest men generally stayed at home while poorer men did the fighting and dying would lend considerable support to the now conventional interpretation of the Confederate war effort and immediate postwar era. A corollary to this interpretation is that poorer southerners eventually reached the bitter conclusion during the war that they were fighting it not because they and their considerably wealthier fellow Confederates had interests in common but because they had been duped into working against their own interests by fighting to advance those of an entrenched planter aristocracy. Moreover, even if few wealthy men actually avoided military service, a considerable body of popular opinion held that many had done just that. Presumably, that conviction and the alienation inspired by it survived the war and helped to shape the politics of the immediate postwar years.[4]

Finding that the wealthiest class of white southern men served in Confederate forces at a rate comparable to that of the eligible population as a whole would significantly undermine the conventional interpretation. At the very least, such a finding would raise the possibility that the presumably widespread resentment expressed by the "rich man's war, poor man's fight" epithet may not have been so widely held, after all. More specifically, service by wealthy men at a rate similar to that of the general eligible male population would call into question the conventional interpretation's collateral implications about popular morale during the war, the reasons for the Confederacy's collapse, and the character of southern politics in the war's immediate aftermath. These concerns are the subject of this essay, which presents a rigorous quantitative analysis of the military service and postwar political power of the slave-owning elite in Mississippi, a state that played an important part in the Confederacy's war effort.

Mississippi was second, and only just so, to South Carolina in the proportion of the total population that was enslaved and in the proportion of the free population that held slaves. The state had the third, after Louisiana and South Carolina, highest proportion of great planters—those who held fifty or more slaves—among its slaveholders.[5] The intensity of its military effort, as measured by the number of troops sent to fight for the Confederacy, was considerable, amounting, according to some unsystematic estimates, to perhaps between 70,000 and 78,000 men, many more than a simple majority of the state's white male population of military age.[6] In these ways, and also because of the extent and intensity of the fighting that occurred within its borders, Mississippi's involvement in the war was acute.

The greater part of the evidence considered here consists of three sets of data. One of these, available on the web, is a list of Mississippi's 2,180 largest slaveholdings in 1860 in the twenty-seven counties (of the state's total of sixty) that had a significant number of large slaveholdings.[7] The determination of the military service or its avoidance by eligible men in this group of the wealthiest Mississippians bears directly on the accuracy of the "rich man's war" characterization of the Confederate war effort. So, too, does a determination of the proportion of young men from wealthy families who served in the army. That proportion is the result of an examination of a second set of data consisting of a comprehensive list of the graduates of the University of Mississippi's last five antebellum classes, from 1856 through 1860, inclusive.[8] The third group of data are two lists of every member of Mississippi's House of Representatives and Senate during the last two years before the war, 1859 to 1861, and during the first two years following the war's end, 1865 to 1867.[9] The use of the data in this group permits a test of the proposition that planters' wartime behavior, including their alleged shirking of military service, sparked intense popular disillusionment and resentment toward the planter class. Presumably, such alienation manifested itself at the ballot box, so that we may reasonably expect that the proportion of seats in each chamber of the state legislature held by planters immediately after the war decreased sharply from what it had been immediately before the war.

These data sets offer a useful vantage point from which to assess, rigorously and quantitatively, the validity of the rich man's war, poor man's fight interpretation of Mississippi's war, especially that interpretation's integrally important assertion that the wealthiest slaveholders served in the military at a rate significantly below that of the eligible population as a whole. Of the state's 2,180 largest slaveholdings, 821 of them were in the hands of men young enough to be eligible for military service under the draft law; of this number, 539, or just under 66 percent, served.[10] The 66-percent rate of military service of Mississippi's eligible largest slaveholders is not only well within the revised range of service rates for the Confederacy's general population but approaches the upper bound of that range. In other words, far from shirking military service, nearly two-thirds of the state's wealthiest men of military age—and some beyond the age of conscription—served in the army. Many, if not most of them, including those in reserve units, saw combat as the fighting penetrated the state's borders.

The generally accepted characterization of the type of military service engaged in by the wealthiest men of eligible age is that they sat out the war in the relative safety of local defense companies, home guard companies, or reserve regiments—in short, in units that had little prospect of seeing combat. That notion is mistaken on two counts. First, almost all of the 539 largest slaveholders of military age who served in the army did so in regular, front-line combat units. Of 422 men enrolled in ten local defense or home guard companies organized in the state's counties with largest slaveholders, 24, or 5.7 percent, were themselves largest slaveholders. Of those twenty-four, only thirteen, or just over 3 percent of the 422 men, were young enough for conscription.[11]

The second misconception about the local defense and home guard units is that able-bodied men of prime military age filled their ranks. Although some of those units fit that description, many others did not. One that did was Fant's Company, a unit of thirty-seven men that had been organized for Noxubee County's local defense. Of the twenty-nine members of the unit for whom a census listing was available, twenty men, with an average age of twenty-five, fell within the age range for conscription into the regular service. But only one of those twenty ranked among the largest slaveholders in a county where more than 18 percent of all slaveholders and 58 percent of all planters were largest slaveholders.[12]

If Fant's Company was an example of the stereotypical local defense unit, then Gordon's Company of Local Guards of Wilkinson County presented one of a very different cast. This company numbered twenty-eight: a captain, three lieutenants, and twenty-four privates. In 1864, when the age of conscription rose to fifty, only two of the company's members were eligible for the draft: one of these was forty-one, the other was forty-five. The other twenty-six members were well into their fifties and even sixties, and none of the members of the company, of whatever age, were among the county's largest slaveholders.[13]

Still another misconception about home guard and local defense companies is that there were many of them. Of the 133 companies organized in Mississippi, only 24, or just over 18 percent, were small home guard or local defense units.[14] Even so, many of those companies saw combat as federal forces moved upon and into the state. In any event, the combined enrolled strength of all of the state's local defense and home guard companies was 953 men, a number that amounted to at most 1.4 percent of the total number of Mississippians who served in Confederate forces.[15] Whatever the ultimate purpose and utility of such units, they provided a refuge from harder service for only a few eligible men among Mississippi's general population and for virtually none of the state's planter elite.

The most privileged people in the South at the beginning of 1861 were probably the young men who had graduated from its major universities. Sons of wealthy planters and farmers, merchants, doctors, and, in a few instances, clergymen, the collegians had grown up in comfort. The financial circumstances of the fathers of the University of Mississippi's classes of 1856 and 1857 illustrate this point.[16] Of the thirty-two fathers whom I was able to locate in the census records, twelve were listed as planters, thirteen as farmers, three as doctors, two as clergymen, one as a merchant, and one as a teacher.

With the exception of the teacher and the merchant, whose real estates were valuated respectively at $500 and $1,700, the fathers of the graduates were rather well off when they sent their sons off to the university. The average value of the real estate of the planters was just over $18,000 and that of the farmers was $7,930, while the average values of the real estates of the doctors and clergymen were $3,667 and $2,750, respectively. The average of all thirty-two fathers' real estates was $10,569, a rather substantial amount in 1850 and the equivalent of about $313,889 in 2011 dollars, clear evidence that almost all of the university's students came from families of considerable means.[17]

These scions of wealth and privilege became the sort of young men who, according to the "rich man's war, poor man's fight" interpretation of the Confederate war, remained civilians or, if that proved impossible, found refuge from the war in local defense or home guard units. In fact, the young men studied here did almost precisely the opposite. Rather than avoid service or serve at home, away from the fighting, they enlisted in regular units that saw extensive combat. As table 1 illustrates, just under 93 percent of the members of the last five antebellum graduating classes of the University of Mississippi, 1856 through 1860, served with Confederate forces. Of the 126 students from Mississippi who graduated in those years, 117 went into the army, and, apparently, none of those 117 served in local defense or home guard units.

Whatever the reasons that impelled so many of Mississippi's recent university graduates to serve in the Confederate forces, their service further undermines the rich man's war, poor man's fight interpretation of the Confederate war effort. For veterans who had served with or under those graduates, the notion that men like their university-educated comrades had shirked their duty to the Cause could not have been especially persuasive. The graduates' service, like that of the largest slaveholders, is significant not only for our understanding of the character of the war waged by the Confederacy but also for comprehending the political life of Mississippi—and likely that of the other Confederate states—immediately after the war.

During the first two years after the war, the states of the former

TABLE 1

Military Service by the Last Five Antebellum Graduating Classes
of the University of Mississippi, 1856–1860[a]

Class Year	Number of Graduates	Number Served in CSA	Percentage Served in CSA
1856	24	17	70.8
(34)	(25)	(73.5)	
1857	33	27	81.8
(36)	(29)	(80.6)	
1858	27	24	88.9
(39)	(31)	(79.5)	
1859	16	16	100.0
(19)	(19)	(100.0)	
1860	26	25	96.2
(27)	(25)	(92.6)	
1856–60	126	117	92.9
(155)	(124)	(80.0)	

Sources: Number of graduates in each graduating class is derived from *Historical Catalogue of the University of Mississippi, 1849–1909* (Nashville, TN: Marshall & Bruce Company, 1910), 123–34. Figures on number of graduates who served in Confederate military forces are derived from H. Grady Howell Jr., *For Dixie Land I'll Take My Stand! A Muster Listing of All Known Mississippi Confederate Soldiers, Sailors and Marines*, vols. 1–3 (Madison, MS: Chickasaw Bayou Press, 1998), and U.S. National Parks Service, "Soldiers and Sailors Database," www.itd.nps.gov/cwss/.

General note: The number of graduates in any class are those who received the A.B. degree. Excluded are those who received a degree in law, those who did not graduate with their class, and those who were "pursuing selected studies."

[a] For each graduating class, the numbers without parentheses refer to the number of students whose homes were in Mississippi; the numbers within parentheses include Mississippi residents, as well as students whose homes were in other states.

Confederacy operated under the provisions of presidential Reconstruction. That policy encouraged them to hold elections for state and federal legislative offices. Although Congress ultimately rejected almost all congressmen and senators sent to Washington by the former Confederate states, those states' white politicians and voters were still able to reconstitute their own legislatures. As had been the case before the war, an electorate of white male voters chose the members of Mississippi's House of Representatives and Senate.[18]

Had there been widespread popular resentment of Mississippi's planter elite, whatever the reasons, that sentiment would probably have expressed itself at the polls. That is, the proportion of seats held by planters in the state legislature during the two years after Appomattox should have been significantly lower than the corresponding proportion during the years immediately preceding the war. A comparison of the House and Senate chambers of the legislature during the last two years before the war and the first two years following it does suggest an erosion of the position of planters in the legislature. But that erosion was more apparent than real.

As table 2 indicates, the share of seats held by planters in the House of Representatives did, in fact, decrease from 40 percent to just over 30 percent, while the planters' share of Senate seats fell from not quite 45 percent to almost 39 percent. One may, of course, see in these results evidence of a significant reduction of planters' political power in Mississippi, a reduction presumably caused by a popular resentment of planters heightened during the war. Yet, even considered in that light, the reduction was not substantial: planters still held almost a third of the seats in the state legislature in the years immediately following Appomattox.

Although these results ostensibly lend support to the view of the war as a rich man's war but a poor man's fight, they actually present a somewhat distorted view of the situation. One of the likely reasons for the reduction in the ranks of planters in the state legislature was that the state's postwar population of men who, in 1860, had been planters had decreased from what it had been before the war. The reduction was particularly acute among the great planters, that is, those who had held fifty or more slaves. Many of them, as well as lesser planters, had died of natural causes, been killed in the war, or moved elsewhere since 1860. So much is evident from an examination of the 1870 federal census's enumeration of population. All told, roughly two-thirds of the men who had been Mississippi's great planters in 1860 no longer lived in

TABLE 2

Incidence of Planters in the Mississippi State Legislature, Before and After the War

| | House of Representatives[a] | | |
	No. Members Found in Census	No. Planters among Members Found in Census	Proportion of Planters of Members Found in Census
Prewar (1859–61)	95	38	40.0%
Postwar (1865–67)	83	25	30.1%

| | Senate[b] | | |
	No. Members Found in Census	No. Planters among Members Found in Census	Proportion of Planters of Members Found in Census
Prewar (1859–61)	38	17	44.7%
Postwar (1865–67)	31	12	38.7%

Sources: Members of the Mississippi House of Representatives and Senate are from Dunbar Rowland, LL.D., Director, Mississippi Department of Archives and History, *The Official and Statistical Register of the State of Mississippi, 1908* (Nashville, TN: Press of the Brandon Printing Company, 1908), 46–124, "Members of Mississippi Legislature, 1817-1908." Whether a member of the state legislature was a planter was determined by finding his name in the free and slave population schedules in *U.S. Census (Eighth Census), 1860.*

General note: As the figures in the table indicate, several members listed in Dunbar's roster were not found in either of the population schedules of the 1860 census. In most cases, their absence from the census was more apparent than real and was likely due to differences in the spelling of their last names in the census and in Dunbar's roster, differences that prevented identification in the census. No doubt, in some instances, the absence of a legislator's name from the census signified nothing more than the fact that the census enumerator missed him while making his rounds.

[a] Two members of the House of Representatives served in both the prewar and postwar legislatures and are included in the total number of members for each period.

[b] One member of the Senate served in both the prewar and postwar legislatures and is included in the total number for each period.

the state a decade later. Small wonder, then, that the proportion of seats held in the state legislature of 1865–67 by those who had been great planters had fallen by 67 percent, that is, by about the same percentage as the reduction in the number of former great planters who still lived in Mississippi in 1870.[19]

Far from indicating an erosion of political power, these results suggest that Mississippi's planter aristocracy substantially maintained its political position in the immediate postwar period, despite the disruptions and hardships occasioned by the war and defeat. The electorate that voted for planter candidates consisted largely of yeoman farmers and former small-scale slaveholders. Before the war, white supremacist ideology and fear of the consequences of the abolition of slavery may well have inclined such voters to support planter candidates as bulwarks, actual and symbolic, against a potential floodtide of change. Race figured prominently in postwar politics, as well. Whatever the voters' reasons for electing planters to state offices, the retention of political viability by planters after Appomattox argues against our placing too much stock in the idea that class antagonisms defined and steered southern society during the war and in the years immediately following its end.

Instead, we should probably conclude, at least with respect to Mississippi, that, far from having been discredited during the war, planters emerged from it still esteemed by their less affluent neighbors. Bitter individuals might speak of a rich man's war but a poor man's fight, but that indictment did not persuade voters. Indeed, in light of the high rate of military service by the largest slaveholders, how could it have done so? Many of the electorate knew from first-hand experience as soldiers that large numbers of wealthy planters had fought alongside them in the ranks or, as officers and noncommissioned officers, had led them in combat. For such voters, as well as for those who had stayed at home during the war but knew planters who had gone to fight, planter candidates after the war enjoyed a hard-won political legitimacy, one that transcended class tensions.

A central tenet of the rich man's war, poor man's fight interpretation of the Confederate war is the assertion of class conflict. That conflict is said to have simmered below the surface of southern society even before the war and to have intensified and expanded during the war. Ultimately, it broke through a veneer of Confederate unity, undermining the war effort and helping to shape postwar politics in the South. Presumably, at the core of this alienation was antipathy toward the planter elite. Perhaps there is something to this assertion, at least in the political arena of stump speeches and public assertions of ideology, but in the more concrete, practical domain of law making there is little evidence to support it. As tables 3a and 3b indicate, the record of legislation enacted in the years just before the war, when the proportion of planters in the legislature was at its highest, is comparable to the legislature's record in the years of presidential Reconstruction immediately after the war, when the presence of planters was less prominent.

In both periods, Mississippi's state legislators devoted similar amounts of attention to promoting economic development by chartering railroad, manufacturing, mining, and banking corporations. Of the 758 acts passed by the legislature during the period of presidential Reconstruction, 120 or 16 percent addressed various aspects of development. In the last two years before the war, the state's legislature had passed a total of 409 acts, of which 75 or 18 percent concerned development. The prewar and postwar legislatures' emphasis differed most markedly in the area of education, including public schools, private schools, and higher education. The prewar legislature devoted almost exactly twice as much of its attention to such matters as did the immediately postwar legislature. A possible reason for the relative reduction in the attention paid to education by the immediate postwar legislature may have been its perception that economic development was a more pressing concern.

These results suggest that class antagonism directed at the planter elite probably played a much less significant part in the defeat of the Confederacy and in the shaping of immediate postwar politics than has often been suggested by historians.[20] That observation is certainly consistent with the evidence concerning Mississippi during the years of war and presidential Reconstruction. For white Mississippi, the war had not just been a poor man's fight. It had been a rich man's fight, as well.[21]

---★---

APPENDIX: DATA AND METHODS

Three sets of data constitute the bulk of the evidence examined here. One of these, available on the web, is a list of the state's largest slaveholders in 1860 in each of twenty-seven of the state's sixty counties. A second set is a comprehensive list of the graduates of the last five antebellum classes, from

TABLE 3a

Acts Passed by Mississippi's Legislature to Promote Economic Development just before the War, just after the War, during Reconstruction, and just after Reconstruction

Period Number	Total	All Economic Development[a] (no. percent)	Industry and Misc.[b]	Public Education	Roads and Turnpikes	Railroads	Higher Education	Banks	Academies
1859–60	409	75 (18)	5	27	6	23	2	1	11
1865–67	758	120 (16)	5	11	8	25	8	20	13
1873	468	118 (25)	12	19	5	44	16	21	1
1880	381	89 (23)	27	23	4	18	9	3	5

TABLE 3b

Summary of Acts Passed by Mississippi's Legislature to Promote Economic Development, including Education, just before and after the War and during and after Congressional Reconstruction

	(1)	(2)	(3)	(4)	(5)	(6)	(7)	(8)	(9)
Period	Total Number Passed	Number for Economic Development[a]	Number for All Types of Education[c]	Number for Public Education	(2) as Percent of (1)	(3) as Percent of (1)	(3) as Percent of (2)	(4) as Percent of (2)	(4) as Percent of (3)
1859–60	409	75	40	18	18	10	53	24	45
1865–67	758	120	32	16	16	4	27	13	50
1873	468	118	36	25	25	8	8	21	69
1880	381	89	37	23	23	10	40	26	62

Sources: Laws of the State of Mississippi, Passed at a Regular Session of the Mississippi Legislature, Held in the City of Jackson, November, 1859 (Jackson: E. Barksdale, State Printer, 1860); Laws of the State of Mississippi, Passed at a Regular Session of the Mississippi Legislature, Held in the City of Jackson, November, 1860 (Jackson: E. Barksdale, State Printer, 1861); Laws of the State of Mississippi, Passed at a Called Session of the Mississippi Legislature, Held in the City of Jackson, October, 1866, and January and February, 1867 (Jackson: J. J. Shannon & Co., State Printers, 1867); Laws of the State of Mississippi, Passed at a Regular Session of the Mississippi Legislature, Held in the City of Jackson, Commencing January 21, 1873, and Ending April 19, 1873 (Jackson: Kimball, Raymond & Co., State Printers, 1873); Laws of the State of Mississippi, Passed at a Called Session, of the Mississippi Legislature, Convened in the City of Jackson, October 20th, 1873 (Jackson: Kimball, Raymond & Co., State Printers, 1874); Laws of the State of Mississippi, Passed at a Regular Session of the Mississippi Legislature, Held in the City of Jackson, Commencing January 6th, 1880, and Ending March 6th, 1880 (Jackson: J. L. Power, State Printer, 1880).

[a] As used in the table, "economic development" embraces manufacturing, mining, insurance underwriting, telegraphs, canals, roads, railroads, banks, public and private schools, and higher education.

[b] "Industry and miscellaneous" denote manufacturing, mining, insurance, telegraphs, and canals.

[c] Included here are acts to incorporate private academies, seminaries, institutes, and colleges, as well as acts to fund and regulate public schools and to establish state universities.

1856 through 1860, inclusive, of the University of Mississippi. The third group of data is a comprehensive listing of each member of Mississippi's House of Representatives and Senate during the last two years before the war, 1859 to 1861, and during the first two years following the war's end, 1865 to 1867. None of these groups represents a statistical sample of some larger group; instead, each group contains all members of that group. For example, the group of recent university graduates includes every graduate of the University of Mississippi for the years 1856 through 1860, inclusive.

Of Mississippi's sixty counties in 1860, three—Hancock, Sunflower, and Washington—made no returns in the census of the number of slaveholders among their free population. The twenty-eight counties for which lists of the largest slaveholders are available on the website reflect primarily the decisions of the genealogists who abstracted them from the slave schedule of the manuscript census. The logic underlying those decisions is clear and compelling and imposes a rather rigorous standard for inclusion of counties on the list of those with largest slaveholders. With only one exception, the twenty-eight counties selected had a substantial number of great planters among their slaveholders. The single exception was Simpson County, which, although included by the website in the roster of counties with largest slaveholders, had no abstracted list of largest slaveholders. Instead, the compiler of the data for Simpson County simply provided a list of all slaveholders, rather than a list of the largest slaveholders or even just a list of planters. Consequently, Simpson County, which had all of twenty-nine planters, only four of whom were great planters, does not properly belong in the list of counties with largest slaveholders and is excluded from the analysis presented here.

The one factor that all of the other twenty-seven counties had in common, and one that likely influenced the genealogists' decision to include them in the list of counties with significant numbers of "largest planters," was that each of the included counties had at least twenty great planters among its slaveholders. Although not criteria for inclusion, two characteristics derived from the data for all sixty counties sharply distinguish the twenty-seven included counties from the thirty-three other counties. First, in the included counties, planters represented more than 26 percent of all slaveholders, while planters in the other counties accounted for less than 10 percent of all slaveholders. Second, 31 percent of all planters in the included counties were great planters, while only about 15 percent of all planters were great planters in the other counties.

The prerequisite for calculating the proportion of the largest slaveholders who served in the military was a determination of which of those men were of military age during the war. To make that determination, I traced each man's name in the manuscript population schedule of the 1860 census and recorded his age, his occupation—almost all were listed as either farmer or planter—his real and personal estates, and the names of his sons who reached military age before the end of the war. Those slaveholders who were at least forty-seven years old in 1860 would have been too old during the war for conscription, though they could have enlisted. I then checked these names, as well as those of the remaining slaveholders who were forty-six years old or younger in 1860, against Confederate service rosters to identify those who served in regular military units, those who served in local defense or home guard companies, and those who never served. Table A.1 presents, for each of the 27 counties, the number of largest slaveholders, the average number of slaves owned by them, the number of largest slaveholders eligible for service, the number who served, and the percentage of the eligible number who served. Table A.2 presents for each of the same twenty-seven counties the relative incidences, expressed as percentages, of planters, great planters, and largest planters of all slaveholders.

The lists of university graduates lent themselves to the same basic approach, and, again, the goal was the determination of the number of members of the University of Mississippi's five graduating classes who served in Confederate forces. That information permitted a calculation of the proportion of each of the University of Mississippi's last five antebellum graduating classes that served. All told, there were 581 students, including graduates, students who pursued "select studies," and students who did not complete their degrees but were still listed by their institutions under their respective classes. The results reported in table 2 are based only on the number of actual graduates in each of the five classes.

Finding the members of Mississippi's state legislature of 1859 to 1861 in the free population and slave schedules of the 1860 census was a fairly straightforward matter. It entailed using the procedure followed with respect to the largest slaveholders. The task of finding the members of the state legislature of 1865 to 1867 in the population schedule of the 1870 census was considerably more difficult for two reasons. One of these was the unsettled conditions in Mississippi in the years after the war, years of increased population mobility.

Basic Data on Slaveholding in Mississippi, 1860

County	Slaves	Slaveholders	Planters	Great Planters	Largest Planters
Adams	14,292	688	170	84	39
Amite	7,900	628	110	25	37
Attala	5,015	637	52	10	0
Bolivar	9,078	297	159	43	39
Calhoun	1,823	371	9	0	0
Carroll	13,808	963	210	44	72
Chickasaw	9,087	702	276	30	54
Choctaw	4,197	616	44	2	0
Claiborne	12,296	424	176	89	110
Clarke	5,076	430	71	21	21
Coahoma	5,085	230	78	32	45
Copiah	7,965	737	107	22	33
Covington	1,563	204	19	1	0
De Soto	13,987	1,089	215	35	57
Franklin	4,752	354	67	15	0
Green	705	93	4	2	0
Hancock[a]	857				
Harrison	1,015	161	7	1	0
Hinds	22,363	1,421	371	95	135
Holmes	11,975	806	194	48	169
Issaquena	7,244	115	81	44	26
Itawamba	3,528	518	38	4	0
Jackson	1,087	146	15	0	0
Jasper	4,549	503	63	8	0
Jefferson	12,396	425	187	88	181
Jones	407	116	2	0	0
Kemper	5,741	552	74	15	0
Lafayette	7,129	714	93	21	0
Lauderdale	5,088	577	65	11	0
Lawrence	3,696	450	37	6	0
Leake	3,056	470	24	3	0
Lowndes	16,730	1,006	234	76	123
Madison	18,118	965	293	103	139
Marion	2,185	210	27	7	0
Marshall	17,439	1,295	288	58	94
Monroe	12,729	810	189	65	125
Neshoba	2,212	374	16	0	0
Newton	3,379	413	31	9	0
Noxubee	15,496	748	235	96	137
Oktibbeha	7,631	549	115	28	38
Panola	8,557	629	144	25	45
Perry	738	95	8	0	0

County	Slaves	Slaveholders	Planters	Great Planters	Largest Planters
Pike	4,935	587	47	5	0
Pontotoc	**7,596**	**851**	**99**	**12**	**93**
Rankin	7,103	684	99	15	0
Scott	2,959	368	39	1	0
Simpson	**2,324**	**274**	**29**	**4**	**32**
Smith	2,195	331	18	2	0
Sunflower[a]	3,917				
Tallahatchie	**5,054**	**360**	**85**	**22**	**34**
Tippah	6,331	286	79	9	0
Tishomingo	**4,981**	**707**	**53**	**4**	**44**
Tunica	**3,483**	**132**	**59**	**23**	**33**
Warren	**13,763**	**821**	**196**	**80**	**120**
Washington[a]	14,467				
Wayne	1,947	92	23	7	0
Wilkinson	**13,132**	**499**	**166**	**82**	**40**
Winston	4,223	460	48	8	0
Yalobusha	**9,531**	**721**	**155**	**33**	**149**
Yazoo	**16,716**	**699**	**239**	**99**	**85**
All Counties	436,631	30,943	6,032	1,672	2,350

Source: Numbers of slaves and slaveholders are from *Agriculture of the United States in 1860; Compiled from the Original Returns of the Eighth Census, Under the Direction of the Secretary of the Interior, By Joseph C. G. Kennedy, Superintendent of the Census* (Washington, DC: Government Printing Office, 1864), 232. Numbers of planters, generally defined as farmers with twenty or more slaves, and great planters, generally defined to be a planter with fifty or more slaves, are derived from the same source. The number of largest slaveholders is derived from the data on the "largest slaveholders," presented at http://freepages.genealogy.rootsweb.com/~ajac.

General note: Counties in bold are those enumerated in the rosters of "largest slaveholders." Of Mississippi's sixty counties in 1860, the census reported that three made no returns of the number of slaveholders among their free population. The thirty counties for which data on the largest slaveholders are available reflect primarily the choices made by the compilers of the Web site on which they appear. The logic underlying those choices is clear and compelling.

With only a few exceptions, the thirty counties selected had a substantial number of great planters among their slaveholders. More concretely, the proportion of planters among the slaveholders in these thirty counties was more than 27 percent, while the comparable figure for the twenty-seven counties for which no tabulation of largest slaveholders was available on the Web site was slightly more than 9 percent.

[a] Indicates that the census reported no returns of the number of slaveholders or the size of their holdings for these counties.

Incidence of Planters, Great Planters, and Largest Slaveholders in
Mississippi, 1860 (indicated as percentages for selected counties)

County	Percent of Planters of Slaveholders	Percent of Great Planters of all Slaveholders	Percent of Great Planters of all Plants	Percent of Largest Slaveholders of all Slaveholders	Percent of Largest Slaveholders of all Slaveholders
Adams	24.7	12.2	49.4	5.7	22.9
Amite	17.5	4.0	22.7	5.9	33.6
Attala	8.2	1.6	19.2	0.0	0.0
Bolivar	53.5	14.5	27.0	13.1	24.5
Calhoun	2.4	0.0	0.0	0.0	0.0
Carroll	21.8	4.6	21.0	7.5	34.3
Chickasaw	39.3	4.3	10.9	7.7	19.6
Choctaw	7.1	0.3	4.5	0.0	0.0
Claiborne	41.5	21.0	50.6	25.9	62.5
Clarke	16.5	4.9	29.6	4.9	29.6
Coahoma	33.9	13.9	41.0	19.6	57.7
Copiah	14.5	3.0	20.6	4.5	30.8
Covington	9.3	0.5	5.3	0.0	0.0
De Soto	19.7	3.2	16.3	5.2	26.5
Franklin	18.9	4.2	22.4	0.0	0.0
Greene	4.3	2.2	50.0	0.0	0.0
Hancock[a]					
Harrison	4.3	0.6	14.3	0.0	0.0
Hinds	26.1	6.7	25.6	9.5	36.4
Holmes	24.1	6.0	24.7	21.0	87.1
Issaquena	70.4	38.3	54.3	22.6	32.1
Itawamba	7.3	0.8	10.5	0.0	0.0
Jackson	10.3	0.0	0.0	0.0	0.0
Jasper	12.5	1.6	12.7	0.0	0.0
Jefferson	44.0	20.7	47.1	42.6	96.8
Jones	1.7	0.0	0.0	0.0	0.0
Kemper	13.4	2.7	20.3	0.0	0.0
Lafayette	13.0	2.9	22.6	0.0	0.0
Lauderdale	11.3	1.9	16.9	0.0	0.0
Lawrence	8.2	1.3	16.2	0.0	0.0
Leake	5.1	0.6	12.5	0.0	0.0
Lowndes	23.3	7.6	32.5	12.2	52.6
Madison	30.4	10.7	35.2	14.4	47.4
Marion	12.9	3.3	25.9	0.0	0.0
Marshall	22.2	4.5	20.1	7.3	32.6
Monroe	23.3	8.0	34.4	15.4	66.1
Neshoba	4.3	0.0	0.0	0.0	0.0
Newton	7.5	2.2	29.0	0.0	0.0
Noxubee	31.4	12.8	40.9	18.3	58.3

County	Percent of Planters of Slaveholders	Percent of Great Planters of all Slaveholders	Percent of Great Planters of all Plants	Percent of Largest Slaveholders of all Slaveholders	Percent of Largest Slaveholders of all Slaveholders
Oktibbeha	20.9	**5.1**	24.3	6.9	33.0
Panola	22.9	**4.0**	17.4	7.2	31.3
Perry	8.4	0.0	0.0	0.0	0.0
Pike	8.0	0.9	10.6	0.0	0.0
Pontotoc	11.6	**1.4**	12.1	10.9	93.9
Rankin	14.5	2.2	15.2	0.0	0.0
Scott	10.6	0.3	2.6	0.0	0.0
Simpson[b]	10.6	**1.5**	13.8	12.0	110.3
Smith	5.4	0.6	11.1	0.0	0.0
Sunflower[a]					
Tallahatchie	23.6	**6.1**	25.9	9.4	40.0
Tippah	9.6	1.1	11.4	0.0	0.0
Tishomingo	7.5	**0.6**	7.5	6.2	83.0
Tunica	44.7	**17.4**	39.0	25.0	55.9
Warren	23.9	**9.7**	40.8	14.6	61.2
Washington[a]					
Wayne	25.0	7.6	30.4	0.0	0.0
Wilkinson	33.3	**16.4**	49.4	8.0	24.1
Winston	10.4	1.7	16.7	0.0	0.0
Yalobusha	21.5	**4.6**	21.3	20.7	96.1
Yazoo	34.2	**14.2**	41.4	12.2	35.6
All Counties	19.5	**5.4**	27.7	7.6	39.0

Sources: Derived from figures reported in "Free Population Schedule" and "Slave Schedule," *Agriculture of the United States in 1860; Compiled from the Original Returns of the Eighth Census, Under the Direction of the Secretary of the Interior, By Joseph C. G. Kennedy, Superintendent of the Census* (Washington, DC: Government Printing Office, 1864), and list of "Largest Slaveholders" in Mississippi in 1860, http://freepages.genealogy.rootsweb .com/~ajac. Percentages for Pontotoc County (see note below) are derived from a comprehensive listing of all slaveholders in the county, presented at http://msgw.org/pontotoc/census/1860slave.htm.

General Note: Largest slaveholders are listed for only thirty of Mississippi's sixty counties for 1860. These counties are shown in bold. The thirty counties for which no lists of largest slaveholders are posted are, in virtually all cases, those with ten or fewer large-scale slaveholdings. The single exception to that rule is Pontotoc County, for which the Web site did not list largest slaveholders but for which I extracted the names and holdings of the largest planters from a comprehensive list of all slaveholders in the county.

[a] The census reported no returns of the number of slaveholders or of the sizes of their respective holdings.

[b] The apparent superabundance of largest slaveholders among the population of planters in Simpson County is, of course, misleading. The figure of 110.3 percent in the last column is the result of recording errors made by either the census enumerator when executing the slave schedule or the person who transcribed the entries in the slave schedule for the Simpson County listing on the Web site. In either event, the error has little significance because most of the thirty-two largest slaveholders in the county were, in fact, small-scale planters. Only four of them had the fifty or more slaves that qualified them as great planters.

The other difficulty was due to the generally acknowledged defects of the 1870 census, including its omissions and sometimes haphazard and illegible work by the census enumerators in the South. Together, these two circumstances reduced the odds of finding in the census a representative or senator who had served in the legislature in 1865 and 1866.

NOTES

1. An early and detailed discussion of the terms of the Confederate government's successive conscription acts and the opposition aroused by them is Albert Burton Moore, *Conscription and Conflict in the Confederacy* (New York: Macmillan Co., 1924). Moore's examination of the conflict over the acts is primarily concerned with that between the Confederate national government and the governments of the Confederacy's member states. A recent, careful analysis of the practice of hiring substitutes in the Confederacy is John Sacher, "The Loyal Draft Dodger?: A Reexamination of Confederate Substitution," *Civil War History* 57 (June 2011): 153–78. For a more general account, see Charles P. Roland, *The Confederacy* (Chicago: University of Chicago Press, 1960), 87–88; James M. McPherson, *Ordeal By Fire: The Civil War and Reconstruction* (New York: Alfred A. Knopf, 1982), 181–83; and William J. Cooper and Thomas E. Terrill, *The American South: A History* (New York: McGraw-Hill, 1991), 372. For the specific terms of the Conscription Act of 1864, see "Circular No. 8. March 18, 1864" (Richmond: Bureau of Conscription of the Confederate States of America, 1864), 20 pp., Electronic Edition, Rare Book Collection, University of North Carolina at Chapel Hill, http://docsouth.unc.edu/imls/circular8/circular.html.

2. The literature on this point is extensive, and only a few examples are necessary to convey the tenor of the argument. For a succinct statement of the anger inspired by the conscription laws and a description of their corrosive effect on Confederate morale, see David Williams, *Rich Man's War: Class, Caste, and Confederate Defeat in the Lower Chattahoochee Valley* (Athens: University of Georgia Press, 1998), esp. 4–6, 129–30, 210–11. Also see Randall C. Jimerson, *The Private Civil War: Popular Thought During the Sectional Conflict* (Baton Rouge: Louisiana State University Press, 1988), 192–93. Jimerson also distinguishes between popular resentment over Confederate policies that favored the rich and continued loyalty to the Cause (195–96). A different approach to understanding this aspect of the war's character is presented in Peter Wallenstein, "Rich Man's War, Rich Man's Fight: Civil War and the Transformation of Public Finance in Georgia," *Journal of Southern History* 50 (February 1984): 15–42. Also see Steven Hahn, *The Roots of Southern Populism: Yeoman Farmers and the Transformation of the Georgia Upcountry, 1850–1890* (New York: Oxford University Press, 1983), 123; and Roger L. Ransom, *Conflict and Compromise: The Political Economy of Slavery, Emancipation, and the American Civil War* (Cambridge: Cambridge University Press, 1989), 199.

3. For examples of somewhat qualified skepticism concerning the significance for the Confederate war effort of class divisions and resentments due to the conscription laws, see James M. McPherson, *For Cause and Comrades: Why Men Fought In the Civil War* (New York: Oxford University Press, 1997), appendix, table 3, 181. A more conditional view is presented in Larry M. Logue's seminal study, "Who Joined the Confederate Army? Soldiers, Civilians, and Communi-

ties in Mississippi," *Journal of Social History* 26, no. 3 (Spring 1993): 611–23. A more emphatic rejection of the idea that class divisions and resentments played a vital role in the collapse of the Confederacy is to be found in Aaron Sheehan-Davis, "Everyman's War: Confederate Enlistments in Civil War Virginia," *Civil War History* 50, no. 1 (2000): 5–26. Also see Gary W. Gallagher, *The Confederate War: How Popular Will, Nationalism, and Military Strategy Could Not Stave Off Defeat* (Cambridge, MA: Harvard University Press, 1997), esp. 17–23. For a careful study of the situation in a critically important state, see William Blair, *Virginia's Private War: Feeding Body and Soul in the Confederacy, 1861–1865* (New York: Oxford University Press, 1998), 81–107. Blair establishes that the Confederate effort in Virginia collapsed because of the inexorable external pressure from Federal forces and not because of internal dissension and loss of will to continue to fight. He also makes clear that Virginia's government attacked and corrected inequities in the distribution of the war's burdens and moved the struggle toward a rich man's fight."

4. See Williams, *Rich Man's War*, 132, 134–35, 184–86; and Bradley Bond, *Political Culture in the Nineteenth Century South: Mississippi, 1830–1900* (Baton Rouge: Louisiana State University Press, 1995), 133–34.

5. Proportions are derived from a computer-readable data set of the 1860 federal census, available on CD-ROM from the Inter-University Consortium for Political and Social Research (ICPSR), *Historical, Demographic, Economic, and Social Data: The United States, 1790–1970*, ICPSR data sets 0003, 0007, 0008, 0009, 0014, and 0017 (Ann Arbor: ICPSR, 1975).

6. There is considerable uncertainty about the number of troops provided by Mississippi, and most of the figures offered have an uncertain provenance. A report made to the state's governor, Charles Clarke, about six months after the end of the war estimated that 78,000 men had served. Sixty years later, a textbook on the state's history put the number at "over 70,000." The 1865 estimate is quoted on http://www.researchonline.net/mscw/index.htm. The figure of about 70,000 is given in Franklin L. Riley, PhD, *School History of Mississippi For Use in Public and Private Schools* (Richmond, VA: B. F. Johnson Publishing Co., 1915), 260. One recent reference work uses the figure of 78,000 for the state's contribution, while another puts the number at "some 80,000 troops." The former is given in the entry on Mississippi in *The Encyclopedia of the Confederacy*, 4 vols. (New York: Simon & Schuster, 1993), 3:1052. The 80,000-troop estimate is given in the entry on Mississippi in *The Encyclopedia of the American Civil War: A Political, Social, and Military History of the American Civil War*, 5 vols. (Santa Barbara, CA: ABC-CLIO, 2000), 3:1340. An exception to the generally uncertain and unreliable figures on Mississippians' wartime service is an estimate of about 59,000, a figure derived from the estimate of "roughly ninety thousand eligible males in Mississippi" provided by Larry M. Logue and his conclusion, based on his systematic sampling of the 1860 population census schedule for the state, that 65 percent of the eligible population served. See Logue, "Who Joined the Confederate Army," 612, 613.

7. The names of the largest slaveholders in twenty-seven counties are available as "Largest Slaveholders from 1860 Slave Census Schedules and Surname Matches for African Americans on 1870 Census," at http://freepages.genealogy.rootsweb.com/~ajac/.

8. The lists of graduates are available in the *Historical Catalogue of the University of Mississippi, 1849–1909* (Nashville, TN: Marshall & Bruce Company, 1910), 123–34.

9. The rosters of state representatives and senators are provided in Dunbar Rowland, LL.D.,

Director, Mississippi Department of Archives and History, "Members of Mississippi Legislature, 1817–1908," *The Official and Statistical Register of the State of Mississippi, 1908* (Nashville, TN: Press of the Brandon Printing Co., 1908), 46–124.

10. "Largest Slaveholders"; the manuscript free population schedule, *U.S. Census (Eighth Census), 1860,* for Mississippi; and H. Grady Howell Jr., *For Dixie Land I'll Take My Stand! A Muster Listing of All Known Mississippi Confederate Soldiers, Sailors and Marines,* 4 vols. (Madison, MS: Chickasaw Bayou Press, 1998), vols. 1–3; U.S. National Parks Service, "Soldiers and Sailors Database," www.itd.nps.gov/cwss/. The 65-percent rate of service for the largest slaveholders is almost identical to the enlistment rate computed for a 1,010-person sample of eligible Mississippians by Larry M. Logue. See Logue, "Who Joined the Confederate Army?," 613. Logue also notes a higher rate, overall, of enlistments for affluent men than for those devoid of personal property, the latter term, more often than not, meaning slaves (616). But he reports that "Men living in the river counties, regardless of their investment in slaves or any other observable characteristic, were less likely to join the army that were those living elsewhere in Mississippi" (616). For the most part, the results presented here do not bear out that conclusion, except with respect to the state's northwestern counties along the Mississippi River. The river counties in the southwestern part of the state generally had average or higher than average rates of service among their largest slaveholders.

11. Figures on the ten local defense and home guard units are derived from rosters of the companies, available at www.rootsweb.com; from "Largest Slaveholders"; and from the manuscript free population schedule, *U.S. Census (Eighth Census), 1860,* for Mississippi.

12. Figures on Fant's Company are derived from the company's roster, available at www.rootsweb.com, and from "Largest Slaveholders" and from the manuscript free population schedule, *U.S. Census (Eighth Census), 1860,* for Mississippi.

13. Figures on Gordon's Company are derived from the company's roster at www.rootsweb.com and from the census data cited in note 12. I was able to locate all but seven of the members of the company in the 1860 census. Curiously, one of those seven was George H. Gordon, the captain of the company. Failure to locate an individual in the census can be due to any number of causes: spelling and transcription errors by the enumerator and, subsequently, by the person who transcribed the census record into machine-readable form; the fact that an individual's permanent residence was in a county and even state other than the one in which he happened to be living when he enrolled in a military unit; and the overlooking of an individual by the census enumerator while on his rounds. Captain Gordon, though missing from the free population manuscript schedule for Wilkinson County, is enumerated in the slave schedule for the county.

14. See "Local defense companies" table in *War of the Rebellion: A Compilation of the Official Records of the Union and Confederate Armies* (hereinafter cited as *OR*) (Washington, D.C.: Government Printing Office, 1880–1901, series 4, 2:936. The table lists twenty-six local defense companies, but that figure is larger than the actual number of such companies. At least two of the twenty-six companies served not only outside their respective counties but even outside the state: Foote's Company or Mississippi Mounted Men was reconstituted as the Noxubee Cavalry and saw action in Kentucky and Tennessee, including at Shiloh; and Captain Wheeler's Company, Polk Rangers, fought as Company E of the First Mississippi Cavalry. See *OR*; Howell, *For*

Dixie Land I'll Take My Stand, vols. 1–3; and National Archives and Records Service (NARS), *Compiled Records Showing Service of Units in Confederate Organizations*, National Archives Microfilm Publications Pamphlet Describing M861 (Washington, DC: National Archives and Records Service, General Services Administration, 1973).

15. *OR*, series 4, 2:936. The table in the source provided each unit's strength.

16. The classes of 1856 and 1857 were selected for close examination to permit a determination of the financial standing of the families of the graduates. Members of the classes of 1856 and 1857, who had spent four years at the university, would have begun their studies in 1852 and 1853, respectively. Those years were soon enough after the enumeration of the census of 1850 to have made financial information concerning the students' fathers a reliable indicator of the circumstances in which the students were raised. The classes of 1858, 1859, and 1860 would have begun their studies at the university in 1854, 1855, and 1856, years too distant from the census of 1850 for one to be confident that the census data still accurately reflected the circumstances of the graduates' families. Similarly, data in the census of 1860 would be too late to be pertinent.

17. Unlike in the 1860 census, the free population manuscript schedule of the 1850 census did not record "personal estate," which, for planters, would have consisted almost entirely of slaves. Consequently, no attempt is made here to tabulate the size of the slaveholdings of the fathers of the members of the 1856 and 1857 graduating classes, though a tabulation of that sort is possible by looking in the slave schedule of the 1850 census for each of the fathers. The conversion of 1850 dollars into 2011 dollars is from Lawrence H. Officer and Samuel H. Williamson, "Purchasing Power of Money in the United States from 1774 to Present," MeasuringWorth, 2011, www.measuringworth.com/ppowerus/.

18. For an early account of the workings of presidential Reconstruction in Mississippi, see James W. Garner, *Reconstruction in Mississippi* (Baton Rouge: Louisiana State University Press, 1968; a new edition of a work first published in 1901), chap. 3. An analysis of the persistence of planters' political power is to be found in Eric Foner, *Reconstruction: America's Unfinished Revolution, 1863–1877* (New York: Harper & Row, Publishers, 1988), 191–92, 399.

19. The two-thirds figure must at this writing be only an approximation. It is based on detailed data for four counties that had significant numbers of great planters in 1860: Adams (26 great planters), Amite (17), Bolivar (22), and Carroll (30). Of the 95 great planters in these four counties, only 33, or 34.7 percent, of them still lived in the state in 1870. The proportion of former great planters still living in each county varied markedly. Adams County and Amite County had the sharpest declines, 73.1 percent and 82.4 percent, respectively. The figure for Bolivar County was 31.8 percent and that for Carroll County was 46.7 percent.

The task of finding the members of the 1865–67 state legislature in the population schedule of the 1870 census was doubly difficult. One source of difficulty was the unsettled conditions in Mississippi in the years immediately after the war, years of increased population mobility. The other difficulty in locating members of the state legislature was due to the generally acknowledged defects of the 1870 census of the former Confederate states, including its omissions and sometimes haphazard, incomplete, and illegible work by the census enumerators. Together, these two circumstances reduced the odds of finding in the census a representative or senator who had served in the legislature in 1865 and 1866.

Indeed, while I was able to find 92 percent of the members of the prewar House of Representatives in the federal census of 1860, I could find only 74 percent of the members of the postwar House in the census of 1870. The corresponding percentages for the members of the state Senate are even lower: 60 percent before the war and 68 percent after the war.

20. For a discussion of the historiography of this interpretation, see Gallagher, *The Confederate War*, 3–4, 11–13, 21–23, 27–29, 71; also see Blair, *Virginia's Private War*, 3–4, 141.

21. As already noted above, William Blair attributes the transformation of Confederate Virginia's war effort to policies adopted by that state's government that transformed the war in Virginia into a rich man's fight. See Blair, *Virginia's Private War*, chap. 4. Aaron Sheehan-Davis described the war in Virginia as "everyman's war" in "Everyman's War," 5–26.

CHAPTER SIX

Searching for "Some Plain and Simple Method"
Jefferson Davis and Confederate Conscription
John M. Sacher

On March 28, 1862, Confederate president Jefferson Davis proposed to the Confederate Congress a solution to the vexing problem of raising troops. Frustrated by the frequent alterations in Confederate enrollment policy, the conflicts between state and federal laws, and the lack of uniformity in these measures, Davis offered a straightforward solution—Congress should articulate "some plain and simple method" to enroll all white men between the ages of eighteen and thirty-five in Confederate service. He contended that a military conscription would be equitable, as it would ensure "that the burdens should not fall exclusively on the most ardent and patriotic" men who had volunteered to fight for the new nation the year before. And, he matter-of-factly brushed aside any potential constitutional objections in one sentence, declaring "the right of the State to demand, and the duty of each citizen to render, military service, need only to be stated to be admitted."[1]

Less than three weeks later, the Confederate Congress heeded Davis's call. On April 16, 1862, it passed the first national conscription act in American history. Facing a tremendous manpower deficit—the Confederacy had less than one third the number of white males of military age that the Union possessed—the South could ill afford to have prospective soldiers avoid military service. Not only did the act conscript white males between the ages of eighteen and thirty-five, but it also extended the service of those already in the army from twelve months to three years or the duration of the war. Following traditional practice, the act allowed eligible men to provide substitutes to take their place in the army, and an April 21 amendment added a list of exempt occupations, including government officials, railroad workers, printers, and teachers. Over the next three years, the Confederacy would struggle to find the ideal balance of men at the battlefront and men on the home front, continually tinkering with the list of exempt occupations and classes. In October 1862, Congress increased the upper age limit to forty-five and greatly expanded the exemption policy. That list of exemptions fills two pages of the *Official Records of the War of the Rebellion,* and it includes the addition of the Twenty-Negro law, which allowed exemptions for overseers. During its 1863–64 session, Congress cut the number of exempt classes in half, eliminated substitution, and conscripted men who had provided substitutes. Plus, it again expanded the lower and upper limits of the age range to enroll those between the ages of seventeen and fifty.[2]

Contemporary critics and historians, especially those who espouse the idea that the Confederacy suffered from internal dissent, have pilloried Confederate government officials generally and President Jefferson Davis in particular for their handling of conscription policy. At best, Davis is depicted as aloof and oblivious to the plight of Confederate citizens, and, at worst, he is depicted as a tyrant bent on accumulating power in his own hands. In reality, a reexamination of the evidence indicates that Davis's handling of conscription did illustrate one of his weaknesses—his failure to communicate effectively with and to inspire the Confederate populace. Yet, this reanalysis also reveals that Davis carefully tried to balance several competing needs: obeying the Confederate Constitution, keeping enough men on the home front and at the battlefront, and winning the war. Unlike many of his critics, Davis appreciated the fact that the Civil War would be won and lost on the battlefield, and with the Union army's supremacy in manpower, Davis had to make sure that the South's battalions were as heavy as possible. In sum, Davis's handling of Confederate conscription demonstrates a nuanced understanding of the needs of the Confederacy. His consideration of the larger picture exceeded that of his contemporary critics and is too often missed or dismissed by historians.

Anyone emphasizing that internal fissures doomed the Confederacy primarily focuses on either violations of states' rights theory or the alienation of non-slaveholders. For either verdict, conscription easily serves as exhibit A. The policy gave the Richmond government the power to seize men from the states and compel them to fight and possibly die for that government. This power surpassed any that the federal government had previously employed, and some Confederates contended that if taken to its extreme—the conscription of state officials—the policy could be used to destroy the states. During the war, Davis's vice president Alexander Stephens privately complained that the conscription policy was "perfectly consistent with the hypothesis that [Davis] is aiming at absolute power." In January 1864, Virginia congressman Waller R. Staples echoed this assessment. Addressing the president's desire to have greater control over details, Staples condemned the idea as "cloth[ing] the President with the powers of an autocrat" and granting him "prerogatives before which those of Napoleon sunk into insignificance."[3]

According to historian Frank Owsley, the father of the "Died of State Rights" theory, conscription would have worked much better "if it had not been opposed so bitterly by the state-rights leaders," who, among other things, designated as many as thirty thousand men as state officials to shield them from conscription. For Owsley, this needless tug-of-war between Richmond and state governments contributed "very materially to the defeat of the Confederacy."[4] Albert Burton Moore, in *Conscription and Conflict in the Confederacy*, the only book-length study of the policy, concurs. He finds that conscription was anathema to Confederates, arguing that "it was not only contrary to the spirit of the people but to the genius of the Confederate political system."[5]

For its detractors, conscription policy, in addition to its assault on state rights, had blatant class biases as well. These special privileges, especially the substitution and Twenty-Negro clauses, allowed the wealthy to remain home while the poor served in the army. In his harsh assessment of Davis, Paul Escott stresses the failure of the Confederate president to build popular commitment to the cause. Conscription, particularly these two provisions, comprises a key element of his thesis that the Confederacy collapsed from within as Davis failed in his attempt to build a Confederate nation both because he neglected the common people and because he lost support of the planter class due to personality clashes. For Escott, Davis "proved insensitive to the problems of ordinary southerners," as "Confederate laws and regulations often favored the wealthy." Consequently, "Davis presided over a disastrous decline of southern morale which doomed his hopes of establishing a new nation." Historian David Williams agrees. He stands as one of the most unequivocal advocates of the "rich man's war, poor man's fight" thesis that conscription was unfair class legislation that undermined the Confederacy. In several books, including his aptly-titled *Rich Man's War*, Williams pulls no punches in his analysis of the Confederacy's defeat, arguing that "class conflict . . . proved to be the crucial factor." In arguing in favor of class conflict, he, too, highlights the conscription law and its substitution and Twenty-Negro law provisions, labeling the latter, "perhaps the most widely hated act ever imposed by the Confederacy" and asserting that it "defined the nature of the war for an entire class of southerners."[6]

These censorious assessments, however, do not capture the complexity of Jefferson Davis's handling of conscription. Whereas Williams even goes to the extreme of grandiosely arguing, "Despite overwhelming opposition from plain folk and state officials, the Confederacy refused to reconsider its draft policy," the reality is precisely the opposite. Davis continually reflected upon, reconsidered, and proposed alterations to the draft policy in direct response to conscription's foes. To better assess Davis, one must examine the evolution of his thoughts and actions over the course of the war. Such an examination reveals a president well aware of both state rights and the potential for class conflict in the Confederacy. Davis did not ignore those who grumbled about conscription but instead tried to address their concerns to improve conscription policy. In fact, Davis shared many of their apprehensions as he called for "harmonious as well as zealous action" in addressing the army's manpower needs. Unfortunately for Davis, this request proved to be an oxymoron; regrettably, all "zealous" action was bound to be seen by some southerners as not "harmonious" with their interests.[7]

President Davis's first public announcements on conscription came in March 1862, when he proposed the measure. In describing Davis as approaching conscription "both boldly and timidly," William J. Cooper accurately captures the president's difficulties in his initial call. George Rable agrees as he chastises Davis for failing to issue "a ringing call to arms" or to deal "with possible objections to a draft." Davis provided only the briefest explanation for the need for conscription and clearly underestimated the potential challenges the policy faced. Instead, he abruptly dismissed any objections to the policy with his assertion that power to conscript "need only to be stated to be admitted." Clearly, he could have done more to address or at minimum acknowledge state rights concerns. In a letter attacking conscription's violation of the Confederacy's fundamental doctrine and its creation of "a military despotism," Georgia's governor Joseph Brown, soon to become Davis's most vocal nemesis in regards to conscription, sarcastically assessed Davis's rhetorical strategy. He grumbled to Vice President Alexander Stephens, a fellow Georgian and opponent of conscription, that Davis had not even bothered with "the tyrant's plea of necessity for the passage of the act."[8]

In stark contrast to Davis, the Confederate Congress highlighted military needs with the preamble to the Conscript Act stressing "the absolute necessity of keeping in the service our gallant Army, and of placing in the filed a large additional force to meet the advancing columns of enemy." If Davis had placed more emphasis on the sacrifice the war demanded, especially in light of the enemy's presence at the gates of Richmond in the spring of 1862, he might have engendered a greater acceptance of this expansion of government power. In other words, had Davis channeled Lincoln's folk wisdom, he might have used the Union president's analogy that sometimes it is necessary to sacrifice a limb to save a life, but it is never wise to sacrifice a life to save a limb. Of course, Davis was not Lincoln, and he offered very little in the way of justification.[9]

While Davis did not address this sacrifice, some congressmen cavalierly brushed aside any constitutional objections as irrelevant. Senator John Clark of Missouri bluntly declared, "in time like these the sovereignty of the States must be secondary to the sovereignty of the people." And, arguing on behalf of conscription, Texas senator Louis Wigfall lectured his state rights colleagues to "cease this child's play," as he asserted that "there was no limitation" on the Confederate government's power to raise armies. He added, "No man has any individual rights, which are in conflict with the welfare of the country." Four months later, in his diary, Texas congressman Franklin Sexton recounted the congressional debate. "I voted for the conscript law with some doubt as to its constitutionality—& with regret," but he "believe[d] that it had save[d] the country" and that his constituents in Texas accepted it. Later in 1862, Davis's fellow Mississippian Ethelbert Barksdale, in advocating on behalf of conscription, expressed his willingness "to throw aside the constitution" if necessary to win the war. In other words, these members of the Confederate Congress willingly sacrificed the limb of state rights to save the life of the Confederacy.[10]

Davis, however, avoided such a comparison not only because he lacked Lincoln's political savvy but also because he did not believe the Confederacy was sacrificing a limb. He viewed conscription neither as undermining state rights nor as unconstitutional, as it stemmed directly from Congress's power to raise armies. Plus, enrolling men into state units and allowing men who volunteered prior to their conscription to choose their unit paid homage to state and individual liberty in the Confederacy. In a letter to South Carolina's governor and executive council rebuking their efforts to exempt men from the national draft, his frustration on this constitutional point boiled over. In disbelief that anyone could think a state could limit this federal power, Davis angrily chided, "I am a loss how to illustrate so plain a proposition" as conscription's constitutionality. Yet, others did force him to illustrate it. The bitter, extremely quotable, epistolary debate between Davis and Governor Brown of Georgia offers the best opportunity to examine Davis's rationale for conscription. Their constitutional discussion was intended for the public as well as themselves, and Davis had it published in pamphlet form in 1862. Historians delight in rediscovering the irony that he and other conscription supporters mimicked the broad construction arguments of men such as Alexander Hamilton and John Marshall in their defenses of conscription.[11]

In this exchange, Brown, who saw himself in the mold of Jefferson and Madison, wrote longer letters, and he wrote more often. He maintained that conscription gave the Richmond government power "to destroy her State Government." When Davis objected to that characterization, the governor re-iterated that the question involved "the very existence of State Government" and that conscription was "at war with all principles for the support of which Georgia entered into this revolution." While stating that he was willing to postpone discussion of conscription's constitutionality until a time when "it may less seriously embarrass the Confederacy," Governor Brown repeatedly labeled the act unconstitutional. On top of that, he found it to be unnecessary, especially as Georgia had provided the Confederate army all the men they requested without resorting to a draft.[12]

Although Davis insisted that "it was no part of my intention to enter into a protracted discussion," he was not one to back down from a written challenge. In this case, Davis believed that failing to respond to Brown's postal assault involved "consequences . . . too momentous to permit me to leave your objections unanswered." The president could not resist the chance to lecture Brown about the constitutionality and necessity of the act. First, in every letter of the exchange, he reminded Brown that power to conscript did not come from the power to call out the militia (which is where Brown insisted it lay) but instead stemmed from the power to raise armies. Second, as for its constitutionality, Davis pointed out that a large majority of both houses of Congress and every cabinet member, including attorney general Thomas H. Watts, agreed with Davis on the law's constitutionality. Watts and Davis concurred that the Constitution granted Congress the power to raise armies, and it did not limit the methods to be used to do so. Third, Davis found the law to be necessary and proper. In fact, in his words, it was not only necessary but "it was absolutely indispensable." Fourth, he concluded his final missive in this exchange with a reminder that he, too, adhered to the doctrine of states' rights. The right of states to render judgment when the federal government usurps its power "is too familiar and well settled a principle to admit discussion," but he could not "share the alarm and concern about State rights . . . which to me seem quite unfounded."[13]

While Davis strenuously advocated for the constitutionality of conscription, he never contended that this decision was solely his. He agreed that the courts had a say in the matter, and in the Confederacy, which lacked a national supreme court, this view would come from the state court systems. In a November 1, 1862, letter to North Carolina's governor Zebulon Vance, Davis hoped that the judiciary would resolve conscription issues in the only two places where it had been directly challenged: in Georgia and at the Virginia Military Institute (VMI). The latter institution, which considered itself akin to a Confederate West Point, desired to have its students exempted from conscription. If Davis was worried about the state courts' decision, his fear would be assuaged by the end of the month. By then, the president could contend, perhaps with a bit of relief, "that the decision of the supreme court of Georgia may be regarded as conclusive on the constitutional question."[14]

In the case of *Jeffers v. Fair*, the Georgia Supreme Court echoed Davis's view, declaring that "compulsory enrollment is a proper incident of the power to raise armies." When the judges searched the constitution for any restrictions on this power, they found none. Even if that were not the case, they added, the "necessary and proper clause" would sanction conscription. The *Jeffers* decision did slightly protect state rights in limiting who could be conscripted. It precluded the Confederate government from drafting state officials or interfering with individual states acting "in the exercise of their proper functions." In other words, as long as conscription did not destroy state government, it was considered to be constitutional. Davis must have celebrated this thorough vindication from Governor Brown's own supreme court, particularly as it concluded that it had reached its decision unanimously and "without any lingering doubt."[15]

Across the Confederacy, other state supreme court justices might have possessed more lingering doubts than the Georgia justices, but no state court ever ruled conscription to be unconstitutional. In each state, the justices unequivocally endorsed President Davis's position and rejected Governor Brown's. In Alabama, in *Ex Parte Hill*, the court ruled that "The Confederate government . . . has the unquestioned right to call the male residents of the Confederacy into service." In Mississippi, the judges addressed the potential flaws in allowing any state interference with conscription. If a state governor or legislature could exempt one citizen, then they could exempt all citizens. So, accepting state interference would be "absolutely and totally contradictory" to the Constitution and would, in effect, "paralyze the war-power of the Confederate government."[16]

While many historians focus on Governor Brown, he is not representative of Confederate governors generally. He brought out the worst, most rigid side of Jefferson Davis. If one instead examines Davis's correspondence with North Carolina's Vance, often portrayed as the Confederacy's second most obstructionist governor, a more flexible Davis emerges. In a November 1, 1862, letter to Vance, Davis assessed the first six months of conscription. In response to Vance's concerns regarding how conscripts would be assigned to units, Davis first praised the governor for sustaining every war measure. Then, with a tint of gallows humor, he reflected that "the Conscript Act has not been popular anywhere out of the Army." Davis nevertheless emphasized that in fairness to the soldiers who had their twelve-month enlistments extended, Congress passed conscription as "a means equitable to distribute the burthen of public defence." The reaction, aside from Georgia and VMI, had been positive, as "popular sentiment . . . supports any measures necessary to . . . secure our political independence." After defending the popularity, equity, and legality of conscription, Davis then agreed to Vance's request that North Carolina troops be allowed to choose their units.[17]

In July 1863, Davis and Vance continued their exchange. After apologizing for taking three months to answer Vance's March 1863 letter, Davis explained that "it has been my desire to comply as far as possible with the wishes and views of the Governors of the several States in all cases where there seems to be any fair doubt as to the intention of Congress." In this case, the issue involved the status of constables and justices of the peace. Davis offered a creative solution. While explaining that he could not add occupations to Congress's exemption list, he offered the suggestion that putting these men in home guard units while allowing them to perform their ordinary duties most of the time would meet the letter of the law. Furthermore, Davis agreed that in gray area like these, he would order conscription officers "to defer to you . . . where it could be done without positive infraction of the law." This correspondence, in which Davis seeks to find middle ground between federal and state rights, clearly lacks the bitter tone of his hostile, pedantic constitutional debate with Governor Brown.[18]

In looking at conscription and federalism, the cooperation and compromise exemplified in the Davis-Vance exchange is more indicative of Davis's correspondence with state governors than his caustic relationship with Brown. In 1863, Davis debated the overseer exemption with Florida's governor John Milton. Milton had expressed his anxiety regarding how an alteration in the exemption of overseers would affect the harvest in Florida (and how it would conscribe his own overseer). While instructing Milton that he could not change the law, Davis informed him that the Bureau of Conscription had been ordered "to grant liberal details of overseers until the crops could be made and gathered." Milton might have reflected on this give-and-take later in the year when, in his opening remarks to Florida's legislative session, he instructed the state's assembly that it was more important to concentrate energies on the enemy rather than "to criticize and defeat the purpose of the Government of our choice, administered by the statesmen of our selection."[19]

Overall, Davis had more positive than negative interactions with Confederate governors in regards to conscription. Generally, governors concurred with Milton that defeating the enemy was more important than overly sensitive debates over conscription's constitutionality. Often, while admitting their personal unease regarding conscription, these governors accepted Davis's arguments in favor of the measure and urged compliance. In Alabama, Gov. John G. Shorter—despite his private worries that if conscription was necessary, the cause was doomed—stressed that "Harmony between the State and Confederate authorities is a matter of utmost importance." In a May 1862 message to his state legislature, Virginia governor John Letcher declared that he considered conscription to be unconstitutional, yet he "urge[d] upon the people [of Virginia] a prompt and cheerful response." In his edited collection of essays on Confederate governors, W. Buck Yearns concurs that with a few exceptions, the state leaders followed knee-jerk protests with cooperation, and one should be wary of condemning them for their words when their deeds did not indicate animosity toward the national government.[20]

If during the Civil War the president sought to persuade the governors of conscription's constitutionality, after it ended, he sought a broader audience. In looking for Davis's strongest feelings on conscription, one can examine his postbellum *The Rise and Fall of the Confederate Government,* published in

1881. Here, Davis praises the act for improving the army, and he still expresses his surprise that "the law upon which our success so greatly depended was assailed with unexpected criticism," especially in regards to states' rights. In particular, he reflects on his constitutional debate with Governor Brown and even reproduces in full his longest letter from this exchange. Apparently, he believed that his argument easily won over Brown and the rest of the South, for in *The Rise and Fall,* he reflects that the opposition "soon became limited" as the law's "good effects were seen in the increased strength and efficiency of our armies."[21]

Unquestionably, the act brought men into the army, but Davis's postwar opinion that he easily won over the act's opponents does not do justice to his own actions over the next two-and-a-half years. A closer examination of his record in regard to conscription reveals a president cognizant of the plight of the Confederacy's common people and of their fears regarding conscription. Davis, however, faced a Herculean task, for it was probably impossible to make conscription universally popular. By definition, conscription demanded sacrifice, and he struggled to convey this message. In December 1862, in a rare public speech in his home state in Mississippi, Davis offered a defense of conscription policy, and this speech demonstrates his inability to inspire the public. He maintained that the April act did justice to those in the army, who were willing to stay in the field as long as the stay-at-homes, "who had thus far been sluggards in the cause," should be forced to join them. Ironically, within the same paragraph in which Davis twice called these men "sluggards," he changed his tune and without further explanation declared that "it is no disgrace to be brought into the army by conscription." Davis regretted that the conscription act had suffered from "erroneous" and "harsher criticism than it deserves." Alluding to his debate with Georgia's Governor Brown, he added, "let it never be said that there is a conflict between the States and the Confederate government, by which a blow may be inflicted on the common cause." Instead, he viewed the federal relationship between Richmond and Mississippi as a harmonious one, and he hoped that this trend would continue.[22]

Next, Davis turned his attention to the exemptions in the October 1862 revision of the conscription act. He lectured his audience that exemptions kept men at home whose services on the home front would be more useful to the country and to the government than their service in the army. Lamenting that critics of exemption policy in general and the Twenty-Negro law in particular had resorted to a class-based attack, he reminded his listeners of the simple lesson that throughout history "the poor do, indeed, fight the battles of the country." At the same time, he added that "most of the wealthiest and most distinguished families of the South have representatives in the ranks" and that the Twenty-Negro law was needed to provide a police force to keep slaves under control. After defending even the most controversial parts of the conscription act, Davis ended his discussion of the measure on a different note, predicting that "the Exemption act . . . will probably be made the subject of revision and amendment."[23]

Two weeks later, at the opening of Congress's 1863 session, Davis made good on his pledge as he urged Congress to revise the exemption law. Having heard "serious complaints" about it from "eminent and patriotic citizens whose opinions merit great consideration," Davis requested that Congress make some alterations. His charge to the body, however, made apparent the near impossibility of such a task. He made the supposedly simple request "that some means will be devised for leaving at home a sufficient local police without making discriminations, always to be deprecated, between different classes of citizens." But, he offered no suggestions as to how this could be accomplished and ignored the incredible difficulty of devising a policy that would allow some men to remain at home but would not engender some type of discrimination. By definition, conscripting some men while allowing others to remain at home involved either discrimination or at least the appearance of discrimination.[24]

While Davis offered no exact suggestions at this point, in the next two years, he would offer specific amendments to the conscription policy, and for some Davis's "cures" would be worse than the disease. On one hand, his plan could be seen as an effort to end special privileges. On the other hand, it could be seen as a further expansion of federal government power and of the government reneging on a previous promise to men on the home front. Perhaps surprising to some of conscription's critics, Davis's uncomplicated solution to the perceived injustice of conscription was to give the army and executive branch of the national government even *more* power over exemptions. He decried occupational exemptions as "unwise" and "indefensible in theory." Instead, what he preferred was a conscription of all men into the army with the government then offering individual details to return men to their communities. In short, he expressed his preference for a true conscription policy. Although *conscrip-*

tion and *draft* are often used interchangeably, they have different definitions. In the latter, individuals are selected generally via some type of lottery for armed service. In the former, all men within the age range are assumed to be in the army unless they are granted a detail or exemption. In other words, the entire society is mobilized for war, but some are assigned to the army and some are assigned to the home front.[25]

Davis's commitment to this wholesale conscription policy can be seen in *The Rise and Fall of the Confederate Government.* In his discussion of conscription, he quotes only two documents: (1) the aforementioned 1862 letter to Brown and (2) his 1864 message to Congress calling for an end to exemptions. In this message, the president returned to a theme he had addressed in his December 7, 1863, message to Congress. He declared that "the exemption from service of entire classes should be wholly abandoned." In other words, no group—whether teachers, printers, preachers, overseers, millers, or drugstore owners—should have an automatic exemption. In words that sound like they came from the staunchest challengers to conscription, the president stresses the importance of the "defense of home, family, and country . . . as the paramount political duty of every member of society." And, he agrees with conscription's critics that "nothing can be more invidious than an unequal distribution of duties or obligations."

In highlighting the protection of home, Davis observes that exempting entire classes of people was inefficient. Class-based exemptions, Davis argued, were based on the improbable assumption that somehow the Confederacy possessed the exact number of each exempt class (no more, no less) needed on the home front and that this number was perfectly distributed across the South. Not only did he consider that assumption absurd, but he also added that exemptions of entire classes encouraged fraud as potential conscripts either pretended to practice exempt occupations or established fake schools, churches, drugstores, and so on, in order to stay out of the army. Instead of wholesale exemptions, the government would detail only those men truly needed on the home front. Thus, if a town had three blacksmiths but needed only one, the one would be detailed and the other two enrolled in the army rather than exempting all three. This true conscription would grant the government more precise control in allocating assets between the battle and home fronts. Such a policy would also, in the president's view, be more equitable than an exemption-based plan.[26]

Congress moved hesitantly toward Davis's plan. Some members wanted to protect certain classes, and others were leery about giving total control of the Confederacy's manpower to Davis and the army. Davis's first plea in December 1863 resulted in a halfway measure that reduced the number of exempt classes and increased the president's power to detail men. Also, Congress altered the Twenty-Negro law in an effort to tie it more directly to aiding the home front. In order to make sure that the measure rewarded agricultural production and not just wealth, Congress changed the number from twenty total slaves to fifteen field hands. It further stipulated that families with an exempt over-seer must provide the government with a specified amount of food and sell their surplus at fixed rates to soldiers' families. In June, however, it passed an amendment that included an expansion of the editorial exemption. Previously, it applied only to newspapers, but Congress wanted to extend it to editors of magazines and other periodicals. Seeking to reduce, not increase, exemptions, Davis swiftly vetoed the measure, labeling it "impolitic" and expressing his concern that the precedent it set would "be productive of evil effect."[27]

In March 1865, Congress passed its final exemption law, and President Davis promptly vetoed it as well. He argued that the plan would not add any men to the army, since it exempted all artisans and mechanics employed by the government. More important, the measure demonstrated that he and Congress viewed conscription from opposite perspectives. While Davis worried about class exemptions, Congress was more concerned about an abuse of executive details. Consequently, the bill revoked all individual details and exemptions that Davis and the secretaries of war had previously granted. Davis could not accept this challenge to his authority. Two days after his veto, he made his final address to Congress regarding exemption policy. Calling on Congress to postpone its adjournment, Davis expressed his disappointment that his suggestion to "abolish all class exemptions has not met your favor," though he still considered it "a valuable important measure," both to add to the army and to "abat[e] the natural discontent and jealousy created . . . by the existence of classes privileged by law to remain in places of safety while their fellow-citizens are exposed in the trenches and the field."[28]

Davis shared the common man's view of the inequality of the Confederate exemption policy, and he concurred with their attitude toward principals and substitutes. In this case, the president and Congress worked together to alter the provisions regarding substitution. In a July 1863 letter to fellow

Mississippian and general Reuben Davis (no relation), he concurred that "substitution has done much harm and been prolific of crime." Six months later, President Davis would urge Congress to cancel substitution, as "dissatisfaction has been excited among those who have unable or unwilling to avail themselves of the opportunity . . . of avoiding military service." In addition to ending substitution, Davis requested that Congress conscript principals—the men who had provided substitutes. This latter contention proved more controversial, and principals maintained that the government had entered into a contract to accept substitutes in their place. In an argument that yeoman could support, Davis claimed that wealthy principals had only received a special privilege and had not entered into a contract, and therefore they would now face conscription. Congressmen agreed with Davis's logic, ending substitution on December 28, 1863, and eight days later, they called for the conscription of principals.[29]

Discussions of exemptions, details, and substitution demonstrate that in assessing Jefferson Davis's record on conscription, one must be careful not to measure him against an impossible standard. Contemporaries and historians who criticize Davis's handling of conscription fail to point out a better method, and his congressional opponents prevented the implementation of his preferred policy of eliminating all exemptions. No president could have made conscription popular among all southerners. Conscription demanded an expansion of national power at the expense of the states. And no one could have devised a system that all would have found equitable. Some men needed to remain at home while others served in the army. Undoubtedly, at least some of the friends and relatives of those in the army were bound to resent the men who had the privilege to remain in their homes with their wives and children. Adding to these complications, Davis had to enact conscription in a brand-new nation that faced a numerically superior opponent and thus had to mobilize as many men as possible.

Yet, despite these obstacles, Davis's handling of conscription could be judged a qualified success. The Confederacy never experienced anything like the draft riots in New York and other northern cities. Unlike Lincoln, Davis did not have the luxury of allowing men (or even entire communities) to pay a $300 commutation fee to avoid service or of looking the other way as men wholesale avoided the draft. The Confederacy needed every soldier it could find, and it successfully managed to place as much as 75 to 85 percent of its military age white population in the army. At times, Davis might have been guilty of self-righteously dismissing constitutional critics such as Governor Brown of Georgia, but state courts supported his position. And, when critics carped about the class biases of conscription, Davis responded by proposing alterations in the policies designed to create an equitable system.

Davis's most significant problem in addressing conscription involved his underestimation of the controversy it would engender. The "plain and simple method" that he requested in March 1862 was a chimera. Assuming that others recognized the necessity of conscription, he did not lay much groundwork for the initial measure. Similarly, having no intention of destroying state rights or establishing a dictatorship, he did not understand how anyone could question his motives. When people assailed the policy, he sometimes reacted acerbically. Simply put, Davis recognized that victory depended on getting all men, not just the eager volunteers, to do their part. For him, though not for his critics, fairness necessitated assigning the entire military-age population to either the military or to war-supporting tasks. Davis's record, including his conscription policy, must not be evaluated in light of Confederate defeat. Instead, it must be evaluated in light of what was possible. Therefore, Davis's conscription policy should be assessed as effectively balancing the needs of the battlefront and the home front.

NOTES

1. Jefferson Davis to the Senate and House, March 28, 1862, in James D. Richardson, ed., *A Compilation of the Messages and Papers of the Confederacy, Including the Diplomatic Correspondence, 1861–1865* (Nashville: United States Publishing Co., 1904), 1:205–6.

2. For a copy of the April 1862 conscription law, see *The War of the Rebellion: A Compilation of the Official Records of the Union and Confederate Armies*, 128 vols. (Washington, DC: Government Printing Office, 1880–1901), ser. 4, 1:1095–97 (hereinafter *OR*). For the October 1862 alterations, see *OR*, ser. 4, 2:160–62. For the best discussions of the alterations in Confederate conscription laws, see Albert Burton Moore, *Conscription and Conflict in the Confederacy* (1924; reprint, Columbia: University of South Carolina Press, 1996) and William L. Shaw, "The Confederate Conscription and Exemption Acts," *American Journal of Legal History* 6 (October 1962): 368–405.

3. Alexander Stephens to Herschel V. Johnson, April 7, 1864, in *OR*, ser. 4, 3:280; Staples quote in E. Merton Coulter, *The Confederate States of America, 1861–1865* (Baton Rouge: Louisiana State University Press, 1950), 322.

4. Frank L. Owsley, *State Rights in the Confederacy* (1925; reprint, Gloucester, MA: Peter Smith, 1961), quotes on 279 and 75.

5. Moore, *Conscription and Conflict in the Confederacy*, 354 (quote).

6. Paul D. Escott, *After Secession: Jefferson Davis and the Failure of Confederate Nationalism* (Baton Rouge: Louisiana State University Press, 1978), quotes on 269 and 272; David Williams, *Rich Man's War: Class, Caste, and Confederate Defeat in the Lower Chattahoochee Valley* (Athens: University of Georgia Press, 1998), quotes on 1, 4.

7. Williams, *Rich Man's War*, 133; Message to the 2nd Session of the 1st Confederate Congress, August 18, 1862, in Richardson, *Messages and Papers*, 234.

8. William J. Cooper Jr., *Jefferson Davis, American* (New York: Knopf, 2000), 384; George E. Rable, *The Confederate Republic: A Revolution Against Politics* (Chapel Hill: University of North Carolina Press, 1994), 139; Jefferson Davis, March 28, 1862, in Richardson, *Messages and Papers*, 20; Governor Joseph Brown to Alexander Stephens, May 7, 1862, Alexander Hamilton Stephens Papers, Emory University.

9. *OR*, ser. 4, 1:1095.

10. Proceedings of the Confederate Congress in *Southern Historical Society Papers*, 52 vols. (Richmond, VA: William Byrd Press, 1876-1959), vol. 45 (1925), 26–27 (Clark and Wigfall quotes); vol. 46 (1928), 108 (Barksdale quote); Mary S. Estill, ed., "Diary of a Confederate Congressman, 1862–1863," *Southwestern Historical Quarterly* 38 (April 1935): 277–78 (Sexton quote).

11. For Davis to South Carolina's Governor and Executive Council, September 3, 1862, see *OR*, ser. 4, 2:74. For historians' view, see Joseph H. Parks, "State Rights in a Crisis: Governor Joseph E. Brown vs. President Jefferson Davis," *Journal of Southern History* 32 (February 1966): 3–24; David P. Currie, "Through the Looking-Glass: The Confederate Constitution in Congress, 1861–1865," *Virginia Law Review* 90 (August 2004): 1257–1399.

12. Brown to Davis, April 22, 1862 (quotes); Brown to Davis, May 9, 1862 in *Correspondence Between Governor Brown and President Davis on the Constitutionality of the Conscription Act* (Atlanta: Atlanta Intelligencer, 1862).

13. Davis to Brown, July 10, 1862 (first and last quote); May 29, 1862 (second quote) in *Correspondence Between Governor Brown and President Davis*. The Confederate house voted 53 to 26 in favor of conscription and the senate voted 19 to 5 in favor. For Watts's opinion, see Rembert W. Patrick, ed., *The Opinions of the Confederate Attorneys General, 1861–1865* (Buffalo, NY: Dennis & Co., Inc., 1950), 94–98.

14. Davis to Zebulon B. Vance, November 1, 1862, in Frontis W. Johnston, ed., *The Papers of Zebulon B. Vance* (Raleigh: State Department of Archives and History, 1963), 1:296, and Davis to Vance, November 28, 1862, in *OR*, ser. 4, 2:216. The Virginia government contended that VMI had a greater value to the Confederacy if its cadets remained on campus training rather than in the army. The Confederate government, which exempted teachers but not students, rejected this exemption, and the Virginia court would side with the national government.

15. *Jefferson v. Fair*, 1862, Georgia State Archives. The Confederacy never formed a supreme court, so the state courts represented the highest level of judicial review.

16. *Ex Parte Hill* (1863); *Davis Simmons v. J. H. Miller* (1864). For a discussion of the state supreme courts and conscription, see Donald J. Stelluto, "'A Light Which Reveals its True Meaning': State Supreme Courts and the Confederate Constitution" (PhD diss., University of Maryland, 2004).

17. Davis to Vance, November 1, 1862, in *The Papers of Zebulon B. Vance*, 1:296.

18. Davis to Vance, July 14, 1863, *OR*, ser. 4, 2:633. Gordon McKinney makes a similar point regarding Vance and Davis's cordial relations in *Zeb Vance: North Carolina's Civil War Governor and Gilded Age Political Leader* (Chapel Hill: University of North Carolina Press, 2004), esp. 131–44. He also points out that Vance smartly reserved his harshest attacks on Richmond for letters to other members of the government. David D. Scarboro agrees that Vance was able to achieve concessions from the national government in "North Carolina and the Confederacy: The Weakness of States' Rights during the Civil War," *North Carolina Historical Review* 56 (April 1979): 133–49.

19. Davis to Milton, September 1, 1863, in Lynda Crist, Mary Dix, and Kenneth Williams, eds., *The Papers of Jefferson Davis* (Baton Rouge: Louisiana State University Press, 1997), 9:363–64; Milton to the Florida Legislature, November 17, 1863, in *Journal of the Proceedings of the Senate of the General Assembly of the State of Florida* (Tallahassee, 1864).

20. Shorter in John B. Robbins, "Confederate Nationalism: Politics and Government in the Confederate South, 1861–1865" (PhD diss., Rice University, 1964), 106–7. Letcher quote in *Charleston Mercury*, May 7, 1862. W. Buck Yearns, ed., *The Confederate Governors* (Athens: University of Georgia Press, 1985).

21. Jefferson Davis, *The Rise and Fall of the Confederate Government* (1881; New York: Da Capo, 1990) 1:434–40 (quotes on 434 and 439).

22. "Speech at Jackson," in Crist et al., *The Papers of Jefferson Davis*, 8:568–60.

23. Ibid.

24. Davis message to Congress in Richardson, *Messages and Papers*, 1:295.

25. Davis, *The Rise and Fall of the Confederate Government*, 440.

26. Jefferson Davis, "Address to Congress," November 7, 1864, in *The Rise and Fall of Confederate Government*, 440. For his December 7, 1863, message, see Richardson, *Messages and Papers*, 1:370.

27. For Davis's June veto, see *OR*, ser. 4, 3:472–73. For a discussion of exemption policy, see Moore, *Conscription and Conflict*, 83–113.

28. Richardson, *Messages and Papers*, 540 (veto), 547–48 (final message on conscription).

29. Jefferson Davis to Reuben Davis, July 20, 1863, in Crist et al., *Davis Papers*, 9:290; Moore, *Conscription and Conflict*, 41–44. While state judges consistently endorsed conscription's constitutionality, some, especially Richmond Pearson in North Carolina, had greater objections to the conscription of men who had provided substitutes. Moore, *Conscription and Conflict*, 46–48.

PART III

THE LEGACY OF WAR AND ITS MEMORY

CHAPTER SEVEN

Old South, New South

The Strange Career of Pierre Champomier

Richard Follett

"**E**verybody knows *le vieux* Champomier," announced Eliza Ripley in her account of antebellum New Orleans. "He mingles with all," she observed, "conspicuously carries his memorandum book and pencil, and we all know he is 'on business bent.'" Pierre Champomier was a distinguished figure within the pantheon of southern economic and social history. For eighteen years, between 1844 and 1862, Champomier traversed the rivers and bayous of southern Louisiana visiting every sugar planter in the state and compiling production data and technical information on Louisiana's sugar industry. Every spring, he recorded, computed, and published in a small, paper-covered book the name and address of every planter, the amount of sugar made on each individual estate, and the production facilities on every farm. "Champomier's report," Ripley concluded "was considered as authentic as need be for the planter to know what his neighbor's crop actually amounted to, and the city merchant to adjust his mortgages and loans on a safe basis." It was a compendium of the American sugar industry and testimony to Champomier's enduring commitment to the region's economy and its commercial development.[1]

Champomier's labors were not in vain, for in the years following the Civil War Louis Bouchereau and his son Alcee Bouchereau continued the work of sugar reporting. Like their predecessor, they recorded plantation ownership, crop yields, and detailed technical information on each sugar-producing estate, primarily in Louisiana though additionally in Texas. Compiled into annual reports that cover the years 1844 to 1917, these remarkable records provide an unbroken series on the commercial operation of one of America's definitive plantation crops. Indeed, no other plantation staple was so meticulously recorded for such a long period of time as was America's sugarcane industry. Recently digitized at the University of Sussex, England, and freely available as fully searchable digital resources, the Champomier and Bouchereau sugar records reveal in micro and macro detail the economic performance of an entire plantation sector. The annual records enumerate the histories of land ownership, business consolidation, persistence, and change among the plantation elite, along with capital acquisition, technology transfer, the shifting dynamics of plantation land use, and the impact of the Civil War and emancipation on a leading plantation economy. In short, Champomier and Bouchereau's sugar reports provide a unique window into the social and economic history of American sugar and an unparalleled perspective on the most industrialized and capital intensive of the U.S. plantation regimes.[2]

But who was Pierre Champomier and did his tireless work to document the American sugar industry prove emblematic of the modernizing impulses of mid-nineteenth century society? Sadly, Champomier left no personal records through which we might examine his life or his motivations to begin data collection. In his annual published reports, however, the self-made statistician revealed the rationale behind his labors. Alongside pages of carefully tabulated data recording the outputs of every cane farmer, Champomier provided substantive commentary, with particular attention directed toward plantation agriculture, labor, technology, sugar markets, and international and domestic competition. He wrote authoritatively on the industry, providing producers, investors, merchants, and bankers with a detailed compendium on the success and failures of each planter, and his advice and commentary provided farmers with information and guidance to enhance their competitive advantage and to survive the vagaries of the world market. Champomier's attention to business data was certainly not unique, as price-currents were readily available in the main commercial cities, New Orleans included, but Champomier was exceptional in extending the statistician's work back to the individual farm and plantation. With his pencil and notebook at the ready, Champomier was a networked symbol of the market age. Even with all his efforts at mastering data, however, progress and modernity did not advance lockstep in the antebellum South. Like other commercial investors and promoters (notably in the railroad industry), Champomier encountered trenchant conservatism and commercial reticence within the plantation and mercantile elite of New Orleans and its environs. Even in America's most capital-rich plantation sector, Champomier recorded a checkered history of stagnation and change where modernity advanced in uncertain and insecure ways. The neat lines and ordered numbers of the sugar reports appeared rational and businesslike; they were spreadsheets well before that term was coined, but as this essay makes clear, appearances can often be historically deceptive. Irrespective of the tidy columns in Champomier's little books, the antebellum sugar trade proved chaotic and disorderly, with production data revealing the topsy-turvy fortunes of the planter class. The annual sugar reports thus captured and reflected the tensions of production, the vagaries of the market, and both the controlled and uncontrollable aspects of antebellum commerce. To be sure, the reports reduced those instabilities into orderly figures, but as sugar planters well understood, boiling down numbers, like reducing sugar juice to create raw brown sugar, was anything but a precise art. Champomier was certainly not the first or the last sugar analyst or data collector, but his career reveals the numerous and contradictory tensions of nineteenth-century trade and the impossibility then, as now, of truly mastering business success.[3]

Sugar was, of course, an exceptional crop, with unique production and commercial pressures upon it. Only a few parts of the United States possessed the climate and topography required for commercial cane sugar production. Indeed, until the innovation of modern frost-resistant cane varietals in the early twentieth century, the prevalence of a long frost-free growing season limited the geographical extent of cane production. The lower Mississippi Valley offered most of the climatic advantages enjoyed by cane-growing societies further south, but even here, Louisiana's semitropical environment was hardly ideal for cane farming. Icy winds occasionally whistled down the Mississippi River's wide sweeping corridor, freezing cane buds or more dangerously damaging the maturing canes in the late autumn, oxidizing the cane juice, and rendering it commercially valueless. Every year, sugarcane growers faced an agricultural dilemma. They could plant the majority of their seed crop in January and harvest it some nine or ten months later, but the slave crews who entered the fields in mid to late October harvested immature cane with lower sucrose content than that produced by their Caribbean rivals. Alternatively, farmers could wait a few weeks more, maturing their canes but pitting their fortunes against the weather. Most planters ultimately chose to cultivate their canes until mid to late October before ordering the slave crews into the fields for the annual harvest. After an eight-month growing season and facing a still volatile climate, slaves worked relentlessly to gather and process the canes before the first killing frosts descended.

Once the grinding season began, operations continued round the clock as cane cutters advanced over the fields supplying the mill with freshly cut canes at breakneck speed. Enslaved workers then fed the canes through the mill and extracted the sugar juice. The evaporation process took place over four open kettles, each of which varied in size before reaching the smallest, or battery, where granulation began. As a roaring furnace kept the kettles at the correct temperature, skilled sugar makers added lime to the boiling juice to remove impurities. Workers then skimmed the clarified juice before ladling it into the next kettle for evaporation. In the last kettle, the sugar maker carefully watched the cane juice begin to granulate, its thick grainy appearance signaling the final and crucial stage of production. The sugar maker would then order the semi-molten juice to be struck before laborers transferred the clarified sugar into wooden vats, known as coolers, where the sugar would crystallize over the course of twenty-four hours. It was then packed into large wooden hogsheads (containing between one thousand and twelve hundred pounds of sugar) with holes in their bases and left to drain until the molasses separated from the brown crystalline sugar. Planters then either shipped the sealed hogsheads to market to be consumed raw or transported it for refining in one of several northern cities. At every point in the harvest production schedule, planters held speed at an absolute premium as they strove to fashion reliable work crews who would efficiently harvest the annual crop and synchronize field operations with those in the mill house.

While the grueling pace of the agricultural year peaked during the harvest months, plantation labor continued unchecked during the spring and summer months. Immediately after the cane was processed in late December, work began seeding and planting the next year's crop—a task that seldom matched the intensity of harvest labor but one that nonetheless involved extensive and arduous work through the late winter months as farmers hurried to maximize the already foreshortened growing season. Not every field required replanting, but whether sowing newly seeded plant cane or tending second- or third-year ratoons, the sapping pace of agricultural life did not relent as planters drove their work crews to labor as swiftly as possible. In the spring and summer, work continued until the shoots were robust enough to survive without constant attention. During the lay-by season, routine plantation maintenance took over, as workers toiled to maintain the protective river levees, cultivate corns, or collect timber to fuel the steam-powered sugar mill come harvest. The overlapping duties placed continuous pressure on a labor system that worked to a strict production agenda during the grinding and planting seasons. Speed and workplace reliability accordingly commanded immediate attention, as few estate managers could afford the potentially disastrous impact of delays in a time-conscious industry.

To combat these production constraints, Louisiana's planters invested heavily in land, labor, and machinery. By 1850, some 125,000 enslaved African Americans toiled on 1,500 estates across southern Louisiana. Those slaves produced almost all the cane sugar manufactured in the United States, supplying approximately half of the American demand for sugar. On average, large sugar planters owned 110 slaves, 1,600 acres of land, and machinery valued between $14,000 and $27,000 (five times the mechanical capital of the largest cotton planters). These cane lords produced three-quarters of the sugar and owned two-thirds of the land and slaves in south Louisiana. By 1861, sugar planters owned some of the largest slaveholding units in the country. As America went to war, they produced over 450,000 hogsheads of sugar. It was the largest and last sugar crop made entirely with slave labor and the crowning moment of the antebellum sugar masters.[4]

Production, however, necessitated speed and disciplined organization. As Timothy Flint observed, the managerial order on a Louisiana sugar plantation resembled "a garrison under military discipline." Everything, he observed is "managed by system." By the mid-antebellum decades, planters intensified the labor order still further by investing in a highly capital-intensive plantation system. They purchased steam-powered sugar mills to grind cane swiftly, dragooned gang labor, and synchronized field operations with those in the mill house. The introduction of steam power in the 1820s, and its widespread application by the 1840s, ensured that planters who plowed ahead with the steam revolution enjoyed production gains and advantages accrued by economies of scale. Steam-powered mills ground the cane faster and more efficiently than the previous technology; the new mills featured higher grinding capacities, ensuring that planters could confidently cultivate more cane than previously; and the faster mill speed ensured that planters could wait until the final moment before ordering the cane cut and ground at the double-quick. These changes prompted a speed-up on the work floor as slaves toiled round the clock to meet the voracious demand of the new mills. Steam power resolved many of the environmental limits on production, and it made the Louisiana sugar industry competitive with its neighbors in the tropics. Federal tariff protection provided a further lifeline to planters. Import duties on foreign sugars cocooned Louisiana planters from ruinous, free-market competition with cheaper Caribbean producers. Tariff rates oscillated during the prewar decades, allowing Cuban sugar to gain an increasing share of the market in the 1850s, but with Louisiana's pro-sugar Whig congressmen lobbying hard to protect import duties, planters enjoyed profit margins of between 6 and 12 percent on good sugar harvests. The problem, however, lay in the unpredictability of harvest yields.[5]

The path toward technical modernity, however, faced still further obstacles—above all, the mounting costs of technology and labor, growing international competition, and reticence toward the enormous expenses of industrial sugar production. Such caution on the behalf of the planter class was not unfounded. Until the introduction of centralized grinding facilities in the 1880s, when farmers sold their cane to a collective mill for rolling, almost all Louisiana sugar planters possessed their own milling facilities. Since even modestly priced steam sugar mills proved relatively costly for all save the very rich, machinery investment proved to be an expensive though essential outlay for every sugar producer. Most planters by midcentury had grasped the technical panacea of steam, but the same planters who oversaw the steam revolution proved slow converts to the hugely expensive vacuum-processing facilities that appeared in the 1850s. (They were not fully adopted by Louisiana planters until the postbellum era.) These multiple-effect evaporators used the heat generated by the exhaust of a steam engine, rather than the direct heat of a furnace, to reduce the sugar juice to granulation point. The earliest vacuum pans dated to the mid-1810s and were substantially advanced by French engineers Louis-Charles Derosne and Jean-Francois Cail, who developed a series of evaporating pans that employed the principle of latent heat. In Louisiana, Norbert Rillieux—a free person of color in New Orleans—patented his multiple-effect vacuum pans in 1843. The use of steam vacuums minimized the risk of scorching or discoloring the sugar and produced a higher-grade, whiter sugar than the standard plantation grade produced by open kettles.

By 1846, a small group of planters, numbering no more than thirty, had adopted vacuum technology. The high price of "fancy grade" sugar and the enhanced 1842 tariff proved instrumental in fueling confidence among the very wealthy, who sought to benefit from the six-cent import duty paid on white and powdered sugars. Plantation grade raw sugar, by contrast, retained only a 2.5-cent rate. The 1842 tariff had a disproportionate, pump-priming effect on the sugar elite, who invested up to $30,000 to acquire a multiple effect evaporator. The price tag was too high for most producers, who continued to produce sugar with the open kettle technique, albeit with steam-powered mills. Some planters additionally experimented with partnerships and mergers to enhance their capital bases, but even these lacked the financial liquidity to advance the industry substantially. Technically, therefore, the Louisiana sugar industry underwent two evolutionary stages during the period Champomier undertook his data collection. The first of these stages featured the replacement of horsepower with steam power for the grinding of sugar and the introduction of a gang labor system that would furnish the antebellum sugarhouse with a steady supply of canes. The second stage of technical evolution gathered momentum slowly. Wealthy planters experimented with the vacuum evaporation of sugar in the 1850s, but it would be several decades more before cane industrialists moved ahead en masse with these innovations.

The enormous costs incurred with vacuum processing and the volatility of the prewar industry certainly contributed to the slower pace of technical evolution in the 1850s. The planters' desire for economic independence additionally ensured that Louisiana's cane elite funneled resources into private capital acquisitions; less frequently they cooperated with their neighbors to purchase expensive machinery as collectives or associations. Price and expense contributed to the planters' disinclination to purchase vacuum evaporators, though it was also the singular absence of associationalism in the sugar belt and the myopic individualism of the cane planters that underpinned the sporadic and rather sluggish approach many planters adopted to the second stage of economic evolution in the 1850s.[6]

Fortunately, the debate over whether the antebellum South was definitively modern or premodern no longer divides the historical community as it once did. As Anthony Kaye argues, the Old South was not an "anachronistic, seigniorial society." Rather, it was a "variant on modern capitalism" that exhibited aspects of economic and social modernity, even while it remained rooted to slavery and nonmarket relations of production. Antebellum southerners recognized that their way of life was a product of the rapid, dynamic processes of market integration, but they also remained wedded to a social ethic based on mastery, individualism, and independence. As a generation of scholarship has now shown, the culture of American slaveholding ultimately bred jealous independence, a short-sighted focus on the individual, authority, and upon personal liberty. Acquisitive and market-oriented, expansionist slaveholders spoke a lingua franca of modernity but tempered it with paternalism, planter hegemony, and a region-wide commitment to the preservation of liberty, slavery, and republican precepts of independence and virtue. Nowhere was this truer than in the Mississippi Valley where slaveholding magnates, a slaveocracy or plantocracy in fact, transformed early national Louisiana into a large and expansive slave society. Slaveholders were at the helm of this economic transformation. The expansion of the cotton and sugar kingdoms in the old Southwest required a monumental increase in enslaved labor (which the internal slave trade from Virginia and Maryland supplied) and global market integration too. Capital, credit, and commodities assumed standardized forms as the ethics of exchange bound riverfront farms in Mississippi and Louisiana with the urban hubs of nineteenth-century industrialization—London, New York, and Manchester. Slavery was itself transformed by the intersection of capitalism, forced labor, and international commerce.

Indeed, so substantial were these transformations that historians would do well to adopt Dale Tomich's formulation of "second slavery" to capture the step-change in market integration. At the vanguard of this transformation were the planter class, but as Jonathan Daniel Wells indicates, a professionalized southern bourgeoisie rode shotgun to the slaveholders' market revolution. Wells has assiduously detailed the rise of a southern middle class, chronicling their efforts to organize and professionalize diverse professions in the antebellum South. But for all its apparent symbols of economic progress, the Old South lagged far behind Great Britain or the American North in the race to modernity. Slavery lent a peculiar tenor to southern social relations, proslavery sectionalism eschewed the nation-state as a vehicle for national progress, and its politicians led a failed revolution to establish a slaveholders' republic that stood foursquare against the prevailing international tide of free labor. Southern planters and their middle-class merchants, however, found little incongruous in their regional devotion to slavery and the market age. Indeed, the picture now emerging from many contemporary historians is of a region that embraced modernization where rational (including risk-averse) business practices prevailed, a bourgeois middle-class flourished, and its wealthiest citizens thrived as part of the global economic order. Simultaneously, the southern elite championed the individualism of the independent farmer, harangued the federal government, and held resolutely to a definitively sectional identity, at least in the lower South. For all their complexities and occasional inconsistencies, the southern middle class and their slaveholding neighbors believed that slavery and modernity could coexist in tandem, if not in harmony.[7]

Louisiana's sugar industry exposed the conceptual and practical limits to antebellum modernization. As I have argued elsewhere, Louisiana cane planters were doubtlessly capitalist in their economic vision and invested in highly developed plantations, but they simultaneously embraced a social ethic based on mastery over land, labor, and sugar and a myopic focus on the individual. The sugar elite accordingly invested in more slaves or steam-powered mills, but they ultimately embraced a blinkered, estate-focused brand of southern capitalism. It enabled them to produce large crops and ruthlessly exploit their slaves, but it provided little scope for the associationalism that recent historians have characterized as a leitmotif of capitalist societies. Rather, the planters' self-absorbed commercialism ensured that, irrespective of individual plantation wealth and progress, the sugar parishes remained in a transitional stage, pockmarked by hundreds of well-established, capital-intensive estates but ultimately lacking the infrastructure of an advanced modernizing society.

Born in France in 1794, just one year before Etienne Boré became the first man successfully to granulate sugar in New Orleans, Pierre Antoine Champomier was uniquely placed to chronicle the determinative and marginal components of the southern plantation economy. Champomier's attention to the crop and the development of the sugar industry was unparalleled. It derived from his commercial expertise and his unwavering commitment to "the importance of correct knowledge in regard to the crops." A New Orleans commodities merchant and sugar broker himself, Champomier detailed in his *Fourth Report of the Sugar Crop of Louisiana*, "the minute and accurate statistics of each estate." Such information would inform every planter of "the movements and results of each other" and "stimulate individual industry, enterprise, and emulation" among landholders. From his reports, Champomier calculated that "it can thus be inferred what may be expected in prices; what another year will develop; how we are comparing with other sugar countries." Turning agriculture into a precise discipline was never easy in the cane country, but Champomier's reports attempted to provide rational, ordered tables for statistical and judicious analysis. As T. B. Thorpe of the Louisiana Agriculturists' Association announced in 1846, planters and merchants needed to "make agriculture, as mathematics, an exact science." New Orleanian James De Bow agreed, noting that the dearth of "correct and reliable statistics" proved particularly serious in the southwestern states. "Nothing," De Bow rejoined, "is more important . . . than knowledge," and he applauded European nations for elevating statistical research "into the dignity of a science." Responding to this injunction, Champomier embraced De Bow's advice to "benefit the nation" by imitating Yankee ingenuity and collating a "minute statistical report." Like census enumerators who reduced the complexity of an individual farm into a table of data or tirelessly computed the entire output of a parish, county, or state into a single sheet, Champomier celebrated the individual and collective value of the reports, noting that no-one could oppose his data collection, save those "who would abolish the whole principle of census taking, whether Federal, State, or Parish."[8]

Little is known about Champomier, the individual. Without his remarkable crop reports, the elderly French man would have no doubt have been forgotten. But for eighteen years, between 1844 and 1862, Champomier rendered "a lasting service to the country of his adoption," the *New Orleans Times Democrat* enthusiastically recalled. As Champomier admitted, touring every cane sugar–producing farm in the state was an "onerous" task and one that occupied him for three months a year. Plying the bayous of Louisiana from north to south on the steamer *Belle Creole,* Champomier either visited or corresponded with every sugar-producing planter in each parish, noting the owner or business operating name (in case of partnerships and incorporations), the name of the plantation, and, most significantly, the output of sugar in hogsheads. Added to this, Champomier recorded the technology used to grind the cane on each estate, employing the relatively simple terms "horse" or "steam power." The term *steam power* encompassed a wide array of mechanically powered sugar mills, and Champomier included additional data on estates that utilized the latest evaporating processes for the manufacture of sugar, notably, the Rillieux apparatus, single and double effect evaporators, and vacuum pans. He recorded the geographic position of each estate, its location on rivers and bayous, its proximity to post offices, and its distance to New Orleans. All of his data was collated by parish and recorded in tables that listed individuals and titles, plantation names, technology, locations, and output. Along with appendices, Champomier also provided a short page-long survey of Texas cane sugar production, reporting individual farm output, much as he had done with Louisiana. These were in turn published every spring as a pamphlet called "Statement of the Sugar Crop of Louisiana [by year]," priced five dollars, and printed by Cook, Young, & Co. of New Orleans.[9]

Champomier introduced and concluded his reports with a brief synopsis on the state of the industry, noting the relative size and quality of the crop and any adverse meteorological or flood conditions affecting the annual yield. He additionally detailed the technical state of Louisiana's cane industry, noting the number of facilities utilizing various technologies and the prognosis for the following crop, based on his assessment of the seed cane and ratoons. Based on past performance or predicted sugar returns, he occasionally counseled and censured planters for their crop management. Finally, Champomier also included a brief section in his annual report on the relative position of the Louisiana industry, vis-à-vis its domestic and international competitors. He thus recorded the imports, exports, and stock of imported and domestically produced sugar and estimated U.S. consumption levels. Additionally, he reported on the state of the New York and East Coast sugar markets and listed the relative supply of sugars from the Caribbean and Latin America. Like his contemporaries in the sugar trade, Champomier focused his attention on Cuba, Louisiana's closest competitor for supply of the U.S. domestic market.

These key aspects of production and market information provided Louisiana planters with an annual compendium on the state of their industry and reports with which to enhance their competitive advantage. Importantly, too, the annual data collection gave local and national merchants a portrait of the cane industry that detailed with precision the emerging and dwindling business concerns of individuals, businesses, and specific geographic locales. The reports, moreover, provided state and national politicians with a condensed overview of the industry and its broader value (notably in shipping, insurance, and technology) to other sections of the American economy. As the most capital-intensive agricultural enterprise in the country (one that far outstripped capital investment in any other branch of U.S. agriculture), Louisiana's cane sugar industry was a ready market for steam engines, boilers, grinding mills, and evaporators, most of which were produced by foundries in the northern states. He listed the number of mills manufactured in various cities and noted the regional dimension to this trade. Champomier's detailed technical reports thus provided vital local intelligence on the state of the industry, its requirements, and its contribution to the broader national economy.

Published in New Orleans, Champomier's findings were annotated and condensed still further for report and comment in the *New Orleans Price Current,* the leading periodical *De Bow's Review,* and the national trade periodical *Hunt's Merchants' Magazine,* as well as republished in U.S. congressional papers (notably, *the Annual Report of the Commissioner of Patents and in the Report to the Secretary of the Treasury*). His reports were not only unique in their detail but provided planters, factors, and trade merchants, in Louisiana and elsewhere, with a brief regional business portfolio. As James De Bow noted in July 1851, planters and merchants "should liberally sustain the arduous labours of Mr. Champomier . . . the extent of his services to the state cannot be lightly passed over." Three years later, De Bow published his weighty three-volume compendium, *The Industrial Resources of the Southern and Western States.* Again, he was effusive in praise for Champomier, noting that while errors were no doubt present in his reports, "they are altogether too unimportant to affect the general results. Nothing so reliable can be had from any other source." Musing on the role of his reports, Champomier concluded that his work was "highly appreciated by many intelligent planters and merchants, by the citizens of other states and the federal officers, by whom these services have been noted."[10]

That notoriety appears to have gained Champomier a singular reputation! As Eliza Ripley recalled, the Frenchman was eagle-eyed, his pencil ever sharpened, and his notebook at the ready. Encountering the "ubiquitous M. Champomier with his everlasting book and pencil" on board the *Belle Creole,* Ripley fled the elderly man when he opened conversation (in French) with the line: "Can you tell me the exact amount of—?" Frequently seen with his snuff box and telling "amusing stories" in "broken English," Champomier was, the *New Orleans Daily Picayune* stated, a "worthy old fellow-citizen" well known to older residents of the city. Like other settlers who flocked to the lower Mississippi Valley in the aftermath of the War of 1812, Pierre Champomier left Maryland, where he had first settled after arriving from France, and headed to Louisiana soon after the state had secured its statehood. Well before he began to collect data on the regional sugar industry in the 1840s, Champomier had established himself as an eager businessman and broker who profited from New Orleans' role as the commercial entrepôt of the continental interior. His sugar reports, however, soon became the "standard authority" on the trade and a source of "considerable revenue" to the Frenchman. His "business integrity" was (apparently) unimpeachable, and like so many others whose interests were inextricably bound to the slave plantation complex, he remained a "steadfast partisan" of the Confederate States. He returned, paralyzed and in ill health, to France, where he died on August 27, 1868.[11]

Underpinning Champomier's undoubted reputation was, of course, his exceptional position as the preeminent commentator on the sugar trade. His statistical portrait of the region far exceeded the sporadic records of the decennial U.S. census and condensed data from the Board of Trade and the Cotton Exchange. The statistical reports, moreover, imposed a business-oriented culture upon the often disorganized sugar industry. As William P. Bradburn of the *Plaquemine Southern Sentinel* underscored, the risk of misfortune perpetually imperiled the planter class. Noting in June 1850 that "people seem run mad upon the culture of staple product," Bradburn bemoaned, "they turn the farmer's life into that of a gambler and speculator. They are dependent upon chance, and an evil turn of cards—a bad season, a fall in prices, or some such. " Planter Moses Liddell concurred, declaring, "I am rather sick of sugar growing, there is such a succession of labor to perform the whole season round and so much anxiety prevails . . . Every year improvements are to be made, repairs to be done, new fixtures to be added."[12]

Liddell's anxieties were well placed. According to Frederick Law Olmsted, the peripatetic New York journalist who toured the cane fields in 1853–54, sugar planting was "essentially a gambling operation . . . if three or four bad crops follow one another, [the planter] is ruined." These concerns were not unfounded; Louisiana's temperamental climate made sugar cultivation a difficult and hazardous concern, while federal tariff protection required constant Congressional lobbying. Tariff support was "a question of life and death for us," insisted planter Alexander Porter who, like his fellow sugar elite, watched the importation of foreign sugars with disdain and no small measure of alarm. Cuban imports in particular rose through the prewar years. In 1840, for instance, Cubans exported almost 50 million pounds of sugar to the United States; a decade later this figure had surpassed 125 million pounds, and during the 1850s, Havana and New York–based shippers conducted a flourishing trade. In 1851 alone, longshoremen working on the Hudson and East Rivers unloaded 94,000 hogsheads of sugar and 188,000 boxes of sugar (each containing four hundred pounds) from Cuba. Six years later, some 150,000 Cuban hogsheads entered Manhattan, and on New Year's Eve 1860, officials at the Port of New York calculated that 230,000 hogsheads and 165,000 boxes of Cuban sugar had arrived during the calendar year—a grand total of 171,000 tons or 380 million pounds of sugar. Added to that lay another 22,000 tons of Puerto Rican sugar that waterfront workers unloaded onto New York's crowded quays. Louisiana's entire crop of 1860 (228,000 hogsheads) simply could not match the volume of imported Caribbean sugars that stevedores and draymen along the Atlantic seaboard heaved onto carts bound for warehouses and sugar refineries.[13]

Champomier's reports provided an uncomfortable reality check for those in the Greek Revival mansions along the lower Mississippi. His annual statements listed in cold detail the growth of offshore competition. The final pages of each annual statement included a summary on the sugar trade, listing imports, exports, stock in various port cities, and a synopsis of consumption. The tabulation of the New York and St Louis markets gave cold comfort to the sugar elite, for the tiny six-point print offered a unpalatable lesson—Louisiana could not keep pace with American demand, and although the state held on to between 40 and 60 percent of the domestic sugar market through the 1840s, its relative position was slipping, even with the expansion of Texan sugar. To guard themselves against the multiple challenges of the midcentury market, let alone the "viscitudes" of the weather, Champomier implored his readers to record information accurately, to share those results in a timely and proficient manner, and above all, to produce high-quality sugars. Advising the sugar interest of their shortcomings was no easy task in a culture that privileged personal autonomy and tetchy independence, but his advice steered planters toward the production of high-quality and higher-grade sugars. Like others in the trade, Champomier recognized that one of the planters' weakest suits was industry-wide cooperation. Particularly irritating was the tendency of sugar producers to flood the market by shipping large consignments of sugar in early January. Once on the New Orleans levee, port regulations required that sugar had to be sold in thirty-six hours or warehoused at the planter's expense. The effect of these regulations exacerbated the planters' weak position in the market, as factors expedited the quickest sale possible, often to the detriment of price. As the *New Orleans Bee* added, the rules of supply and demand simply did not function along the levee—supply continued, irrespective of demand. Urging cooperation and united action, some editorialists like Robert Wilson of the *Planters' Banner* concluded that the scarcity of mercantile information, the speculative manner of New Orleans commerce, and the planters' tendency to press a glutted market conspired to render the sugar community comparatively powerless against price oscillation. But, as Wilson well understood, the planter class did not help themselves. As one Jefferson parish planter observed, the "fatal habit" of Louisiana's elite, is that "of so many people wrapped up in their own individuality." Readers of the *Capitolian Vis-à-Vis* might have concurred with this prescient observation. Pointedly speaking to the structural problems within the sugar community, the paper's editorialists lamented that "there is neither union, co-operation or friendly association existing, each person pursuing his own plan, prosecuting his own theories, and perpetuating a great deal of mischief." Calling for collaboration and regional association, exasperated newspaper editors counseled the sugar masters to protect their interests from "ruinous competition" by prudent management and sagacious marketing.[14]

However good such advice appeared in principle, Louisiana's sugar planters remained singularly deaf to it. As one editor bluntly put it, the planting community proved "wholly indifferent as well as blind to their own interest." Such myopic individualism was by no means out of character. Indeed, it reflected the self-interest of planters who poured capital and resources into their personal estates but who shied away from collective action. Tangible assets in brick and mortar, muscle and sinew heightened the planters' sense of self and reinforced their wealth and mastery over land, labor, and sugar. Above all, the planters' self-identity remained anchored to the plantation and to their role as slaveholders and labor lords. Capital expenditure on slaves, building, and the latest technology may well have made Louisiana's sugar industry comparatively modern, but the individualistic values that underpinned such an approach proved ill suited for cooperation and the increasingly competitive market in which sugar producers operated.[15]

As planter James Hanna of Terrebonne Parish observed in 1858, the failure of associationalism had enduring consequences. "There is probably no interest in the United States, of the same importance, so much neglected by those engaged in its culture, or so much preyed upon . . . as the sugar interest of Louisiana," Hanna rejoined, "and there is probably none which so much requires combined energy and care in the promotion of its interests. While all other branches of industry are cared for by the associated efforts of those engaged in them, we are content to let the sugar interest float along on the current of daily events, and let it take its chance for good or ill, giving ourselves, collectively, very little concern about it." Hanna's lament aside, the disciplined lines of Champomier's reports attempted to bring order to the chaos of American sugar, and the dispassionate data bespoke a culture wholly different from that lambasted by the Terrebonne agriculturist. The regimented managerial accounting provided planters, merchants, and regional boosters with the detailed business information to promote the sugar interests and defend the productive capacity of plantation slavery and the contribution of slaveholding sugar planters to the wealth and development of the United States.[16]

Promoting Louisiana's interests, however, was no easy task. The New Orleans business community remained, like the city and its planters, divided into American and Creole factions. These ethnocultural divisions were spatial, too, with American traders and merchants occupying the Second Municipality, above (upriver from) Canal Street, while Creoles and Francophones like Champomier clustered in the First Municipality, a district that included much of the original colonial city and is now known as the Vieux Carré or French Quarter. Long-standing cultural divisions and mutual enmity "injure[d] civic enterprise" within the city, Frederick Law Olmsted observed, and hindered unity of action. Above all, as historian Scott Marler indicates, New Orleans merchants functioned in a "shared but isolated business culture" characterized by indifference and complacency. Local boosters, of course, attempted to rally business confidence with outlandish predictions of commercial growth. New Orleans, the *Picayune* declared in February 1838, was "destined to be the greatest city in the Western Hemisphere." But behind these bullish claims lay unease. The city's riverfront docks and levees proved inadequate, and the city enjoyed an unflattering reputation for its high costs. Wharfage, storage, and even transportation charges from New Orleans remained persistently high through the antebellum years and more costly than those levied in competitor port cities. The considerable volume of trade (particularly in cotton and sugar) should have given Crescent City merchants a competitive advantage over traders elsewhere, but despite their privileged position, New Orleans merchants failed to offer lower overall costs than those available in Charleston, Mobile, or New York.[17]

Louisiana's capacity to squander its commercial opportunities, whether in trade or natural resources, was unique neither to its commercial class nor to the antebellum period. The city's business culture, however, was partially responsible for many traders' lackadaisical approach to New Orleans' competitiveness. More particularly, factors and traders operated in atomized, speculative markets where individualistic behavior predominated among the city's mercantile elite. The planter's tendency to ship sugar en masse exacerbated these atomistic tendencies, but so too did the lack of unity among city businessmen. Ethnocultural divisions split the commercial community, preventing unified action on important issues of market reform. American investors and business leaders held prejudicial views of their Creole neighbors. As James Robb, the prominent banker and railroad promoter observed in *De Bow's Review*, the city had two classes of merchant: the "toiling, diligent merchants" and the "large property-holders, who live upon the princely revenues of their estates, acquired by inheritance, lucky speculation, or by long and successful business." The latter class, he deduced, "always opposed all public improvements and enterprises" and did little to "advance the city" or the regional economy. Parasitical in nature, these unproductive rentier capitalists were, Robb maintained, overwhelmingly Creoles, while the more productive derived from American stock.[18]

Robb's critique was hardly new, but it fueled nativist animosities in a city that was already physically, ethnically, and commercially divided. Robb's attention to the absence of local improvements, New Orleans' moribund railroad links, and its weak manufacturing sector exposed the city's relative underperformance. New Orleans, moreover, lacked a definitively industrial class, and as Olmsted tellingly observed on his return to the Crescent City, there was no "*atmosphere* of progress and improvement" in the slave states. "At the North," the New Yorker observed, "there was a constant electric current of progress, which no man could resist being moved by. At the South, every second man was a non-conductor and broke the chain. Individuals at the South were enterprising," Olmsted concluded, "but they could move only themselves." Champomier might have nodded in agreement, for while the elderly Frenchman attempted to bring stability and accountability to the instabilities of Louisiana sugar, his annual reports detailed a history of individualism, innovation, and stagnation within the sugar trade. Like Olmsted, he must have recognized that every second man was indeed a nonconductor who broke the chain of progress in the antebellum South.[19]

Whether Champomier explicitly sought to refute Robb and other Americans' scathing critique of the Francophone business class remains unanswerable in the absence of his private papers, but his attention to business detail commanded him palpable respect among fellow New Orleanians and the planting community he so diligently served. His annual report helped cross the perceived Rubicon of Francophone indolence and American energy by servicing a single industry where commercial and trade difficulties affected all, irrespective of their ethnocultural roots. As James De Bow candidly observed in 1851, the entire planting and mercantile community was in Champomier's debt, so "valuable" were the annual pamphlet and his "instructive remarks." Urging planters and merchants to "liberally sustain the arduous labors of Mr. Champomier which . . . can scarcely be rewarded adequately," De Bow gushed, "the extent of his services to the state cannot be lightly passed over . . . We risk nothing in saying that no other individual would assume the same toil for the same consideration."[20]

Selfless, meticulous, and reliable, Pierre Champomier may well have been a "conductor" of modern business information in the Old South. He certainly exuded the progressive protean energy that Olmsted praised, and his sugar reports attempted to "move" others toward sensible, risk-averse estate and crop management. Scholars keen to portray the Old South as a progressive bastion of business modernity might alight on Champomier's story as an illustration of a Whiggish, commercial middle-class man who aped the morals, manners, and aspirations of his northern free-labor urban counterpart. Aspects of that account are accurate, but as this essay makes clear, Champomier faced a tide of reticence, market anxiety, and self-interest which undermined collective progress. Modernity advanced, but it did so in fits and starts. There was no single electric current of progress in the slave South, and despite his best efforts, even the busy statistician could not keep the circuit buzzing or the voltage up. Individualism trumped collectivism in the pell-mell search for profits and stability, plantation values impinged on business affairs, and global competition haunted sugar producers.

Champomier understood that world with remarkable acuity; he recognized that slavery had proven remarkably adaptable in the sugar country, and its success (and horrors) underpinned the wealth of the region's slave lords and commercial traders. But Champomier was a product of a hybrid society, a place where modern and premodern values circulated, where slavery and precapitalist modes of production coexisted with dynamic commercial practices, and where modern-minded and globally interconnected individuals fretted over, or simply ignored, their dwindling commercial position. As Champomier's career demonstrated, the antebellum South and its greatest commercial port were never really "old," nor were they ever truly "new." The South was in fact both, a culture and economy where traditionalism and progress coexisted, where the politics of slavery held sway, where steam power and global markets in sugar and human beings defined lives, and where Pierre Champomier could watch old and new merge with surprising, if at times uncomfortable, ease.

NOTES

1. Eliza Moore Chinn McHatton Ripley, *Social Life in Old New Orleans, Being Recollections of my Girlhood* (New York: D. Appleton, 1912), 183–84, 189. On urban businessmen in the antebellum south, see Jonathan Daniel Wells, *The Origins of the Southern Middle Class, 1800–1861* (Chapel Hill: University of North Carolina, 2004); Frank Towers, *The Urban South and the Coming of the Civil War* (Charlottesville: University of Virginia Press, 2004); Scott P. Marler, *The Merchants' Capital: New Orleans and the Political Economy of the Nineteenth-Century South* (Cambridge: Cambridge University Press, 2013); Clement Eaton, *The Mind of the Old South*, rev. ed. (Baton Rouge: Louisiana State University Press, 1967).

2. Richard Follett, *Race and Labor in the Cane Fields: Documenting Louisiana Sugar, 1844–1917*, May 2008, www.sussex.ac.uk/louisianasugar; Richard Follett, Rick Halpern, Alison Bambridge, and Alex Lichtenstein, "Documenting the Louisiana Sugar Economy, 1845–1917: An on-line Database Project," *Journal of Peasant Studies* 35 (October 2008): 801–10.

3. No previous account of Champomier's career has been published; indeed, there is practically nothing publicly available about him, save his obituaries and sugar reports.

4. On cultivation, harvesting, and processing, see Richard Follett, *The Sugar Masters: Planters and Slaves in Louisiana's Cane World, 1820–1860* (Baton Rouge: Louisiana State University, 2005), 14–45; J. Carlyle Sitterson, *Sugar Country: The Cane Sugar Industry in the South, 1753–1950* (Lexington: University of Kentucky Press, 1953); Glen R. Conrad and Ray F. Lucas, *White Gold: A Brief History of the Louisiana Sugar Industry, 1795–1995* (Lafayette: University of Southwestern Louisiana Press, 1995), 14–22; Karl Joseph Menn, *The Large Slaveholders of Louisiana—1860* (New Orleans: Pelican, 1964), 6–31. One hogshead contained between one thousand and twelve hundred pounds of sugar.

5. Timothy Flint, *History and Geography of the Mississippi Valley*, 2 vols. (Cincinnati: E. H. Flint, 1833), 1:244–45; Richard Follett, "Slavery and Plantation Capitalism in Louisiana's Sugar Country," in J. William Harris, ed., *The Old South: New Studies of Society and Culture* (New York: Routledge, 2008), 37–57.

6. On antebellum technology and slavery, see Follett, *The Sugar Masters*, 90–150; Sitterson, *Sugar Country*, 112–56; John Heitmann, *Modernization of the Louisiana Sugar Industry, 1830–1910*

(Baton Rouge: Louisiana State University Press, 1987), 1–48. Postbellum developments are carefully addressed in Richard Follett, Eric Foner, and Walter Johnson, *Slavery's Ghost: The Problem of Freedom in the Age of Emancipation* (Baltimore: Johns Hopkins University Press, 2011); Heitmann, *Modernization*, 49–114; Louis Ferleger, "Farm Mechanization in the Southern Sugar Sector After the Civil War," *Louisiana History* 23 (Winter 1982): 21–34.

7. Anthony E. Kaye, "The Second Slavery: Modernity in the Nineteenth Century South and the Atlantic World," *Journal of Southern History* 75 (August 2009): 628; Dale Tomich, *Through the Prism of Slavery: Labor, Control, and World Economy* (Lanham, MD: Rowman and Littlefield, 2004), 56–71; Michael O'Brien, "Afterword," in L. Diane Barnes, Brian Schoen, and Frank Towers, *The Old South's Modern Worlds: Slavery, Region, and Nation in the Age of Progress* (New York: Oxford University Press, 2011), 306; Jonathan Daniel Wells, "Professionalization and the Southern Middle Class," in Susanna Delfino, Michelle Gillespie, and Louis M. Kyriakoudes, *Southern Society and Its Transformations, 1790–1860* (Columbia: University of Missouri Press, 2011), 157–75; Walter Johnson, *Rivers of Dark Dreams: Slavery and Empire in the Cotton Kingdom* (Cambridge, MA: Harvard University Press, 2013), 3–17. There is a vast literature on slavery and modernization; for examples of recent work that present slavery as a complex hybrid of capitalist and precapitalist values, see Christopher Morris, *Becoming Southern: The Evolution of a Way of Life, Warren County and Vicksburg, Mississippi, 1770–1860* (New York: Oxford University Press, 1995); Mark M. Smith, *Mastered by the Clock: Time, Slavery, and Freedom in the American South* (Chapel Hill: University of North Carolina Press, 1997); Jeffrey R. Young, *Domesticating Slavery: The Master Class in Georgia and South Carolina, 1670–1837* (Chapel Hill: University of North Carolina Press, 1999); Daniel Dupre, "Ambivalent Capitalists on the Cotton Frontier: Settlement and Development in the Tennessee Valley of Alabama," *Journal of Southern History* 56 (May 1990): 215–40; James David Miller, *South by Southwest: Planter Emigration and Identity in the Slave South* (Charlottesville: University Press of Virginia, 2002); William Kauffman Scarborough, *Masters of the Big House: Elite Slaveholders of the Mid-Nineteenth-Century South* (Baton Rouge: Louisiana State University Press, 2003); Follett, *Sugar Masters*, 151–94; Tom Downey, *Planting a Capitalist South: Masters, Merchants, and Manufacturers in the Southern Interior, 1790–1860* (Baton Rouge: Louisiana State University Press, 2006).

8. *Proceedings of the Agriculturists' and Mechanics' Association of Louisiana, Annual State Fair, January 5, 1846* (New Orleans: B. M. Norman, 1846); U.S. Patent Office, "Annual Report of the Commissioner of Patents for the Year of 1848," 30th Cong., 2nd sess., *House of Representatives Doc. No. 59* (Washington DC: Wendell and Van Benthuysen, 1849), 511; Champomier, *Statement 1850–51*, iii.

9. *New Orleans Times Democrat*, May 8, 1910.

10. *De Bow's Review* 11 (July 1851): 70; J. D. B. DeBow, *The Industrial Resources of the Southern and Western States*, 3 vols. (New Orleans: Office of De Bow's Review, 1853), 285–86; Champomier, *Statement, 1850–51*, iii.

11. Ripley, *Social Life in Old New Orleans*, 183–84; *New Orleans Daily Picayune*, September 17, 1868.

12. *Plaquemine Southern Sentinel*, June 22, 1850; Moses Liddell to John R. Liddell, July 28, 1845, Moses and St. John Richardson Liddell Family Papers, Louisiana and Lower Mississippi

Valley Collection, Hill Memorial Library, Louisiana State University, Baton Rouge (hereinafter LLMVC).

13. Frederick Law Olmsted, *A Journey in the Seaboard Slave States in the Years 1853–1854*, 2 vols. (1856; reprint, New York: G. P. Putnam's Sons, 1904), 2:318–19; W. H. Stephenson, *Alexander Porter: Whig Planter of Old Louisiana* (Baton Rouge: Louisiana State University Press, 1934), 27. On Caribbean competition (especially New York), see DeBow, *The Industrial Resources of the Southern and Western States*, 2:312, and P. A. Champomier, *Statement, 1851–1852*, 49; *Statement, 1857–1858*, 41–42; and *Statement, 1860–1861*, 41–42. On debates over Cuban annexation, see R. E. May, *The Southern Dream of a Caribbean Empire, 1854–1861* (Baton Rouge: Louisiana State University Press, 1973), 46–76.

14. Champomier, *Statement, 1851–1852*, v; Champomier, *Statement, 1853–1854*, v; *Franklin Planters' Banner*, February 16, 1856, and December 30, 1847; *New Orleans Bee*, quoted in *Port Allen Sugar Planter*, December 26 and 12, 1857; *New Orleans Daily Picayune*, October 22, 1858; *Baton Rouge Weekly Comet*, October 9, 1853; *Plaquemine Southern Sentinel* March 6, 1852, and *Port Allen Capitolian Vis-à-Vis*, August 23, 1854.

15. *Franklin Planters' Banner*, July 28, 1855.

16. *Port Allen Sugar Planter*, January 23, 1858; *De Bow's Review* 20 (1856): 226.

17. Frederick Law Olmsted, *Cotton Kingdom*, 302; Scott P. Marler, "Merchants and the Political Economy of Nineteenth-Century Louisiana: New Orleans and Its Hinterlands" (PhD diss., Rice University, 2007), 100, 41 (comparative wharfage costs); *New Orleans Picayune*, February 20, 1838. On the importance of Creole-American divisions in New Orleans, see Joseph G. Tregle Jr., *Louisiana in the Age of Jackson: A Clash of Cultures and Personalities* (Baton Rouge: Louisiana State University, 1999). Champomier's home address was 71 Conti Street; see the 1861 *New Orleans City Directory*, http://files.usgwarchives.net/la/orleans/history/directory/1861c.txt

18. *De Bow's Review* 11 (1851): 77–78; Harry Howard Evans, "James Robb, Banker and Pioneer Railroad Builder of Antebellum Louisiana," *Louisiana Historical Quarterly* 23 (January 1940): 170–258.

19. Olmsted, *Journey*, 275–76.

20. *De Bow's Review* 9 (July 1850): 111; *De Bow's Review* 11 (July 1851): 70.

CHAPTER EIGHT

Continuity Recast
Judge Edward McGehee, Wilkinson County, and the
Saga of Bowling Green Plantation
Samuel C. Hyde, Jr.

Scholars have long debated just how much the Civil War transformed the South. Other than the undeniable destruction of legalized slavery, few aspects of these debates have offered much certainty. Did the very pillars of the Old South—the plantation system, the dominance of the elite, and white supremacy, all arguably sustained by a pliant class of yeoman farmers—survive the war and thrive virtually unchanged in the New South? Or did conditions in the postwar South represent a significant departure from those of the antebellum era?

Entire schools of thought have focused on the degree of continuity in political leadership that crossed the divide of war as well as the amount of economic power the prewar elite maintained in the aftermath of the conflict. Similar debates have focused on the endurance of deference as a defining quality of life from the antebellum period to the postwar era. Other questions have centered on the changing nature of race relations, class antagonisms, and perspectives of one another, North and South, as the nation transitioned into and emerged from war and upheaval.

Scores of studies, including C. Vann Woodward's seminal *Origins of the New South,* have offered perspectives on the transformation of identity as the Old South gave way to the New. Most such studies have employed a broad approach designed to include a study area large enough to suggest that conclusions could be applied to the entire South. The large study design, though useful in its own right, frequently relies on generalities that may obfuscate specifics. A complimentary method is the micro-study that not only allows the researcher to test the general conclusions but frequently reveals precise details of issues and events that may be less evident in larger studies.[1]

A dramatic set of circumstances that prevailed in Wilkinson County, Mississippi, and climaxed in October 1864 offers an opportunity for examining questions related to the transformation of identity in the South through the prism of a defined test case sample. Situated in the extreme southwestern corner of Mississippi, Wilkinson enjoys a storied past. Bordered by the Mississippi River near the confluence of the Red River, the county boasted some of the richest farmland in the nation. By 1850, planters there produced a whopping 26,381 bales of cotton—second in per capita yield in the state, which made it one of the most productive counties in the South. The county's immediate proximity to the famed river port at Natchez made it a principle pathway for numerous market trails that extended from the hub of the Natchez Trace along a variety of corridors to the South's one great metropolis, New Orleans.[2]

Created in 1802, Wilkinson became the fifth county organized in the new Mississippi Territory. It was named for General James Wilkinson, who came to Natchez in 1798 and later created the military post at Fort Adams, which served as the U.S. port of entry on the Mississippi River prior to American acquisition of the Orleans Territory. As such, Fort Adams and the surrounding Wilkinson County environs served as a hotbed of intrigue during the early American Republic. The region's strategic location and reputation as a site of political schemes and machinations led Fort Adams to serve as the site of the fictional trial of Philip Nolan, the unfortunate associate of Aaron Burr and despised antihero of Edward Everett Hale's classic *The Man Without a Country*.

Notwithstanding the political turbulence occasioned by the county's location on the great river and its shared border with the chronically chaotic territory of West Florida immediately to its south, Wilkinson enjoyed the power, prestige, and abundance common to many such well-endowed regions of the plantation South. The rich alluvial landscape attracted some of the earliest white settlers to that region of the Mississippi. The collection of import and export duties, along with the substantial garrison located at Fort Adams, generated revenue, offered security, and stimulated development. The county seat, Woodville, was home to the first cotton mill established in Mississippi. Chartered in 1850, the Woodville Cotton Factory produced $92,635 worth of cotton and woolen goods on the eve of war in 1860, which was the highest level of production of any plant in Mississippi. Woodville also served as the terminus of the West Feliciana Railroad, which connected the cotton-rich region to the nearby Mississippi River port of Bayou Sara, Louisiana. Initiating operations in 1842, the West Feliciana RR enjoyed status as the first railroad in Mississippi and the first standard gauge line in the United States.[3]

Incorporated in 1811, Woodville was home to a veritable host of politicians, military men, and government officials, not the least of whom was Jefferson Davis. In his youth, the future one and only president of the Confederate States of America called Woodville home while he attended the Wilkinson Academy. The Davis family maintained a large plantation in the area. Originally called Poplar Grove, the name of the plantation was later changed to Rosemont due to the extensive rose gardens maintained on the property. After losing his first wife, Sarah Knox Taylor Davis, to malaria, one of the consistent scourges of the region, Davis spent several years in seclusion in Wilkinson County before embarking on a career that would eventually land him as the political leader of the Confederacy.[4]

A list of prominent individuals hailing from Woodville and the immediate environs would read like a who's who of dignitaries from early Mississippi history. In the year 1830 alone, Woodville had the distinction of being called home by U.S. senator George Poindexter, Mississippi governor Gerard C. Brandon, and lieutenant governor Abram M. Scott.[5] The talented and powerful people in the Woodville area demanded access to educational and literary services typically absent in vast regions of the rural South. In addition to the Wilkinson Academy, the community boasted the Woodville Female College, the Woodville Bank, and a newspaper, the *Woodville Republican,* whose continued operation since 1823 has earned it the distinction of being the longest operating business in the state. Nearby Centenary College offered a reputable outlet for higher education, while numerous churches, including stately Bethel Methodist church, provided succor to the faithful.

Remarkably, cotton factory to railroad, educational facilities to churches, and economic engines to political position, with the exception of the *Woodville Republican,* each of these ventures was tied to the efforts of one man—Judge Edward McGehee. Born in Oglethorpe, Georgia, in 1786, McGehee personified the story of self-made ascent to power in the antebellum Old Southwest. At age twenty-one, he moved to Wheeling, in western Virginia, where he first exhibited understanding of the tools necessary to be successful in the South— amassing land and labor served as the object of his adventure. Aware that increasing numbers of slaveholders in that region of Virginia were interested in selling their bondsmen, McGehee used money advanced by his father to buy seven slaves, a horse, and a flatboat. After procuring provisions to sustain his small party for a lengthy journey, he traveled down the Ohio River and into the Mississippi en route to Fort Adams.[6]

While stopped to rest and resupply at Fort Adams, McGehee explored the hinterlands. Impressed by the soil quality and the lush undisturbed forests, he purchased land along nearby Thompson's Creek and determined to make the region his home. He constructed a small log cabin before returning to Georgia, where he married his first wife, Peggy Louisa Cosby. After a short visit with his family, McGehee returned to Mississippi with his new wife and a small library. Before his death in 1880 at the ripe old age of ninety-three, McGehee would marry three times and father nineteen children. To accommodate his ever-growing family, the judge constructed a series of homes in Wilkinson County, the most lavish of which was a three-story brick mansion, replete with four columns, which McGehee named Bowling Green.[7]

Constructed in 1833, Bowling Green epitomized the opulence and power that characterized the antebellum slaveholding elite. A high fence surrounded much of the plantation property; McGehee kept deer preserves so that he could take guests hunting. Several large ponds were stocked with fish for the family dinner table. Visitors noted that Red Devon cattle grazed on hundreds of beautiful park-like acres and that in the deeper parts of the woods roamed hundreds of hogs, "not razorbacks but improved Berkshire hogs." The hogs and their wallows were looked after by one of McGehee's slaves known as Old Prince, "a faithful and efficient man," who refused to live in the slave quarters, preferring instead to reside alone in a house built near the woods.[8]

Life at Bowling Green provided comfort and plenty in every regard for the McGehee family; it also stood as a physical manifestation of the family's power to command deference from those around them. By every account, Edward McGehee was an extraordinarily gifted speaker with legendary powers of persuasion. Arguing before the Louisiana legislature in 1831 in support of the charter of the West Feliciana Railroad, McGehee left the audience spellbound. James H. Muse, a young lawyer from East Feliciana Parish, Louisiana, was awed by his performance. "I was never so favorably and deeply impressed on first acquaintance with anyone as I was with Judge McGehee. In his conversation, his demeanor, and general bearing, combined with the simplicity and gentleness of a child, the seriousness of a sage, and the dignity of a prince . . . Of course he obtained what he desired at the hands of the legislature."[9]

In addition to highlighting his abilities of political persuasion, the railroad debates revealed McGehee's power in relation to his neighbors. Recalling the dispute over the railroad some years later, the judge's grandson James Stewart

McGehee confided that some residents of Wilkinson County adamantly refused to have the line pass through their property. Indeed, resistance to the construction of railroads proved a constant challenge for promoters, who were required to overcome fears that new transportation networks would lead to a changed way of life or would be dangerous. James S. McGehee noted that in Wilkinson County the railroad opponents were not small farmers but planters owning two or three thousand acres, "and they were as powerful as feudal barons of the middle ages, who could very effectually block any enterprise of this kind almost indefinitely." Judge McGehee was forceful, rationally arguing the pros and cons of the proposed line, and eloquent. In a note to a wavering William Haile, he wrote, "you convinced me so completely that the road should and could be built that nothing you may say in opposition to it now can alter my course or end my efforts to build it." In the end, the railroad was completed, and McGehee earned the lion's share of the credit.[10]

His power of persuasion, along with his wealth and standing in the community, made Edward McGehee an excellent candidate for elected office. Even so, he encountered challenges to his entry into the sordid world of politics—primarily the shortage of hours in a day. In 1860, on the eve of war and during the most active period of his life, McGehee owned at least eight plantations in addition to Bowling Green. He spent the entire day, every day but Sunday, riding on a horse or in his favorite carriage from spot to spot supervising the work of more than five hundred slaves who resided in 122 cabins scattered across his vast properties, which totaled more than 29,000 acres. He also supervised production at the Woodville Cotton Factory, served on countless educational boards and religious committees, acted as international agent for the local bank, and functioned as co-manager of the railroad. McGehee acknowledged the ever-mounting burden that daily confronted him in a letter to his son: "the railroad business in addition to my former business occupies my time three days of each week. When I get home I am so much fatigued that I cannot write."[11]

Despite such varied demands and limitations on his time, his well-established talents and manifest resources led him toward political office. First elected to the Mississippi House of Representatives from Wilkinson County in 1825, McGehee tirelessly advanced internal improvements such as transportation and communication networks. His efforts later set the stage for his collusion with Samuel F. B. Morse to construct the first telegraph line in Mississippi. The state legislature later appointed him vice chancellor for Wilkinson County, a position equivalent to probate judge, and forever after he was known as Judge McGehee. His power, prestige, and accomplishments soon propelled the judge into national political circles. Upon his ascension to the presidency in 1848, Zachary Taylor tapped McGehee to serve as his secretary of the treasury. McGehee declined the offer, preferring to remain in Mississippi, where he seemed to enjoy virtually uncompromised power.[12]

The notion of power has long intrigued scholars of the antebellum South. Such observers have long debated the question, "Whose South was it?" According to one well-known school of thought, the Old South belonged to the slaveholding elite. Powerful planters who exercised absolute political dominance, or hegemony, extended their power over the South through their control of the economic infrastructure that functioned almost exclusively for their benefit. The common folk's ambition to emulate, if not outright advance to the ranks of the slaveholding elite, provided the planters with a powerful mechanism of social control that marginalized the emergence of any competing avenues for advancement among the poorer people. In short, the planters controlled the politics, economy, and very culture of the antebellum South. Or, as succinctly articulated by historian Eugene Genovese, the planters enjoyed "the habit of command."[13]

A different vision of the South emerged in the writings of the so-called Owsley School of historians. In the late 1940s, history professor Frank Owsley and a cadre of students challenged the notion of planter dominance in the antebellum South. Owsley and others argued instead that a vibrant middle class, far more numerous than those who enjoyed planter status, maintained an identity separate and distinct from the South of the great plantations. This group did not command the same level of popular interest as planters, due to their comparatively plain way of life, but the Owsley School argued that anyone who consulted census statistics and other primary source records could see their relative wealth and understand the power of their numbers. Proponents of the plain folk ideal of the South argue that the slaveholding elite's need to control their bondsmen necessarily forced them to compromise, at least socially, with common whites in order to sustain their political power.[14]

Wilkinson County exemplifies the dilemma for understanding identity in the antebellum South. While the county itself and many individual residents exhibited extraordinary wealth, the status of some locals was quite the opposite. In 1850, Wilkinson ranked thirty-seventh among Mississippi's fifty-nine counties in total number of farms. Despite the comparatively low number, the county's farms ranked twelfth in value statewide, producing the second highest per capita yield in cotton. As for population, Wilkinson County's 3,624 white residents and 13,260 slaves ranked thirty-fourth and fifth, respectively, in the state. The demographics clearly conform to that typical of a wealthy plantation county. They also reflect the relationship between power and privilege. Despite enjoying a reputation for educational opportunities, less than half of the school age children in Wilkinson County attended either public or private school—a fact that suggests the privilege of education did not extend far beyond the plantations.[15]

McGehee's expanded neighborhood likewise reflected the disparity. In addition to the family home of Jefferson Davis, other not-so-distant neighbors to Bowling Green included the plantations of Duncan Stewart and John A. J. Hamilton, Colonel Vincent D. Walsh's opulent Rosemound Plantation, and a collection of equally impressive plantations styled Woodlawn, Rosehill, Holly Hill, and Laurel Hill. The plantations in the area varied in the number of bondsmen they maintained. Yet whether one spoke of Elgee Chambers and his 501 slaves or of the 70 slaves on the plantation of A. M. Turnbull, it was abundantly evident that a multitude of wealthy planters lived in Wilkinson County. A caustic letter published in the *Natchez Courier* lamented, "we live under an oligarchy that has not yet dared to trust the people with a say as to its consent." Such an argument is revealing of the level of control exercised by McGehee and his powerful neighbors. But there were other neighbors. James S. McGehee recalled that on the northwest border of Bowling Green lived "Mr. and Mrs. Wicker very old and very poor people. Their place was small and worn out and Mr. Wicker tried to make a living by canvassing among the neighbors for the sale of household articles." Similarly, the nearest neighbor to the south was the Lemon family, "who were poor in an area where all the white people were wealthy but they retained the respect and high regard of every member of that community."[16]

It is open to debate whether James McGehee's observation reflects the presence of W. J. Cash's "proto-Dorian bond" or relates to the fact that during the war Mr. Lemon killed his planter neighbor John Hamilton when Hamilton tried to enforce a government order to burn cotton rather than let it fall into the hands of the Federals. What is certain is that the names Lemon, Wicker, and the like never appear in any role suggesting status in Wilkinson County before or during the war. Instead, a different name remains omnipresent in virtually every role indicating power and privilege in Wilkinson County—Edward McGehee.[17]

Judge McGehee served as a political leader, commanded vast economic power, assumed the lead in technological and industrial development, and served on or facilitated scores of religious, civic, and educational enterprises. Ever the paternalistic patriarch, he sent his servants to assist less fortunate neighbors or to aid in community projects, never hesitating to admonish those he assisted to support his own projects. He likewise improved the lives of Wilkinson County residents by securing the improvement of existing roads and the construction of a railroad to get goods to market. Control of, or influence over, the means of access to market served as an important component of planter power in some regions of the antebellum South, such as the neighboring Florida parishes of Louisiana. James S. McGehee reflected that the judge and his regional peers "might be likened to a nation of princes . . . raised on such a magnificent plane that their ideas were almost too colossal for application." Yet whether the position McGehee and a small group of similarly endowed planters maintained constitutes hegemony remains debatable. That he and his associates enjoyed the pinnacle of power in the South is indisputable. Power rooted in the concomitant qualities of paternalism and deference characterized Wilkinson County and much of the South on the eve of war.[18]

As the calls for secession arose across the South in the winter of 1860–61, many prominent individuals in Wilkinson County found it hard to abandon the old Union. Edward McGehee was among this group. Unlike some southerners who remained committed to the Union in the early months out of love for the United States, the judge understood that secession would likely lead to a war that the South could not win. As a well-traveled man, McGehee understood the vast resources of the North and realized that defeat would be bad for business in every regard. Yet when secession came, the judge cast his lot with the Confederacy. He allowed his sons and grandsons to join the Confederate army and converted his cotton mill at Woodville to production of uniforms for the southern soldiers. He even purchased two brass six-pounder cannons and presented them to the first Confederate unit organized in the county.[19]

Like the surrounding area, Wilkinson County witnessed massive support for the Confederacy. In addition to serving as the boyhood home of the fledgling nation's only president, the county produced five Confederate generals along with three full companies of infantrymen known as the Jeff Davis Guards, officially Company D, 21st Mississippi Infantry Regiment; the Wilkinson Rifles, Company K, 16th Mississippi Infantry Regiment; and the Hurricane Rifles, Company E, 21st Mississippi Infantry Regiment. A second Wilkinson Guards unit served as Company D, 38th Mississippi Mounted Infantry. Other Wilkinson contributions to the Confederacy included a cadet corps, home guard unit, and a company of "state troops" known as Minute Men. The extraordinary enthusiasm for the cause encouraged volunteerism among the regional youth. In a letter to his sister shortly before his departure, John G. Smith asked that no tears be shed for him if he died because it would be "for one of the best causes we have ever experienced." Traveling across Mississippi shortly after the state's secession, the Englishman William Howard Russell noted, "the enthusiasm for the southern cause among all the people is most remarkable—the sight of the flag waving from the carriage windows drew all the populations of the hamlets and the workers in the field, black and white, to the side of the carriage to cheer for Jeff Davis and the southern confederacy." Similarly, the faculty minutes of one of Judge McGehee's favorite beneficiaries, Centenary College, reflected the mass enlistments in the Confederate army, declaring succinctly on October 7, 1861, "students have all gone to war. College suspended and God help the right."[20]

Located near the Mississippi River along key market trails from Natchez to New Orleans and home to a significant industrial enterprise that produced goods for the Confederate army, Woodville seemed poised to attract the attention of the Federals. Though the first months of the war passed rather uneventfully, in the spring of 1862 a two-pronged disaster befell the western Confederacy that threatened the prevailing harmony in Wilkinson County. In April 1862 an impending invasion of northern Mississippi provoked the Battle of Shiloh, which resulted in heavy losses that for the first time brought the bloody cost of war home. Despite the severe casualties, the Federal Army remained unbroken and continued to menace the lower Mississippi Valley, offering the residents no respite from the fear of invasion.

Of even greater concern to regional residents, in the same month a powerful Union fleet forced its way past the forts below New Orleans and captured the great river port. As refugees and soldiers streamed north from the Crescent City, panic followed. Writing from St. Helena Parish, Louisiana, just south of the Mississippi State line, Abigail Amacker despairingly confided to her diary, "the Federals have taken New Orleans, the hour seems very dark for us, God grant we may have peace shortly . . . we fear starvation just now more than the Lincolnites." A few days later, she confirmed the deteriorating state of affairs in the region: "to be subjugated to be slaves would not be worse than this. Starvation stares us in the face and defeat too."[21]

Immediately following the fall of New Orleans, Federal warships steamed up the Mississippi, capturing Baton Rouge and Natchez with only token resistance before being turned back by powerful Confederate batteries at Vicksburg. The Federal occupation of Baton Rouge and Natchez placed Wilkinson County in a perilous position. Following an abortive August 1862 attempt to retake Baton Rouge, the Rebels fortified the bluffs at Port Hudson, Louisiana, less than thirty miles from Woodville, in an effort to maintain control of that portion of the river situated between the two cities. Determined to secure Baton Rouge and Natchez by intimidating the surrounding population, the Federals launched frequent raids into the interior, which in turn provoked reprisals from local partisan and guerrilla units. In the summer of 1863, a Federal raid through Woodville left the McGehee Cotton Factory in ruins.[22]

As the war dragged on, the Federal raids assumed a more ominous character. Increasing numbers of citizens were seized by Federal soldiers as potential Confederate supporters and sent to Federal prisons in Baton Rouge or New Orleans without a word of notice to their families. Anxiously commenting on the frequent raids near her home, local resident Anna Jennings asserted, "the greatest outrages are committed throughout the country and we tremble as to our fate." Exasperated by his inability to control the marauding, Lt. Col. J. H. Wingfield, commanding the 9th Louisiana Partisan Rangers, complained to his superior, "the depredations committed by the enemy are of the most shameful character on private property and on the persons of our fellow citizens and helpless women and children." Even some Federal officers expressed dismay at the behavior of their own troops. Gen. Thomas Williams, commanding at Baton Rouge, complained to Union headquarters about the excessive depredations committed by the Wisconsin and Michigan regiments under his command. "These regiments, officers and men appear to be wholly destitute of moral sense and I believe that they believe in the face of all remonstrances that they regard pillaging not only as a right in itself but a soldierly accomplishment."[23]

By the summer of 1863, powerful Union armies were tightening the noose around the Confederate strongholds at Port Hudson and Vicksburg. James S. McGehee recalled that the family at Bowling Green could hear the guns booming night and day as the fighting about Port Hudson intensified. In an effort to starve the Rebels into submission and to disrupt the illicit trade that continued in the region, the Federals issued General Orders No. 33. This set of orders allowed for enhanced efforts on the part of Union troops to seize or destroy foodstuffs and any other materials that might benefit the Confederates. The orders advanced the misery of local residents. Exasperated by the aggressive Federal actions, a grieving mother near Woodville declared, "You can never imagine my hatred for the Yankees. I despise everything that is connected with them in any way. From henceforth and forever I will school mine to despise more than I now do if it is possible the Yankees, but my hatred for them is so intense I don't think I can increase it."[24]

In an effort to bring some relief to the residents, in the spring of 1864 the Confederates dispatched Col. John S. Scott to command the newly reorganized Department of Southwest Mississippi and East Louisiana South of the Homochitto, which included Wilkinson County and environs. During service in command of the 1st Louisiana Cavalry Regiment in Tennessee and Virginia, Scott had proven to be a cunning and courageous yet controversial figure. A native to the region, he was well familiar with the geography and shared the residents' outrage at the Federal operations in the area. Accordingly, he moved quickly to consolidate his new command. Through aggressive recruiting and conscripting efforts, he raised a new battalion for service in the department. Scores of refugees from New Orleans and others eager to fight the Yankees were drawn to the charismatic leader. The years of deprivation and war nonetheless proved apparent. Local resident Serrano Taylor described the appearance of Scott's army: "We have refugees from New Orleans in Colonel Scott's command—barefoot—a coarse shirt and pants, unwashed for months—for they have no change." Similarly, Jane McCausland Chinn asserted that the new Confederate force on which the local residents rested their hopes for victory consisted of "old grey bearded men, soldiers in their prime with fiery angry looks, and flustered young lads."[25]

Despite the limitations confronting him, Scott moved aggressively to contain Federal raids and secure the region. In a series of hit-and-run actions during the late spring and early summer of 1864, cavalry operating under Scott's command disrupted Federal communications and supply trains between Baton Rouge and Natchez. They also repeatedly established mobile batteries along the Mississippi and shelled Federal steamers and transports. A Federal raid dispatched to destroy his base of operations failed when Scott ambushed the Union column and defeated it. In a bold August 1864 maneuver, Scott's cavalry forced the surrender of the Union stockade at Doyle's Plantation near Baton Rouge.[26]

Scott's offensive maneuvers created consternation among Union commanders in the region. Outraged Federal officials placed a $10,000 bounty on Scott's head. But in a substantive military sense, his efforts did little more than provide temporary relief and a bit of hope for the local population. The primary result of Scott's actions was the dramatically intensified Federal war on the civilian population, which related directly to Scott's attitude toward guerrilla operations.[27]

Little evidence exists to indicate that Scott actively called for guerrilla warfare, but that he tolerated its methods is indisputable. Recognizing the odds that faced him, Scott sanctioned the participation of citizens in the war effort as necessary to contain the "marauding" of the Federals. In the fall of 1864, the *Amite City Daily Wanderer*, one of the few newspapers still publishing in the region, echoed Scott's position. The *Daily Wanderer* reminded readers that Spain had survived the burning of its cities and the destruction of its armies to prevail over the French by adopting guerrilla tactics. Through the summer and early fall of 1864, increasingly aggressive guerrillas preyed upon Union forces operating in the area, often in full cooperation with Scott's cavalry and his mobile batteries along the Mississippi River. In response, the Federals planned an operation to rid the region of all Confederate forces once and for all—a decision that would seal the fate of Bowling Green and forever transform the family of Edward McGehee.[28]

The residents of southwestern Mississippi had experienced deprivation and want since the first months of the war. They had also experienced periodic Federal raids and impressment of draft animals and crops by Confederate authorities. But nothing they had experienced prepared them for the ferocity of the operation initiated in the first week of October 1864. The plan called for a major offensive operation originating from the Union bases at Baton Rouge and Natchez. Powerful cavalry columns supported by infantry and backed by artillery were to advance from the two cities in a pincer movement across

Wilkinson County and the Feliciana parishes of Louisiana. The columns would meet near the state line south of Woodville and then disperse in sweeping movements across the region, destroying anything of value that could be of use to the Confederates.[29]

As the columns advanced, the Rebels scrambled their available forces in an effort to contain them. Scott's main body of cavalry attacked and turned back one Federal column advancing across West Feliciana Parish, Louisiana, south of Woodville. In response, Union gunboats in the Mississippi River began intensive shelling of the towns of Bayou Sara and St. Francisville, Louisiana, prompting panicked residents, including former Louisiana governor Robert Wickliffe, to prevail upon Scott to break off the engagement. Other Confederate units were dispatched to contest the advance of Federal columns marching from Natchez and Fort Adams. Among these small units, a column of cavalry commanded by Col. Daniel Gober was directed to Woodville to protect the civilians and property of that area. On the evening of October 4, 1864, Gober's exhausted cavalrymen stopped to rest along the Bayou Sara Road two miles south of Woodville on the grounds of Bowling Green Plantation.[30]

That same evening Col. E. D. Osband departed Natchez at the head of detachments from the Fourth, Fifth, and Eleventh Illinois Cavalry, the Second Wisconsin Cavalry, Third U.S. Colored Cavalry, and one section each from the Twenty-Sixth Ohio Battery and the Second Illinois Light Artillery, approximately 1,500 men total. Arriving at Woodville in the middle of the night, Osband's troopers surrounded the town and then attacked, taking the few Rebel guards completely by surprise. After destroying more than $100,000 in commissary stores belonging to the Confederate government, along with anything else that could be useful to the Rebels— including the telegraph office and the remnants of Judge McGehee's cotton factory—the column moved a half-mile south of town and made camp.[31]

Less than two miles down the Bayou Sara Road, Judge McGehee had his kitchen servants up early that morning cooking breakfast for Gober's small force. The judge had visited with the officers the previous evening, when they approached Bowling Green to request permission to camp on his land, and had offered to provide them with a hot breakfast before they resumed their pursuit of the Yankees. Unbeknownst to those at Bowling Green, in the early morning hours Osband received intelligence indicating a Confederate force was camped along the road to his south. At dawn the Federals advanced down the Bayou Sara Road.[32] Caught completely unaware by the Federal advance guard as they lined up for breakfast, the Rebels hastened to mount a defense. Led by Colonel J. B. Cook, the Third U.S. Colored Cavalry attacked as the Confederates unlimbered their small battery. In a skirmish that lasted less than thirty minutes, the Federals drove Gober's 123 men from the field and captured all three guns of their battery. What happened next has been the subject of much controversy.[33]

Advised that Judge McGehee had allowed Gober's men to camp on his land and was preparing to feed them breakfast, Osband ordered Cook to burn the house and all outbuildings. As Cook approached the house, it became apparent that the looting of Bowling Green was already underway. Lt. Thomas Edland, who had commanded the company that captured the Rebel battery, reported that as he and Cook approached the house they encountered a "white soldier with an accordion under his arm." When Cook asked him where he got it, the soldier responded "from that house" as he pointed to Bowling Green. Carrie McGehee recalled that she was resting, ill with a fever, in her bedroom on an upper floor when she heard a commotion in the grove north of the house that soon could be discerned as cannon firing. The noise was quickly followed by the sound of battle as her sister Mary rushed into her room crying, "sister the yard is full of Yankees." According to Carrie McGehee, after scattering Gober's command, the Federals "soon returned, swarmed in the yard and house through the windows" smashing china and looting valuables. When her mother tried to stop the rampaging, a Union soldier slapped her violently, "every finger of the negroes hand could be seen in deep red marks on her face yet she remained undaunted."[34] Meanwhile, outside, after Cook announced his intention to burn the residence, he reported that he was approached by an older man "who claimed this would be terribly unjust and I told him I had to obey orders as a soldier. He was quite calm and self possessed as any one I ever saw and was not at any time excited." Cook gave the judge twenty minutes to remove items from the house, arguing that haste was necessary due to his fear that Scott's cavalry might show up at any moment. Cook later confided, "I considered the order to burn the house very cruel and unjustified and I still consider it so. The feeding of Gober's men did not justify it."[35]

When the judge requested courtesy toward the ladies, he was struck in the face with a revolver and rendered unconscious. In the absence of any senior officers, two Union cavalrymen dragged the unconscious judge toward the edge of the woods in an apparent effort to force him to reveal the location of additional valuables. Their efforts would have been in vain, as the judge had prepared well. James Stewart McGehee remembered that his grandfather had earlier identified a couple of rotting fence posts and had instructed a slave to prepare new holes for replacement posts. During the night, Judge McGehee concealed items in the holes and then supervised the positioning of the new fence posts the next morning. Other valuables were concealed in a hole under a large Beech tree on the grounds of Bowling Green. Regardless, all observers reported that the judge was in no condition to reveal hiding places at that moment. When his wife attempted to rescue him, she received a blow to the face from the blunt side of a sword. Some Federal officers blamed the black troops for the looting and brutality shown toward the family. Captain M. H. Chapin, who had also attacked with the advance guard of Federals, reported, "those negroes were as treacherous as the devil and we only had them right when we had them in a good hot fight." Yet others disputed the notion that the black Federal soldiers were responsible for the brutality. Thomas Edland advised that white Union soldiers had been the primary perpetrators, "the white troops did the stealing and burning and then laid it on the colored boys."[36]

Hearing reports that Scott's cavalry was advancing on Woodville, the Yankees departed a profoundly altered Bowling Green. The home and most outbuildings lay in ashes, and Judge McGehee and his wife had been beaten and abused. The judge's son Burris, a Confederate soldier who happened to be in the region gathering horses for the army that day later reported what he had found. As he returned to his unit, he saw smoke billowing from the direction of Bowling Green and hurried to the house: "father was sitting on a workman's table between the big China tree and the south carriage house contemplating the smoking ruins with the left side of his face swollen and bruised centering inward from a wound between the ear and cheekbone made by the cock of an army revolver with which he had been struck as with a club. His appearance was as bad as it was sad."[37]

Word of what had transpired at Bowling Green quickly spread through the region. Eve Brower reported that one of Judge McGehee's slaves came running into her yard, wringing her hands and crying, "they are burning master's house." Brower and a friend hastened to Bowling Green to find "the house in ashes and the family sitting in the yard amid a small pile of clothes." A clearly exasperated and apologetic Gen. George B. Hodge, who had recently arrived in the department as Scott's superior, reported to Confederate president Jefferson Davis that the Yankees "burned the house of your old friend Judge McGehee, and abused the gentleman and his wife. I had but 650 troops in the whole department to meet them with."[38]

The events of October 5, 1864, profoundly affected Edward McGehee, his family, and the region. Indeed, they carried such implications that in the early twentieth century author Stark Young would write his award-winning novel *So Red the Rose*, which was later released as a movie, based on the events at Bowling Green. After the family endured a troubled winter scattered as guests among neighbors and friends, with the exception of a few bushwhackings, the war in the region came to a close in the early summer of 1865. A turbulent Reconstruction era followed, ultimately resulting in the collapse of the Republican government, restoration of one-party Democratic rule, and unquestioned white supremacy.

After more than a decade of war and Reconstruction, southerners yearned for the return of peace and social stability. In some regions of the South, stability was restored under the direction of the prewar elite. In other regions, new leaders drawn from the ranks of business and industry emerged as the champions of a "New South." Still other regions of the South found themselves the victims of the transition from Old South to New. The neighboring Florida parishes of Louisiana, immediately south of Wilkinson County witnessed a restoration of stability in the traditional plantation parishes near the Mississippi River, while in the piney woods parishes, which had always deferred politically to the powerful planters to their east, something far different emerged. Local residents' rejection of the authority of their traditional planter leaders, coupled with the failure of new men to establish effective governance, resulted in utter chaos. The region became home to countless blood feuds and sustained some of the highest rural homicide rates recorded in American history for the sixty years following the close of Reconstruction.[39]

Despite the region's extensive social, economic, and political contacts with the Florida parishes, just across the state line in southwestern Mississippi, the situation was different as the turbulence of war and Reconstruction came to a close. Although occasional acts of violence occurred and political contests remained spirited, the chaos prevailing in the piney woods parishes to the south did not consume southwestern Mississippi. One reason the region avoided the pattern of sustained brutality involved the aggressive position taken by state leaders. Mississippi governors John M. Stone and Anselm McLaurin proved proactive in combating extralegal violence and organized lawlessness, in sharp contrast to their counterparts in Louisiana, who appeared either overwhelmed by the violence or disinterested.[40]

Unlike in the neighboring plantation parishes across the state line, which experienced antebellum sociopolitical conditions almost identical to those in southwestern Mississippi, the prewar elite was not restored to its previous position in the postbellum era. Instead, a reconfigured leadership emerged in Wilkinson County and surrounding environs. Judge Edward McGehee embodied the changed circumstances. As with most residents of the South, the war had been hard on the McGehee family. In 1860, McGehee's real estate had been valued at $195,600, complementing a personal estate valued at $519,850, which included awe-inspiring luxuries alongside the necessities of plantation scale production. By 1870, McGehee reported real estate properties amounting to $24,900 and a personal estate valued at $41,700—a 95 percent reduction in actual wealth. In addition to the loss of his slave properties and residence, the reduction in his agricultural holdings said much about the effects of war. In 1860, the judge maintained livestock valued at $19,800, which included 31 horses, 315 hogs, and 227 cows. By 1870, his livestock, valued at $4,170, included seven horses, thirty hogs, and seventy cows. On top of the massive reduction in personal wealth and the loss of his home, virtually all he had created, including the railroad and his cotton factory, had been completely devastated. It is easy to see why the judge was so profoundly affected by the war's consequences.[41]

Described as "tough, tenacious, and unwilling to sink under the financial reverses and devastation caused by the War," Edward McGehee put forward a bold front. Yet his behavior revealed that he was clearly a changed man and the patriarch of a visibly transformed family. The Judge left the four stately columns of the home he loved standing as a visible reminder of what had happened that fateful October morning, but he did not rebuild the plantation house. Instead, he constructed nearby a far different home, one that reflected the changed circumstances in Wilkinson County and his own identity. The new home was a simple two-story wood frame structure with a wide porch in front. Some observers were taken aback by the simplicity of the new residence compared to the three-story brick mansion that once had been Bowling Green. James McGehee noted that, "comfort and all necessities were everywhere in prodigal profusion but neither luxury nor art ever came within the gates." Another observer reflected that the new dwelling "included everything humanity could need except a good house," stating further that the house was "rude but comfortable." The grounds of the new dwelling included a substantive vegetable garden of several acres, but unlike Bowling Green, it included no flower gardens at all. Local residents noted that the postwar McGehees quickly returned to making money but no longer sought to display wealth and power, a sharp departure from the antebellum character of the family.[42]

As much as the more demure grounds of the McGehee residence reflected the changed circumstances, the interests and behavior of the family reflected it even more. The judge and his sons remained active, but they did not return to politics. The burdens of the war seem to have drained the family of its collective political will. Nor did they assume leadership roles in any new industrial projects or technology schemes. One could easily assume that age served as the primary determinant for the changed interests. Seventy-eight at the close of the war, the judge was clearly past his prime. Even so, his activities did not reflect the limitations of age. Though his outlook on life had changed, he remained extraordinarily energetic. He immediately returned to farming, producing 166 bales of cotton and 3,500 bushels of corn by 1870. Despairing of the reluctance of the freedmen to labor on their former places of bondage, Judge McGehee quietly supported fledgling colonization efforts while at the same time seeking new sources of labor. Shortly after the war, he sponsored the arrival of approximately seventy-five men and women from the North to work on his plantation. James McGehee recalled that this experiment in substitute labor failed partially because of the declining price of cotton but also because "many of these farm hands were simply the scum of the cities who knew nothing about farming and country life and were simply brought there by a leader who was paid by the head. The hands could not take the heat and humidity eating heavy meals several times a day and were always depleted with fevers and digestive troubles."[43]

The judge also took the lead in encouraging agricultural diversification in Wilkinson County. Convinced that the region's obsessive reliance on cotton had contributed to conditions that led to war and destruction, McGehee was a pioneer in the move toward greater emphasis on livestock and products associated with its cultivation. Aggressive Federal forays into the region in the final year of the war resulted in the confiscation or slaughter of a large percentage of remaining livestock. The *Amite City Daily Wanderer* reported in late 1864 that Union raiding parties so effectively eradicated livestock in southwestern Mississippi that, "if absolute want and starvation do not ensue, something akin will certainly follow." Yet barely five years after the close of the conflict, with McGehee in the lead, the county reported impressive gains in livestock holdings. Census records reveal significant advances from the antebellum period in the production of livestock-related commodities such as butter, as well as varieties of hay and other feed grains.[44]

When Edward McGehee died on October 1, 1880, his death prompted an incredible outpouring of praise and gratitude from the people and institutions he had assisted. Observers and media accounts noted that the judge had been even more generous with his neighbors in the later years of his life. The judge was lauded for his vision; one observer noted that no single man had done more to improve the quality of life in southwestern Mississippi, both before and after the war, than Edward McGehee. In his later years, he donated large sums to the Methodist Church, providing funds for the construction of churches from Natchez to New Orleans, including the large Carondelet Street Methodist Episcopal Church, and he gave to the American Bible Society, among other organizations. He assisted regional families by funding the education of their children, and he proved a key financial backer behind Centenary College as it recovered from the war. The list of assets recorded at his death included more than $150,000 in cash, $100,000 in railroad bonds, and properties so vast that he left each of his children and grandchildren an impressive tract of land. Though he no longer projected wealth and power as he had prior to the war, the judge had clearly more than recovered financially.[45]

The judge's sons, especially George and Burris, proved productive in their own right. Both directed successful plantations and supported various philanthropic and educational endeavors. Burris McGehee experimented in agricultural foodstuffs at his Woodlawn plantation, earning the epithet "Father of the Lespedeza Hay Industry." On his farms, Burris produced varieties of oats and hay that would be sold by the ton or carload, along with Red Polled Devon Cross high-grade cattle. When Confederate general John Bell Hood and his wife died of yellow fever during the 1878 epidemic in New Orleans, George McGehee adopted the general's twin daughters Odile and Ida. Though the girls kept the name of their famous father, Ida requested that she be buried at the foot of her beloved adopted father, a wish that was granted.[46]

The postwar McGehees may have distanced themselves from the policy-creating world of politics, but they did not retreat from positions of leadership. Area residents continued to show deference to the family for many years. In a particularly poignant example of the family's enduring influence, a woman named Henney Moton penned a passionate 1893 letter to James McGehee, pleading with him to come to Woodville and save her son Milton from being hanged. "He killed his wife and child, he hit them with a stick but he did not go to do it. So many other murders is out there some kill too [sic] at a time and none to be hung but Milton." Suggesting that the whole community supported her plea, the writer added, "Aunt says that if you want to own her you can do it by buying her and Milton both. If you save him Milton promises to stay with you for the balance of his days." Bemoaning the critical role the family played in the community, James McGehee's wife despairingly wrote to him that she sometimes forgot "how many people and interests are entirely dependent on him."[47]

Developments in southwestern Mississippi from the territorial period through the war and its aftermath reveal a pattern consistent with other regions of the South. The pioneers who carved communities from the wilderness were led by enterprising entrepreneurs who understood the value of land and slaves as they created a class of planter elites who dominated the antebellum South. In the aftermath of war and Reconstruction, some regions witnessed a return to power of the prewar planter elite, while others experienced the emergence of a new class of urban-oriented businessmen and professionals who championed the creation of a New South that embraced white supremacy yet advocated for diversity in investments and production. Events in Wilkinson County, Mississippi, and the saga of the Edward McGehee family suggest that a third category of leaders emerged in the postwar South—a group that had been so profoundly personally affected by the events and implications of the war that they chose to withdraw from politics, though they remained community leaders in many other regards. The war altered their outlook on life so that the near-absolute power they enjoyed in the antebellum era no longer proved attractive to them. They nonetheless retained the deferential respect of regional residents and remained community leaders through paternalism and goodwill. In short, though they no longer sought to shape the destiny of their region to serve their own peculiar needs and those of their peers, they remained as, or more, influential as any politician in shaping local identity. Scholars certainly cannot draw sweeping conclusions from the life of one prominent man or family, but the case of Edward McGehee does reveal another category in our understanding of continuity that is undoubtedly not limited to the judge or to Wilkinson County, Mississippi.

NOTES

1. C. Vann Woodward, *Origins of the New South, 1877–1913* (Baton Rouge: Louisiana State University Press, 1951).

2. J. D. B. DeBow, ed., *Statistical View of the United States: Compendium of the Seventh Census 1850* (1852; reprint, New York: Norman Ross, 1990), 262–65.

3. "The Private Papers of James Stewart McGehee," unpublished ms., 5 vols., James Stewart McGehee Papers, 1:41–45, Louisiana and Lower Mississippi Valley Collections, Hill Memorial Library, Louisiana State University, Baton Rouge (hereinafter cited as LLMVC); Honey and Jeanne Gross, ed., *Journal of Wilkinson County History,* 4 vols. (Woodville, MS: Woodville Civic Club, 1990-98), 2:xiv; John K. Bettersworth, *Confederate Mississippi: The People and Policies of a Cotton State in Wartime* (Baton Rouge: Louisiana State University Press, 1943), 134, 144.

4. William J. Cooper Jr., *Jefferson Davis, American* (New York: Alfred A. Knopf, 2000), 13–16, 19–21, 71–72; William C. Davis, *Jefferson Davis: The Man and His Hour* (New York: Harper Collins, 1991).

5. *Journal of Wilkinson County History,* vol. 4, book 2, xiv.

6. "A Ramble in Autobiography," unpublished ms. in James Stewart McGehee Papers, LLMVC; *Journal of Wilkinson County History,* vol. 4, book 2, xvi. The college for women was named the Edward McGehee College for Girls in 1861.

7. "The Private Papers of James Stewart McGehee," 1:44–46; Stella M. and James N. Pitts, *The Burning of Bowling Green* (McComb, MS: McComb Printing, 1997), 6–7.

8. "A Ramble in Autobiography," 11–12.

9. "The Private Papers of James Stewart McGehee," 1:41; Elizabeth Kilbourne Dart, "Working on the Railroad: The West Feliciana, 1828–1842," *Louisiana History* 25, no. 1 (1984): 35–36.

10. "The Private Papers of James Stewart McGehee," 1:41–43; Dart, "Working on the Railroad," 37–40. For discussion of resistance to railroad construction in the region, see Samuel C. Hyde Jr., *Pistols and Politics: The Dilemma of Democracy in Louisiana's Florida Parishes, 1810–1899* (Baton Rouge: Louisiana State University Press, 1996), 79–82.

11. Manuscript Census of the United States, 1860, Schedule One, "Free Inhabitants," and Schedule Two, "Slave Inhabitants"; "The Private Papers of James Stewart McGehee," 1:100–101; Edward McGehee to Edward J. McGehee, February 15, 1835, J. Burruss McGehee Papers, LLMVC; Pitts, *The Burning of Bowling Green,* 8; John Hebron Moore, *The Emergence of the Cotton Kingdom in the Old Southwest: Mississippi, 1770–1860* (Baton Rouge: Louisiana State University Press, 1988), 228–29; James W. Silver, ed., *Mississippi in the Confederacy: As Seen In Retrospect* (Baton Rouge: Louisiana State University Press, 1961), 34–35.

12. Dunbar Rowland, ed., *Official and Statistical Register of the State of Mississippi 1817–1917, Centennial Edition 1917* (Madison, WI: Democrat Printing, 1917), 250; Gross, *Journal of Wilkinson*

County History, vol. 4, book 1, 335–36; U.S. Supreme Court Ruling, Postal Telegraph Cable Company v. Adams, Revenue Agent State of Mississippi, No. 649 (155 U.S. 688, 15 S. Ct. 268, 39 L. Ed. 311), Jan. 21, 1895; "The Private Papers of James Stewart McGehee," 1:37; Pitts, *The Burning of Bowling Green,* 7–8.

13. Eugene Genovese, *The Political Economy of Slavery: Studies of the Economy and Society of the Slave South* (New York: Vintage, 1967), 13–36. For additional studies highlighting planter dominance in the antebellum South, see William E. Dodd, *The Cotton Kingdom: A Chronicle of the Old South* (New Haven: Yale University Press, 1920); Ulrich B. Phillips, *Life and Labor in the Old South* (Boston: Little and Brown, 1939); Lewis C. Gray, *History of Agriculture in the Southern United States* (Gloucester, MA: Peter Smith, 1958).

14. Frank L. Owsley, *Plain Folk of the Old South* (Baton Rouge: Louisiana State University Press, 1949). For additional studies conforming to Owsley's interpretation of plain folk relevance, see Dickson D. Bruce Jr., *And They All Sang Hallelujah: Plain Folk Camp Meeting Religion, 1800–1845* (Knoxville: University of Tennessee Press, 1974); John S. Otto, "The Migration of the Southern Plain Folk: An Interdisciplinary Synthesis," *Journal of Southern History* 51 (May 1985): 183–200. For studies seeking to define class boundaries in the South, see Randolph Campbell, *A Southern Community in Crisis: Harrison County, Texas, 1850–1880* (Austin: Texas State Historical Assoc., 1983), 31–43; Steven Hahn, *The Roots of Southern Populism: Yeomen Farmers and the Transformation of the Georgia Upcountry, 1850–1890* (New York: Oxford University Press, 1983); Samuel C. Hyde Jr., "Plain Folk Reconsidered: Historiographical Ambiguity in Search of Definition," *Journal of Southern History* 71 (November 2005): 803–21.

15. DeBow, *Statistical View of the United States: Compendium of the Seventh Census 1850,* 260–65.

16. "A Ramble in Autobiography," 22–26; "The Private Papers of James Stewart McGehee," 1:70–71; *U.S. Census (Seventh Census), 1850,* "Slave Schedules"; William K. Scarborough, *Masters of the Big House: Elite Slaveholders of the Mid-Nineteenth-Century South* (Baton Rouge: Louisiana State University Press, 2003), 24–25; John K. Bettersworth, ed., *Mississippi in the Confederacy: As They Saw It* (Baton Rouge: Louisiana State University Press, 1961), 41.

17. Wilbur J. Cash, *The Mind of the South* (New York: Knopf, 1941); "A Ramble in Autobiography," 22–23.

18. "A Ramble in Autobiography," 14–15, 28–29; Dart, *Working on the Railroad,* 36, 47, 52–55. St. Tammany Parish Police Jury Minutes, May Sess. 1846, May Sess. 1849, December Sess. 1845, July Sess. 1847, January Sess. 1852, all in WPA Louisiana Parish Police Jury Minutes Collection, LLMVC; William Pike to Henry Marston, September 10, 1852, Marston Family Papers, LLMVC; James Turnbull to William S. Hamilton, August 27, 1823, William S. Hamilton Papers, LLMVC. For discussion of power being advanced by control of market access, see Hyde, *Pistols and Politics,* 37–43.

19. "The Private Papers of James Stewart McGehee," 1:48–49; Pitts, *The Burning of Bowling Green,* 8; *Woodville Republican,* July 13, 1861, May 11, 1889; Gross, *Journal of Wilkinson County History,* vol. 4, book 1, 1–4.

20. Gross, *Journal of Wilkinson County History,* vol. 4, book 1, 23–205; John G. Smith to his sister, March 12, 1862, D. L. McGehee Papers, LLMVC; Bettersworth, *Mississippi in the Confederacy,* 41; Arthur Marvin Shaw, *Centenary College Goes to War in 1861* (Shreveport: Centenary College of Louisiana, 1940), 3; Silver, *Mississippi in the Confederacy,* 260–61.

21. *The War of the Rebellion: A Compilation of the Official Records of the Union and Confederate Armies*, 130 vols. (Washington, DC: Government Printing Office, 1880–1901), ser. 1, 6:624 (hereinafter cited as *OR*, and unless otherwise indicated, all citations are to series 1); Abigail Means Kent Amacker Diary, April 26, May 9, 1862, O. P. Amacker Papers, LLMVC.

22. *OR*, 15:19–22, 24–25, 122–23; Joseph Corkern to Jeptha McKinney, August 27, 1862, McKinney Papers, LLMVC; Sara Morgan Dawson, *A Confederate Girl's Diary* (New York, 1913), 40–55; Celine F. Garcia, *Celine: Remembering Louisiana, 1850–71* (Athens: University of Georgia Press, 1987), 69–71; Bettersworth, *Confederate Mississippi*, 144.

23. *OR*, 15:22–23, 80, 122–23, 778, 787, 1119; Anna Jennings to Mr. Odel, June 23, 1862, Hennen-Jennings Papers, LLMVC.

24. *OR*, vol. 41, pt. 2, 804; "A Ramble in Autobiography," 5–6; Nannie C. to Stewart, April 1864, Albert Batchelor Papers, LLMVC.

25. Howell Carter, *A Cavalryman's Reminiscences of the Civil War* (New Orleans: American Printing Co., 1900), 104–7, 117; *Amite City Daily Wanderer*, December 8, 1864; Serrano Taylor to Eugene Hunter, June 1864, Hunter-Taylor Family Papers, LLMVC; Reminiscences of Jane McCausland Chinn, "The Burning of the Barns," Typescript, 2, LLMVC; Steven Ellis to Brother, April 9, 1865, Ellis Family Papers, LLMVC.

26. *OR*, vol. 34, pt. 1, 136–38, 877–79, 906, vol. 41, pt. 2, 833, 919, 932; Carter, *Cavalryman's Reminiscences*, 107–9.

27. *OR*, vol. 41, pt. 2, 833; F. P. Wall to Sister, n.d. [1864] describes a reward of $1,000 for the capture, dead or alive, of Naul and of $10,000 for Scott (Jeptha McKinney Papers, LLMVC).

28. *Amite City Daily Wanderer*, November 10, 1864, and *Sunday Wanderer*, February 12, 1865; *OR*, vol. 41, pt. 1, 276–78; John Burruss to Edward Burruss, February 18, 1864, Burruss Papers, LLMVC; Carter, *Cavalryman's Reminiscences*, 113–14.

29. *OR*, vol. 41, pt. 1, 880–83, vol. 39, pt. 1, 831–32; *Covington Wanderer*, October 15, 1864; *Amite City Daily Wanderer*, November 29, 1864; Kate Blount to "My Dear Robby," October 11, 1864, Catherine T. Blount Letters, Wilkinson County Historical Society, Woodville, Mississippi.

30. *OR*, vol. 39, pt. 1, 831–32, 838–42

31. *OR*, vol. 39, pt. 1, 828–33.

32. *OR*, vol. 39, pt. 1, 830–32; J. B. Cook to J. S. McGehee, January 6, 1904, W. C. Miller to McGehee, February 28, 1904, James S. McGehee Collection, LLMVC.

33. *OR*, vol. 39, pt. 1, 829–40; J. B. Cook to James S. McGehee, January 6, 1904, James S. McGehee Papers, LLMVC; *Woodville Independent Venture*, April 6, 1904; "Destruction of the Residence," unpublished ms. by J. B. McGehee, "The Private Papers of James S. McGehee," 1:51.

34. *OR*, vol. 39, pt. 1, 831–32, 836; Thomas Edland to J. S. McGehee, April 24, 1904, W. C. Miller to My Dear Mr. McGehee, February 28, 1904, statement of Carrie McGehee "Facts Concerning the Burning of Bowling Green," Eve Brower to J. S. McGehee, February 22, 1904, all in James Stewart McGehee Papers, LLMVC; Kate Blount to "My Dear Robby," October 11, 1864, Catherine T. Blount Letters.

35. *OR*, vol. 39, pt. 1, 832–836; J. B. Cook to J. S. McGehee, January 6, 1904, James S. McGehee Papers, LLMVC.

36. M. H. Chapin to J. S. McGehee, March 20, 1904, Thomas Edland to J. S. McGehee, April

20, 1904, James S. McGehee Papers, LLMVC; Kate Blount to "My Dear Robby," October 11, 1864, Catherine T. Blount Letters.

37. J. B. Cook to J. S. McGehee, January 6, 1904, Burris McGehee to My Dear Son, February 5, 1904 in James S. McGehee Papers, LLMVC; *OR*, vol. 39, pt. 1, 830.

38. Eve Brower to J. S. McGehee, February 22, 1904, James S. McGehee Papers, LLMVC; *OR*, vol. 39, pt. 1, 836.

39. *Amite City Independent*, November 14, 1874, December 6, 1879; *Baton Rouge Capitolian-Advocate*, April 15, 1888; *Franklinton (LA) New Era*, August 15, 1888; *Amite City Florida Parishes*, July 15, August 5, 12, 1891; Hodding Carter, "Not Much of a Man if He Hadn't," *Southern Legacy* (Baton Rouge: Louisiana State University Press, 1966), 48–63; C. J. Boatner to Steve Ellis, March 12, 1894, Tom Ellis to Steve Ellis, December 4, 1879, Steve Ellis to Tom Ellis, September 23, 1883, M. S. Newsom to Tom Ellis, December 14, 1883, S. M. Robertson to Steve Ellis, August 25, 1893, all in Ellis Family Papers, LLMVC; E. D. Frost to H. S. McComb, November 3, 1875, W. M. Francis and E. D. Frost Outletters Collection, Newberry Library, Chicago; *Kentwood Commercial*, March 30, April 6, 13, December 14, 1895; "Report of the Attorney General," *Louisiana Legislative Documents*, 1860, 3–42, 1877, 1–48; Minutes of the Pike County, Mississippi, Circuit Court, Books A and B, Pike County Courthouse, Magnolia. For a comprehensive survey of the chaotic conditions prevailing in southeastern Louisiana that occasionally spilled over into southwestern Mississippi, see Hyde, *Pistols and Politics*, 180–262.

40. *New Orleans Daily Picayune*, December 1, 8, 9, 29, 1888, January 12, 1889, March 30, April 1, 12, 1894, November 12, 1895, December 27, 1896; *New Orleans Times Democrat*, December 9, 12, 1888; Minutes of the Pike County, Miss., Circuit Court, Book A, 553–55, 563, 565, 569, 575–76, Book B, 11–12, 16, Pike County Courthouse; Francis Williams Griffith, *True Life Story of Will Purvis* (Purvis, MS: Lamar County Historical Society, 1935).

41. Manuscript Census of the United States, 1860, Schedule One, "Free Inhabitants," Schedule Two, "Slave Inhabitants," Schedule Three, "Agricultural Statistics," and 1870, Schedule One, "Population," Schedule Two, "Agricultural Statistics."

42. "A Ramble in Autobiography," 10–11; Pitts, *The Burning of Bowling Green,* 8–10; Kate Blount to "My Dear Robby," October 11, 1864, Catherine T. Blount Letters.

43. Manuscript Census of the United States, 1870, "Agricultural Statistics"; "A Ramble in Autobiography," 30; "Death of Judge Edward McGehee," editorial in *New Orleans Christian Advocate*, October 7, 1880.

44. *Amite City Daily Wanderer*, November 29, 1864; *New Orleans Christian Advocate*, October 7, 1880; DeBow, *Statistical View of the United States: Compendium of the Seventh Census 1850*, 262–63; Ninth Census of the United States, 1870, "Compendium," 752–53.

45. *New Orleans Christian Advocate*, October 7, 1880; "The Private Papers of James Stewart McGehee," 1:70–75, 101–12.

46. Manuscript Census of the United States, 1870, Schedule Two, "Agricultural Statistics"; J. Burris McGehee Papers, multiple letters, box 1, folder 3, LLMVC; Pitts, *The Burning of Bowling Green*, 13.

47. Henney Moton to J. S. McGehee, July 19, 1893, J. S. to My Dear Honey, September 23, 1916, J. Burris McGehee Papers, LLMVC.

CHAPTER NINE

A Monument of Paper for William Lowndes Yancey
Crafting and Obscuring Historical Memory
Eric H. Walther

News of William Lowndes Yancey's death on July 27, 1863, spread quickly across the South and the North. His hometown newspaper, the *Montgomery Advertiser,* explained that Yancey "was to politics of the country [the Confederacy] what 'Stonewall' Jackson was to the army in the field." The *New York Herald* effectively agreed when it condemned the late Yancey as "that arch plotter of this terrible southern rebellion . . . a restless, plotting revolutionist, a noisy fire-eater, an eloquent blatherskite, always in hot water, and never satisfied with anything." In fact, Yancey ranked as one of the most prominent secessionists of the Old South. He also earned a reputation as one of the greatest orators in the country, and late in his career he drew national media attention for almost everything he said and did.

Born in Georgia in 1814, Yancey suffered the death of his father at an early age and bore the abuse of his emotionally and physically volatile mother, who lashed out against children and servants alike and made impossible demands on Yancey throughout her life. Yancey's stepfather, the prominent abolitionist Rev. Nathan S. S. Beman, proved even more violent and troublesome than his mother, creating a domestic environment of hatred, anger, and violence. Yancey grew up in and near Beman's New England, where men like Beman seemed more cold and foreboding than the region's wintry climate. During his youth, adolescence, and early adulthood, Yancey erupted violently and often in public settings. As a teenager in the 1830s, Yancey defended the Union against South Carolina's John C. Calhoun. After marrying and moving with his wife and slaves to Alabama, in the 1840s he won election to the Alabama assembly, served in Congress, built up an extensive network of secessionists in Alabama during the 1850s, and helped split the Democratic Party at their national convention in 1860, effectively securing the election of Abraham Lincoln and sparking disunion. Yancey represented the Confederacy as its first commissioner to England and France and later as a senator, all before his death just days before he turned forty-nine years old in 1863. His reputation as a duelist—according to some, as a murderer—often eclipsed his political accomplishments.

But the full story of Yancey's life has remained obscure—ironically enough—in large part because of his family's efforts to perpetuate his memory.[1] Yancey's sons had trouble coping with life after the Civil War. His namesake, William Earle Yancey, remained in Alabama, laboring as a farmer for fourteen years with mixed results before trying his hand in business. The son of Alabama's leading secessionist eventually secured a position in Birmingham with the Republican Iron and Steel Company. His brothers Dalton and Goodloe went north for a time. The former studied law and looked forward to establishing his practice in New York City, a place crowded in 1866 with young southerners, like him, looking for a fresh start. "Many of them will go home to remain soon, not having succeeded here," Dalton reported to his uncle, Benjamin Cudworth Yancey Jr. "I have just succeeded by the merest chance." Goodloe Harper Yancey enrolled in Poughkeepsie's Eastman Business College, fulfilling his late father's wishes for him to gain a business education.[2] This eighteen-year-old Confederate veteran was determined to succeed in his new profession and studied assiduously, although he complained of the climate in the alien North. He had never imagined snow could be so deep, nor rivers frozen solid so long, and marveled one day that "the thermometer stood ten degrees lower than I imagined it ever was in Iceland." More upsetting to Dalton Yancey than the North's natural climate was its political atmosphere. To his uncle he expressed his disgust at the federal Congress, fearfully, and correctly, predicting that Radical Republicans—northern officials who called for emancipation, enfranchisement of former slaves, and punitive measures for the defeated South—would gain strength. For Dalton, the war had "blasted all our hopes." Under the impression that a history of the conflict was to be written by the nationalist, northern historian George Bancroft, Dalton now also feared Yankees "will attempt to take from us our character & honor." This young ex-Confederate concluded that America "is no place for an honest white man to live." So he vowed to leave.[3]

In the last half of 1865, not long after the cessation of combat between North and South, several former Confederates organized migrations out of the occupied South. Many of these immigrants turned to Mexico, some even before war's end. Matthew Fountain Maury, a former Confederate naval leader, hoped to recruit two to three hundred thousand fellow Virginians to take "negro skilled laborers in agriculture" as peons to recreate Virginia south of the Rio Grande. Of course, that grandiose project failed. Other former rebels set their gaze upon British Honduras and Venezuela.[4] But during that cold winter of 1866–67, Dalton Yancey contemplated a move to Brazil, the place most favored by former Confederates, where slavery remained legal until 1888. Rev. Ballard S. Dunn of New Orleans had obtained a 960-square-mile tract of fertile land in Juquiá, southwest of São Paulo, and had permission from the Brazilian government to use it as a refuge for ex-Confederates who, like Dalton, despaired of life in the United States. Other southerners with the same idea simultaneously established colonies nearby. In Juquiá, each colonist would get 640 acres of land and six months' provisions, farm implements, and seed, and would have six years to repay Rev. Dunn. Colonists had the option of pursuing Brazilian citizenship or retaining their American one, provided they had been pardoned for activities in the Confederate military or government. Dunn offered complete religious toleration. Corn and cotton were likely crops in this colony, though Dalton was more excited about the prospect of growing coffee. He had discussed this venture with his mother and had received her approval; his oldest brother, Benjamin Cunningham Yancey, would join him. Then he needed to convince his uncle, Ben Yancey, to support the scheme— and to provide the one thousand dollar loan necessary for the land and the voyage. Neither flight from Yankee rule nor financial reward, though, was Dalton's prime motivation for this peculiar pilgrimage. His main purpose was to "rear a monument over the ashes of him who has gone, that would be a fit emblem of his greatness, & that would outlive the nation that would dishonor him." This devoted son sought to perpetuate the name and legacy of his late father, William Lowndes Yancey.[5]

The Brazilian experience had mixed results for the Yancey brothers. Benjamin remained for thirteen years, married there, and worked for a time with the Don Pedro Railroad before moving back to the American South, to a Florida orange plantation. Dalton's enthusiasm burned out fast. He came back in the summer of 1868 and picked up his law practice in Georgia, moving to Florida by the 1870s, first to Lake County, then Tampa. Later, he became a county judge and went on to serve in the state senate. Other southerners remained scattered throughout Brazil, and the name Yancey lived on at least until the late twentieth century as one of the most popular first names among

"Confederados" in Brazil. While all of William L. Yancey's sons would become active members of the United Confederate Veterans—formed in New Orleans in 1889 and characterized by reunions of Southern soldiers as well as by white supremacy—in the 1860s they also believed that they had let down their father's memory and still hoped to provide a suitable memorial.[6]

Shortly after the funeral of William L. Yancey in 1863, a friend and fellow secessionist, William F. Samford, broached the topic of a biography with William's brother, Ben Yancey. Before the senator's death the brothers had spoken of such a project, and William Yancey had mentioned his desire to see the man then considered to be the South's greatest author, William Gilmore Simms, write his life's story. That Yancey *ever* considered Simms a candidate to write his biography is laden with irony. When Yancey read Simms's *Richard Hurdin: A Tale of Alabama*, published anonymously in 1838, he condemned the plot as "confused and intricate" and the characters as "badly drawn & unnatural." Years later, as the secession crisis intensified after Abraham Lincoln's election in 1860, Simms dismissed Yancey as "feeble & indecisive," lacking in wisdom and still bound to the Democratic Party.

But before William Yancey died he had also discussed the project with his friend Samford. An academic, newspaper editor, politician, and cotton planter, Samford had already collaborated with Chancellor Andrew A. Lipscomb of the University of Georgia on a glowing sketch of Yancey in 1860 for *Harper's Weekly*. Years later, Ben explained that William Yancey had hesitated only because of his inability to commission the effort. Ben, who never shared his brother's fiscal misfortunes, gladly approved and financed Samford's proposition. All seemed well.[7] Then Samford immediately began the whining that characterized his entire ill-fated effort. He cited bad health. He suggested Lipscomb take over, or Ben Yancey, or both. In a letter begun in November 1863 and not completed for a month, Samford confessed that he had gotten himself in too deep, that "*the great work* of my life" might overwhelm him. He recalled his subject's desire to have Simms write the biography and now hoped to pass along the task to the South Carolina writer. Much to his horror, Samford discovered that the wartime loss of Simms's house and other tragedies had caused Simms to have a personal religious crisis. "Yr. illustrious Brother, was a *Christian*, & his life *cannot* be adequately written by an infidel," Samford, a minister's son, complained to Ben. Again Samford suggested Lipscomb and Ben Yancey write it while he served as editor. In a rather remarkable rationalization of procrastination, Samford closed the year 1863 by concluding, "Perhaps it is *Providential*, that in the matter of the Biography, we *can't hurry*—the thing is *to have the work done & well done.*" The next year was no more encouraging. With his plantation in disarray, his health still bad, and the Union army approaching, Samford now surmised that no one would care to read a biography of Yancey anyway.[8] In that regard, he was probably correct.

But after 1865, with the defeat of the Confederacy a reality, Samford's desire grew to vindicate his and others' decision to secede, and he had a surge of creative energy. He was possibly among the first few southern writers after the war to take on a political, rather than military history, at a time when the lion's share of "Lost Cause warriors" kept their focus on Gen. Robert E. Lee and his army freeing the soldiers from "the bighting [*sic*] influence of slavery." Finally starting to acquire information on Yancey's early life, his congressional career, and the newspapers he had edited, Samford asked Ben Yancey to contact old friends and associates for details and recollections. Benjamin F. Perry, the leading Unionist in South Carolina and the man under whom Yancey had read law in his youth, gladly supplied Samford with a lengthy, detailed memoir.

And then it all stopped. Years passed with little or no progress. Although he originally had insisted on writing without monetary backing (lest the result have "the taint of 'vile dollars' on it"), by 1872 Samford asked Ben Yancey not only to purchase material for his research and to buy him paper but also to loan him money, with his cotton crop serving as collateral. Although Samford never seemed to have much time for the biography, he always found time to rail against the North, president Ulysses S. Grant, and politics in general. Most maddening to his sponsors, Samford complained it was too hot to work in the summer of 1872 and that he was going to either get someone to publish a novel written by his wife or he would pay for it himself. Finally, too embarrassed to directly contact Ben Yancey, Samford had his son do so, and although he slowly repaid his debts, he never finished a biography of William L. Yancey.[9]

On the heels of the Samford fiasco, the Yancey family sat idly by as Joseph Hodgson produced *The Cradle of the Confederacy: Or, the Times of Troup, Quitman and Yancey* (1876), a portrait of three men who defied federal authority before the war: Gov. George M. Troup of Georgia, John A. Quitman of Mississippi, and Yancey. Hodgson was a lawyer in Montgomery before the war, and although he opposed secession, he, like so many others in the South who had not wanted to secede, subsequently served in the armed forces, heading

Alabama cavalry units. In 1863 he delivered a eulogy for Yancey to his men. As colonel of the 7th Alabama Cavalry in 1864 under the command of Brig. Gen. Nathan Bedford Forrest, Hodgson's regiment took heavy casualties during a merciless nighttime attack by Union forces at Brentwood, Tennessee, south of Nashville. He was left with only 64 effective rank-and-file riders from the compliment of 350, including the leader of Company K from Montgomery, the young Dalton Yancey. After the war, Hodgson took up journalism and wrote one book, *Cradle,* a work that he dedicated to one of William Yancey's many adversaries within the Alabama Democratic party—John Forsyth, a newspaper editor in Mobile. Although Hodgson found many admirable traits in Yancey and considered him a man of great integrity and honor, this book roundly criticized Yancey—and indeed all secessionists and Republicans—for blundering into what he now believed had been a great and unnecessary national tragedy. Doubtless he wrote with thoughts of the Battle of Brentwood in mind. This book, of course, was the polar opposite of the uncritical memorial Yancey's family had wanted.[10]

Well before Hodgson's book came out in 1876, other southerners had already sought to rewrite history, whether through the formation of Ladies' Memorial Associations that retrieved and reinterred the remains of over 72,000 Confederate dead or through the creation of veterans' groups, monuments, or writings. Thomas Nelson Page, a Virginian who was only eleven years old in 1865, was a prolific author who produced romantic essays, novels, and poems in the same plantation genre as that of antebellum southern author John Pendleton Kennedy and others. This genre created a mythical South of noble ladies and gentlemen, happy slaves, and a society harmonized by the code of chivalry. In 1866, Edward A. Pollard, wartime editor of the *Richmond Examiner,* published *The Lost Cause: A New Southern History of the War of the Confederates.* Like Page, Pollard concluded that the war had decided the "restoration of the Union and the excision of slavery, but the war did not decide Negro equality."[11]

Over time a few friends of Yancey dabbled with biographical projects. Alabama senator Clement C. Clay gave such a project considerable thought, but nothing materialized. After Benjamin Perry supplied William Samford with a lengthy and heartfelt recollection of Yancey back in 1866, the old unionist used the otherwise wasted piece, virtually verbatim, as his chapter on Yancey in his *Reminiscences of Public Men,* published in 1883. "I knew him well and loved him most affectionately," Perry wrote, but he blamed Yancey more than anyone else in America for starting the Civil War, for the tremendous loss of lives, and for personally ruining the South. Perry's account, of course, was again a far cry from the uncritical or comprehensive hagiography that the Yancey family wanted and that other Confederates had already received.[12]

In 1884, an Alabama author named John Witherspoon DuBose contacted Ben Yancey about the possibility of writing a biography of the secessionist. DuBose suggested that young people in the South could not accurately learn the history of their section, especially its course to disunion, without a biography of William L. Yancey. DuBose proposed that this work would help perpetuate "that civilization for the preservation of which the Confederacy was formed." Originally, DuBose planned a six- to eight-column piece for the *Philadelphia Weekly Times,* but he quickly decided to expand the project to a full biography. When Ben Yancey balked, DuBose approached Ben's nephews, William Yancey's sons. Goodloe Harper Yancey, who had most of his father's papers, and William Earle Yancey were excited but hesitant. They agreed about the value of such a project, but they had invested great time, energy, and grief once before, for naught.[13]

After so many abortive or unsatisfactory efforts, it was only natural for Ben Yancey to ignore DuBose's initial proposal in 1884. But much had changed since the end of the war. Many men of the Civil War era had already passed away, including Robert E. Lee in 1870. The idea of a "Lost Cause," the notion that only a northern superiority of men and munitions had beaten the gallant southern soldiers, had already taken hold and by 1894 would find reinforcement by the United Daughters of the Confederacy (the UDC). Members of the UDC, like the Ladies' Memorial Associations that emerged closer to war's end, erected monuments across the South of men such as Jefferson Davis and Robert E. Lee. But the UDC also engaged in a textbook campaign that resulted in the publication of pro-Confederate histories "as symbols of defiance" (as historian Karen L. Cox has demonstrated) and thus set the stage for DuBose. Unlike those who had come before him, DuBose had credentials, persistence, and motivation, all of which gradually secured the family's support for his project.

DuBose was born in Society Hill in the Darlington District of South Carolina in 1836. Educated by private tutors on his father's plantation, in private schools, and at the extremely proslavery South Carolina College (now the University of South Carolina), DuBose's entire youth was spent preparing to assume his role in his family's slave empire. His father, Kimbrough C. DuBose, had joined the South Carolina militia in 1832–33 during that state's effort to resist federal enforcement of the Tariff of 1832 during the Nullification Crisis. The elder DuBose remained a staunch secessionist and moved to Morengo County, Alabama, in the 1840s.[14] By 1850 he had given his son James Henry 140 slaves. A little later, John Witherspoon DuBose would inherit his own 152 slaves, and other DuBose family members in the county owned another thirty-one slaves. K. C. DuBose had been a friend of William L. Yancey, and John W. DuBose's maternal grandfather, J. D. Witherspoon, had served in the South Carolina legislature with the father of William and Ben Yancey and proudly counted himself a nullifier two decades later. John W. DuBose actively worked for secession as a member of the Morengo County Democratic committee and, with three brothers, enlisted in the Confederate army. All three of his brothers died. The loss of his brothers, the defeat of the Confederacy, and the emancipation of over 320 slaves were, of course, bitter pills to swallow for DuBose. His anger and frustration found an outlet in 1867, when he became an oath-bound member of the Ku Klux Klan. He later was involved in similar white supremacist organizations, the Knights of the White Camellia and the White Shield. He resumed his activity in local politics in 1901, serving as head of the Alabama convict department and helping to administer the notorious convict lease under which, as elsewhere in the South, African American prisoners were leased to whites and not infrequently worked to death.[15]

DuBose started his literary career as an editor of local newspapers, especially the *Birmingham Age-Herald,* and by writing local histories and accounts of minerals and commerce in Alabama. He was also a frequent contributor to the *Southern Historical Society Papers,* first published in 1876, and later to the *Confederate Veteran,* founded in 1894 by the UDC to give voice to ordinary soldiers as well as to white supremacy. One of the most enthusiastic supporters of the *Southern Historical Society Papers,* former Confederate general Pierre G. T. Beauregard, spoke for many former comrades. "After having taken an active part in *making* history," Beauregard explained, the job of his fellow former generals was now to "see that it is correctly *written.*" As DuBose later explained, all Confederate veterans knew: "that the published histories taught in schools and universities or stored on the shelves of American libraries are not only painful to be read by the older people of the South because of their general inappreciation of the truth, and frequent misrepresentation of the facts to the origin and career of the Confederate States, but they tend to poison the minds of the sons and daughters of that generation . . . who strove so heroically . . . to check the march of the invader."[16]

Like fellow white southerners, DuBose was determined to resist the onslaught of modernization and celebrate antebellum southern culture, and he sought to compose a book designed to rewrite the nation's memory of secession and war.[17] Naturally, DuBose's subject would not be President Davis or even popular military leaders but instead his political hero, his family's friend, Yancey. "Yancey was to the cause of secession what Patrick Henry was to the initial [phase] of the [American] revolution," DuBose explained to another historian. "Indeed it is scarcely possible to vindicate the Southern people while the career of Yancey remains unexplained."[18] DuBose genuinely considered the life of Yancey heroic, but he used his opportunity both to elevate Yancey and to diminish the man he blamed almost exclusively for Confederate defeat: Jefferson Davis. In that regard, DuBose placed himself among a minority of white southerners, yet he was not alone. As early as October 1865, former Confederate brigadier general Thomas Jordan, the chief of staff for and champion of General Beauregard, fired an early salvo at Davis's alleged mismanagement of the war in an article in *Harper's Weekly Magazine*, thereby resurrecting the wartime feud between Davis and the Louisiana general. "Jefferson Davis for four years illustrated, like his monarchical prototypes, that no two natures are so widely opposite and unlike as the willful and the wise," Jordan concluded. In 1874, former Confederate general Joseph Johnston also assailed Davis's leadership in his memoir, *Narrative of Military Operations During the Civil War*.[19]

By 1870, Alexander H. Stephens, a reluctant secessionist and Confederate vice president, published his *Constitutional View of the War between the States*, a work that mixed his spirited defense of the Confederacy with his rationale for opposing Davis during the war. From the beginning of the war to its end, Davis seldom consulted Stephens, especially concerning military matters. In the immediate aftermath of the move of the Confederate capital from Montgomery, Alabama, to Richmond, Virginia, neither Davis nor his cabinet met with the diminutive but obstinate vice president, and Stephens clashed frequently with Davis over questions concerning civil liberties, especially the suspension of the writ of habeas corpus and the ordering of conscription—the first draft in American history. Stephens's "unremitting hatred of Davis" escalated over time, particularly after signal Confederate defeats at Gettysburg and Vicksburg in 1863, and later Stephens disagreed over which generals Davis selected for command. "And," according to Stephens's biographer Thomas E. Schott, "though he denied hating Davis—his feelings were 'much more akin to suspicion and jealousy,' he said—his words betrayed more enmity than he owned up to." By 1864, Stephens explained to a confidant that he had never considered Davis a statesman nor even a good man, but rather a person with good intentions, "weak, vacillating, timid, petulant, peevish, obstinate, but not firm." Stephens's massive *Constitutional View*, Schott wrote, was a "ponderous two-volume treatise on the compact theory of government and the legality of secession," and he observed that the work "sparkled with all the brilliance of a polished mudball." Nearly one hundred years later, the American writer Edmund Wilson described *Constitutional View* as a "great, cold, old monument.[20]

Jefferson Davis contemplated the writing of his own account of the Confederacy as early as 1869. First, he had to overcome the great challenge of locating and acquiring the masses of his presidential papers that had been scattered broadly after the fall of Richmond, but he became determined to do "justice to the cause" and initially titled his work "Our Cause." He sought both to vindicate himself and to justify secession and the prosecution of the war. He confided to a friend that his work would "make a valuable contribution to history before I go hence, and thus complete a long life of service to the people of the South"; he also meant to "add whenever I could another leaf to her crown in glory." He wrote from 1877 to 1880, when he completed his two-volume *The Rise and Fall of the Confederate Government*, all 1,279 pages of it, published in 1881. Davis denied the centrality of slavery to the cause of the conflict—a sharp reversal from his position in 1861 that it was the fundamental reason for secession—and argued that the North had waged an uncivilized, destructive war upon the South and then enforced a harsh and dishonorable peace on honorable men who had given their lives for the Confederacy. According to his biographer, William J. Cooper Jr., Davis had "built his monument to his cause."[21]

Davis's self-serving account in *Rise and Fall* must have irked DuBose, and the ending must have particularly incensed him. On page 764 of volume 2, Davis had written that he hoped "that crimination and recrimination should forever cease, and then, on the basis of fraternity and faithful regard for the rights of the States, there must be written on the arch of the Union, *Esto perpetua*" (It shall be perpetual). Arch of the Union? Fraternity with Yankees? Perpetual union? Certainly not for DuBose, disgruntled Confederate veteran and Klansman. Davis had touched several tender nerves for DuBose with his words, but more appalling was that in all those pages Davis mentioned Yancey not once. That omission further bolstered DuBose's determination to topple Davis's monument of paper by erecting his own for Yancey.[22] That Yancey was blamed for the war, mistreated, or ignored by many ex-Confederates demonstrates that the Lost Cause was not monolithic and that history is often written or shaped by many factors, including the petty and the personal.

With this passionate and personal commitment, DuBose plunged into his work. He wrote to several contemporaries asking for their recollections and to borrow documents. He even asked them to share their own pending literary efforts on the Confederacy. Among those he wrote to was Robert Barnwell Rhett Jr., the radical son of South Carolina's premier secessionist, Barnwell Rhett. In 1890, the wife of Benjamin Perry told DuBose that Yancey and all secessionists deserved "all the abuse [that] can be heaped on them for trying to break up the most glorious government ever given by God to man," but there was no place for blame or fault in DuBose's mind or in his book, and he omitted the information in her letter. He remained in close contact with Ben Yancey and his nephews, although Dalton Huger Yancey, William's second-youngest child, still smarted over Samford's failed effort and directly challenged DuBose to finish the paper monument quickly and to the family's satisfaction. DuBose informed the family of his thesis that Yancey devoted his entire life to stopping a revolution against constitutional government— ironically, Stephens and Davis had concluded the same in their books—and he was glad that Ben Yancey concurred. In refreshing contrast with Samford's delays and excuses, DuBose maintained a reasonable production schedule and only occasionally asked the Yanceys for some money. He dutifully sent each chapter to Ben for his approval, and by year's end in 1889, the year Davis died, DuBose sent a completed manuscript to Robert and Son in Birmingham, who published *The Life and Times of William Lowndes Yancey: A History of Political Parties in the United States, from 1834 to 1864; Especially as to the Origin of the Confederate States* in 1892. DuBose hoped that the 752-page biography was "now condensed enough to read easily," although there was so much more of Yancey he wished to say. A cousin, A. K. Yancey of Mexico, Missouri, wrote to DuBose, "I am truly glad that so valuable a contribution to the story of the 'Lost Cause' has fallen into hands so competent." The Yancey family was relieved that they finally had their monument.[23]

While writing the biography, DuBose confided to Ben Yancey, "I observe frequent recent denials of Mr. Davis that he was a leader in the secession movement. We will try to relieve him, by placing the burden & honor of leadership where it belongs—on W. L. Yancey." DuBose even inserted as a note in his biography the reply he received when he asked for General Beauregard's thoughts on Yancey. The general was favorably impressed by the great orator when the two met briefly during the war: "Indeed, I believe that, if he had been selected as our Chief Executive, the result might have been very different. He appeared to me to be a statesman with enlarged views, and no petty jealousies to jeopardize our sacred cause." DuBose's contempt for Davis had not even been diminished by the latter's death on December 6, 1889. To Ben Yancey, DuBose explained, "The universality of the Southern feeling over Mr. Davis' end is not judgment in his favor, but (God be praised) is the proof that our people defy the Yankees and all they can do."[24]

Most of DuBose's tome was hagiography in its purest form, but he also put it to good use settling his score with Davis. DuBose accomplished this partly by invention and partly by making real conflicts between Yancey and Davis appear vastly more important than they were. An example of the former involved a trip that Senator Davis made to New England in the summer of 1858, by advice of his physician, to restore his health by taking a respite from the ferocity of the summer heat and humidity at his home in Mississippi. According to DuBose, while Davis participated in July 4th celebrations in Boston, he allegedly referred to secessionists as "mosquitoes around the ox's horn." In fact, Jefferson and Varina Davis left Baltimore on July 3 and were on the Atlantic Ocean on the Fourth. He was asked to make some remarks to fellow passengers and the ship's crew. (They did not reach Boston until July 6 and left the same day for Portland, Maine.) What Davis actually said was that, despite mounting sectional tensions in the 1850s, the American people remained undivided. "Trifling politicians in the South, or in the North, or in the West, may continue to talk otherwise," but they could never destroy the Union.[25]

When discussing Davis's qualifications for president of the Confederacy, DuBose damned with faint, if not contradictory, praise. He stated that the general public in the South supported Davis "as the most available and proper person to fill it [the presidency]. He had considerable reputation as a soldier, however slight may have been the claims upon which it was founded; his standing as a politician was very great, notwithstanding he had never been a leader in any successful statecraft." Davis was a West Point graduate who fought in the Black Hawk War from 1832–35 and resigned from his only term as congressman in 1846 to command the First Regiment of Mississippi Riflemen during the invasion of Mexico, where he won national acclaim for his gallantry at the Battle of Buena Vista. He also served parts of five terms in the U.S. Senate and as secretary of war under Franklin Pierce. Davis was one the best-known and accomplished Americans, let alone southerners, of his era, but DuBose took it upon himself to rewrite Davis's history.[26]

More importantly, through much of the last fifty pages of his biography, DuBose invented far greater conflict between Davis and Yancey then ever existed, and he simultaneously ignored or minimized the cooperation between the two, as well as their mutual friendship and respect. Since the 1840s, Yancey had made himself known as a staunch and uncompromising champion of state sovereignty and very limited national government power, and although he did not change his mind about these matters during the Civil War, he did modify some of his positions out of pragmatism. When Davis called for conscription (and in so doing distressed Alexander Stephens), Yancey, as a Confederate senator, championed his president consistently on that subject. On his way back to the Confederate Senate in the winter of 1862–63, Davis happened to join him in Raleigh, North Carolina. The two jointly addressed a crowd at the train station. Yancey called on his listeners to disregard partisanship and to support both military and political leaders, then rode the rest of the way to Virginia with Davis. Once back in the Senate, Yancey supported a controversial bill allowing Davis to personally authorize a foreign loan of $50 million without first consulting Congress—one of the minority in the Confederate Congress to do so. The two did clash over the propriety of establishing a Confederate supreme court. Davis backed it, but Yancey objected that such a court would override state sovereignty by establishing a central, national government over the states, just like the federal system of government from which the Confederate states had withdrawn. Yet even that did not deter Yancey from supporting his president whenever he could do so. After Yancey's death, the *New York Times* noted correctly that Yancey had steadfastly refused to lead congressional opposition to Davis.[27]

During Yancey's final months of life in 1863, he did, in fact, clash with Davis more often, yet Yancey never lost respect for his president. On a break from Congress in April 1863, Yancey returned to his home in Montgomery and a bit of a conflict with his son, Dalton. Recently turned eighteen, Dalton begged his father to allow him to enlist in the Confederate army, where two of his brothers already served. Dalton convinced his father that with so many lives already lost and much fighting still ahead he had a duty to serve the country his father had helped to create. So Yancey wrote to Davis asking for an officer's commission for his boy, and he asked his friend and fellow senator Clement C. Clay, a good friend of Davis, to support the request. Davis flatly rejected it.[28] DuBose, in an appendix to his biography, reproduced many of the letters exchanged between Davis, Yancey, and Clay regarding Dalton and other issues during this time. Some letters show that Yancey and Davis, two stubborn men with notorious tempers, offered an occasional olive branch to one another. But DuBose decided not to include a letter from Yancey to Clay—a letter in the possession of Yancey's older brother, Ben—in which Yancey wondered if the times he had publicly disagreed with Davis factored into the president's decisions. Yancey poured out his reaction to Clay and hoped that the breech with Davis would end; "for the sake of a regard of many years standing (for we commenced public life together in the same Congress), I was pained to learn it." To give him credit, DuBose reprinted a letter from Davis to Yancey, written on June 20, 1863, which concluded, "For myself, all of the hostile feeling that I possess is reserved for the enemies of my country, not for those who, like yourself, are devoted to our common cause." He termed Yancey's relationship to him as "worthy of a patriot." Yet DuBose failed to note that on May 26, 1863, Davis decided to go forward with Yancey's recommendation of an officer's commission for Dalton Yancey. Not only that, Davis told Yancey that he would keep private his complaint about Davis's initial negative response and would share it with no one. Even after Yancey died of kidney disease at his home in Montgomery on July 27, 1863, he posthumously reached out to Davis again. In 1858 Yancey and others had worked with the Ladies Mount Vernon Society of the Union in order to raise funds to preserve the decaying home of the first American president. As a token of their thanks, the society gave Yancey the field glass that George Washington used during the Revolution. In his will, Yancey bequeathed the secular relic to the man he considered the primary founding father of his long-dreamed-of Confederacy, Jefferson Davis.[29] Because the *Life and Times* appeared authoritative, perhaps in part because of its length, many accomplished and careful scholars well into the twentieth century, such as William C. Davis and William L. Barney, seem to have taken for granted DuBose's version of Yancey and Davis as adversaries rather than reinvestigating the situation themselves.[30]

The reaction to DuBose's *Life and Times* was immediate and favorable and not just among family members or southern reviewers. The *Philadelphia Times*, *Magazine of American History*, and *Boston Globe* all hailed the accomplishment, the latter characterizing the work as the greatest contribution by a southerner to southern history to date in the region's history. Doubtless encouraged by these responses, DuBose supplemented his biography with newspaper and magazine articles, confirming his status as the preeminent Yancey scholar.[31]

DuBose created quite a legacy. He had invested so much of himself in his book that he could brook no insult to it or his favorite subject. Shortly before publication, in 1891, an article appeared in the *Atlanta Constitution* and the *New England Magazine* about the infamous attack on Yancey by Benjamin H. Hill in the Confederate Senate in 1863. During a heated debate over legislation that would have established a Confederate supreme court, Yancey argued with some merit that such a body would mock the very notion of state sovereignty that gave birth to the Confederacy to begin with. Hill, a former Whig and unionist who had irritated Yancey for many years before the war, supported the legislation. At one point Yancey said something terribly insulting about Hill—exactly what we cannot ascertain because the Confederate Senate met in secret session and no one ever went public about the details of the affair— and Hill responded by hurling a heavy glass inkstand at Yancey, cutting open his cheek and drawing copious amounts of blood. Whatever Yancey said must have been vile because he was censured while his assailant escaped any form of rebuke from fellow senators. When DuBose read this article, he grumbled that it was one "no true Southern man could write." Even before those newspaper articles appeared, Ben Yancey asked DuBose for a copy of the concluding chapters of his late brother's biography, particularly those regarding Jefferson Davis and Benjamin Hill. Just in time for the book's publication, DuBose added to an appendix of his *Life and Times* a document titled "Protest of W. L. Yancey, A Senator From Alabama," to defend his subject, friend, and hero.[32]

Despite these shortcomings, DuBose's accomplishment was so monumental that for nearly a century after his death (he was killed in a railroad accident in Birmingham in 1918) most authors deferred not only to his labor but also to his judgments and scope. Sometimes these authors changed precious little of DuBose's narrative. In 1902 William Garrott Brown included a chapter on

Yancey in his *The Lower South in American History*. An Alabamian with a history degree from Harvard and eventually six other books to his credit, Brown ranked Yancey as one of the "half-dozen men who have had most to do with shaping American history." To DuBose's larger work he added a valuable insight into the real life and times of Yancey: for white antebellum southerners, African slavery "was a constant reminder of mastery, a constant incitement to a heightened appreciation of the liberty that was still . . . not only an enjoyment, but a kind of rank and privilege." Aside from this critical observation of proslavery ideology, Brown offered nothing new about Yancey. In fact, as historian Wendell H. Stephenson observed, Brown's chapter mostly distilled information from *Life and Times*.[33]

Even more closely indebted to DuBose was Joseph Hergesheimer, author of dozens of popular histories in the early twentieth century. Among his most fanciful was *Swords and Roses*. His wonderfully titled chapter "The Pillar of Words" lamented the passing of Yancey's greatness, as well as "the singing contentment and minor tragedies of slavery." Racist romanticism aside, Hergesheimer was clearly guilty of plagiarism. As John T. Fain has demonstrated with side-by side excerpts, Hergesheimer simply cut and pasted together excerpts from DuBose with a few insignificant modifications and no sources cited.[34]

After the turn of the century, George Petrie, a southern historian at the Alabama Polytechnic Institute (now Auburn University), attempted to produce the first scholarly work on Yancey. Petrie's grandfather had delivered a funeral oration for Yancey in 1863, and Professor Petrie made Yancey a special subject of investigation in his upper-division classes. Petrie reexamined all the Yancey material collected by DuBose and collected other documents himself, but he never produced more than one brief essay.[35]

A story circulated among scholars asserted that in Petrie's later years he turned over all the material he had gathered on Yancey, including "a great trunk full" of letters, to Austin Venable, a doctoral student at Vanderbilt University who graduated in 1937. Venable never transformed his brief dissertation into a complete biography but instead published several articles on Yancey based on his work and a brief monograph on the secession movement. Malcolm McMillan, in his "William L. Yancey and the Historians: One Hundred Years Later," wrote in 1967 that the trunk full of Yancey papers had disappeared or had been misplaced. Another historian went further by asserting that Professor Venable still had them. It is true that the forty-five pieces of Yancey material listed by Philip M. Hamer in his *A Guide to Archives and Manuscripts in the United States* (1961) are no longer in the Petrie collection at Auburn, but the "great trunk full" of letters to which Petrie originally referred are most likely the John Witherspoon DuBose materials at the Alabama Department of Archives and History.[36]

A century after Yancey's death, historian Clement Eaton made the Alabamian a key player in his *The Mind of the Old South*. In a chapter called "The Voice of Emotion," Eaton compared Yancey to Adolph Hitler, likening their ability to sway multitudes "almost hypnotically" with appeals to "their resentment, pride, and fear of the future." Although "The Voice of Emotion" ranks among the best short works on Yancey, Eaton merely intended to use it as a vehicle to dramatize "the passionate addiction of Southern people to florid and emotional oratory," not to supplant DuBose.[37]

The best, most careful scholarly challenge to DuBose came in 1968, when Ralph B. Draughon Jr., completed his doctoral dissertation, "William L. Yancey: From Unionist to Secessionist, 1814–1852," at the University of North Carolina, Chapel Hill. By far the most detailed, dispassionate, and analytical treatment of Yancey to that time, the major shortcoming of this piece was its chronological frame. Draughon argued that a relative paucity of manuscript materials after 1852 rendered impossible a complete reassessment of Yancey's life. Certainly, there are fewer extant Yancey documents from the late 1850s than from earlier or later periods (the mysterious missing forty-five pieces of the Petrie collection notwithstanding), and under the constraints of a graduate program it would have been difficult to track down these scattered items.[38] Nevertheless, the greatest significance of Yancey in American history was his role in the secession and the formation of the Confederate States of America, features beyond the scope of Draughon's otherwise insightful critical study. Yancey continued to crop up occasionally as a key player in various studies of the South yet simultaneously managed to escape some historians almost unnoticed. William L. Barney and John McCardell made Yancey a central figure in their respective studies of secession and southern nationalism, as did David S. Heidler in his study of secessionists. J. Mills Thornton Jr. placed Yancey into the context of antebellum Alabama politics in his sophisticated and sweeping *Politics and Power in a Slave Society*.[39] On the other hand, some recent general treatments of the Civil War barely mention Yancey's name, while countless others argue that Yancey was shoved aside in the Confederate republic that he had helped create, despite that he held two prominent positions in that nation: Confederate senator and commissioner to England and France.[40]

DuBose, like the biographers of Alexander Stephens, Jefferson Davis, and other key Confederate leaders, strived to have Confederate history "correctly *written*," to quote Beauregard. But the complexities of the antebellum South and the Confederacy quite naturally muddied the waters of postwar southern political correctness. Late antebellum conflicts between southern Democrats and Whigs, the tensions between the Boarder South, Upper South, and Deep South, the sharp disagreements between secessionists and unionists, all re-emerged after the war. Biographers in the South attempted to produce their versions of a solid and monolithic Confederate South, a South that never existed, as proven in part by their extensive sniping at one another. John Witherspoon DuBose and others set out to write "the truth" about the recent past, a task rendered impossible because of their very human foibles and jealousies.[41]

NOTES

1. *Montgomery Advertiser*, August 5, 1863; *New York Herald*, August 5, 6, 1863; Eric H. Walther, *William Lowndes Yancey and the Coming of the Civil War* (Chapel Hill: University of North Carolina Press, 2006).

2. William Yancey to Caroline Yancey, March 5, 1859, Benjamin Cudworth Yancey Papers, Southern Historical Society, University of North Carolina, Chapel Hill (hereinafter cited as BCY Papers).

3. Thomas McAdory Owen, *History of Alabama and Dictionary of Alabama Biography*, 4 vols. (Chicago: S. J. Clarke Publishing Co., 1921), 4:1820–22; Goodloe Harper Yancey to Benjamin C. Yancey, January 18, February 10, 1867; Dalton Huger Yancey to Sarah Yancey, October 16, 1866, and to Benjamin C. Yancey, February 22, 1867, all in BCY Papers. Dalton Yancey had studied law at the University of Georgia before joining his brother in New York. George Bancroft added four volumes to his original six-volume *History of the United States from the Discovery of the American Continent* (Boston: Little, Brown, 1861–75) but still concluded his study with the year 1782.

4. Gaines M. Foster, *Ghosts of the Confederacy: Defeat, the Lost Cause, and the Emergence of the New South* (New York: Oxford University Press, 1987), 115–17 (Maury quoted, p. 16).

5. Owen, *Dictionary of Alabama Biography*, 4:1820–22; Dalton H. Yancey to Benjamin C. Yancey, February 22, 27, 1867, BCY Papers.

6. Julia L. Keyes, "Our Life in Brazil," *Alabama Historical Quarterly* 28 (January 1966): 276. Eugene C. Harter provided an outstanding account of the various Confederado colonists in Brazil, *The Lost Colony of the Confederacy* (Jackson: University Press of Mississippi, 1986); also see Ballard S. Dunn, *Brazil, The Home for Southerners, or, A Practical Account of What the Author, and Oth-*

ers, Who Visited that Country For the Same Objects, Saw and Did while in That Empire (New Orleans: Bloomfield & Steel, 1866). Other ex-Confederates had similar ideas but different destinations. The best overall discussion is William C. Davis, "Confederate Exiles," *American History Illustrated* 5 (June 1970): 30–43; see also Andrew F. Rolle, *The Lost Cause: Confederate Exodus to Mexico* (Norman: University of Oklahoma Press, 1965), William C. Griggs, *The Elusive Eden: Frank McMullen's Confederate Colony in Brazil* (Austin: University of Texas Press, 1987), and David P. Werlich, *Admiral of the Amazon: John Randolph Tucker, His Confederate Colleagues, and Peru* (Charlottesville: University Press of Virginia, 1990). For activities of Yancey's sons after the war, see *Confederate Veteran* 24 (1916): 246, and Edward C. Williamson, *Florida Politics in the Gilded Age, 1877–1893* (Gainesville: University Presses of Florida, 1976), 176. Also see David W. Blight, *Race and Reunion: The Civil War in American Memory* (Cambridge, MA: Belknap Press of Harvard University, 2001), 158, 289, 290–91.

7. Benjamin Cudworth Yancey to William F. Samford, September 17, 1863, BCY Papers; Willis Brewer, *Alabama: Her History, Resources, War Record, and Public Men* (1872; reprint, Tuscaloosa: University of Alabama Press, 1964), 317; William Garrett, *Reminiscences of Public Men in Alabama for Thirty Years* (Atlanta: Plantation Publishing Company's Press, 1872), 595–97; [William F. Samford and Andrew A. Lipscomb], "Hon. William L. Yancey," *Harper's Weekly* 4 (September 15, 1860): 580–81; see Ralph B. Draughon Jr., "A Note on William L. Yancey's Opinion of W. Gilmore Simms," *Alabama Review* 18 (1965): 132–34, and William Stanley Hoole, "Alabama and William Gilmore Simms," *Alabama Review* 16 (April, July 1963): 188.

8. William F. Samford to Benjamin Cudworth Yancey, October 1, November 12–December 12, 1863, and September 21, 1864, BCY Papers.

9. Samford to Ben Yancey, October 1, 1863; December 12, 1865; July 2, September 15, 1872; William F. Samford Jr. to Ben Yancey, February 3, 1873; Benjamin F. Perry to Ben Yancey, August 27, 1866, all in BCY Papers. Samford lived until 1893; Gary W. Gallagher quoted in Alice Fahs and Joan Waugh, eds., *The Memory of the Civil War in American Culture* (Chapel Hill: University of North Carolina Press, 2004), 45. See Thomas M. Owen, "William F. Samford, Statesman and Man of Letters," *Publications of the Alabama Historical Society* 4 (1902): 462–85, and Malcolm C. McMillan, "William L. Yancey and the Historians: One Hundred Years," *Alabama Review* 20 (1967): 183.

10. Joseph Hodgson, *The Cradle of the Confederacy: Or, the Times of Troup, Quitman and Yancey* (Mobile: Register Publishing Office, 1876); Brewer, *Alabama*, 482; DuBose, *Yancey*, 2:735; "Seventh Alabama Cavalry Regiment," http://www.archives.alabama.gov/referenc/alamilor/7thcav. html; "The War of Southern Independence in Alabama: Research Tools for the 21st Century," http://www.researchonline.net/alcw/unit45.htm, both accessed September 5, 2012; Lonnie Burnett, *The Pen Makes a Good Sword: John Forsyth of the Mobile Register* (Tuscaloosa: University of Alabama Press, 2006).

11. Fred Hobson, *Tell About the South: The Southern Rage to Explain* (Baton Rouge: Louisiana State University Press, 1983), 11, 85–129; Foster, *Ghosts of the Confederacy*, 48–49; Blight, *Race and Reunion,* and *Beyond the Battlefield: Race, Memory, and the American Civil War* (Amherst: University of Massachusetts Press, 2003); William A. Blair, *Cities of the Dead: Contesting the Memory of the Civil War in the South, 1865–1914* (Chapel Hill: University of North Carolina Press, 2003);

David Goldfield, *Still Fighting the Civil War: The American South and Southern History* (Baton Rouge: Louisiana State University Press, 2002); Cynthia Mills and Pamela H. Simpson, eds., *Monuments to the Lost Cause: Women, Art and the Landscapes of Southern Memory* (Knoxville: University of Tennessee Press, 2004); Wolfgang Schivelbusch, *The Culture of Defeat: On National Trauma, Mourning, and Recovery,* trans. Jefferson Chase (2001; Ontario, Canada: Metropolitan Books, 2003); Caroline E. Janney, *Burying the Dead but Not the Past: Ladies' Memorial Associations and the Lost Cause* (Chapel Hill: University of North Carolina Press, 2008); Anne E. Rowe, "Thomas Nelson Page, 1853–1922," http://docsouth.unc.edu/southlit/pageolevir/bio.html (accessed August 9, 2012); E. B. Pollard, *The Lost Cause* (New York: Treat & Co., 1866).

12. McMillan, "Yancey and the Historians," 183; John W. A. Sanford to Goodloe H. Yancey, February 16, 1884, BCY Papers; Benjamin F. Perry, *Reminiscences of Public Men* (Philadelphia: John D. Ail & Co., Printers and Publishers, 1883), 313–17.

13. John Witherspoon DuBose to Benjamin Cudworth Yancey, August 20, 1884, and March 16, 1888; William Earle Yancey to Hamilton Yancey, September 14, 1884, BCY Papers.

14. "A Memoir of Four Families, by DuBose, 1898," John Witherspoon DuBose Papers, Alabama Department of Archives and History; Karen L. Cox, *Dixie's Daughters: The United Daughters of the Confederacy and the Preservation of Confederate Culture* (Gainesville: University of Florida Press, 2003), 68. On the southern textbook campaign of the late nineteenth and early twentieth centuries, see John M. Barr, "The Anti-Lincoln Tradition in American Life" (PhD diss., University of Houston, 2010), 159–67.

15. Janney, *Burying the Dead but Not the Past;* Joel C. DuBose, *Notable Men of Alabama: Personal and Genealogical* (1904; reprint, 2 vols.; Spartanburg, SC: The Reprint Co., 1976), 1:80–82; *U.S. Census (Seventh Census), 1850,* Alabama, Schedule 2, Slaves, Morengo County, 11–13, 20–21, 82–83 ; DuBose to Ben Yancey, August 20, 1884, July 6, 1887, BCY Papers; *Confederate Veteran* 20 (November 1912): 540; Sheldon Hackney, *Populism to Progressivism in Alabama* (Princeton: Princeton University Press, 1969), 265; "John DuBose" in Bham Wiki, http://www.bhamwiki .com/w/John_Du (accessed August 11, 2012). See also Matthew J. Mancini, *One Dies, Get Another: Convict Leasing in the American South, 1886–1928* (Columbia: University of South Carolina Press, 1996), and Mary Ellen Curtin, *Black Prisoners and Their World, Alabama, 1865–1900* (Charlottesville: University of Virginia Press, 2000). DuBose's other publications included *Mineral Wealth of Alabama* (1886); *Report on the Internal Commerce of the United States as to Alabama* (1886); *Jefferson County and Birmingham Alabama: Historical and Biographical* (1887); *The Witherspoons of Society Hill* (1910); and *General Joseph Wheeler and the Army of Tennessee* (1912).

16. "John DuBose"; see *Confederate Veteran,* vols. 22, 24, 25 (1914, 1916, 1917) and *Southern Historical Society Papers,* vols. 27, 32 (1899, 1904); Beauregard quoted in Blight, *Race and Reunion: The Civil War in American Memory* (Cambridge, MA: Belknap Press of Harvard University, 2001), 159. See *Southern Historical Society Papers,* vol. 32 (January–December 1904): 150–51 (quote), *Confederate Veteran* 20 (February 1912): 84–86, 261. Joel C. DuBose, *Notable Men,* 1:80–81, contains a partial bibliography of his father's publications. DuBose to Robert A. Brock, November 8, 1890, Robert Alonzo Brock Correspondence, Huntington Library, San Marino, California.

17. DuBose to John W. Bush, n.d., in *Confederate Veteran* 12 (March 1904): 115–16; DuBose to Alonzo Brock, November 8, 1890, Brock Correspondence.

18. John W. DuBose was a frequent contributor to *Confederate Veteran* (see vols. 22, 24, 25 [1914, 1916, 1917]) and the *Southern Historical Society Papers* (vols. 27 and 32 [1899, 1904]), as well as various newspapers around the country. DuBose to John W. Bush (n.d.) in *Confederate Veteran* 12 (March 1904): 115–16; DuBose to Robert Alonzo Brock, November 8, 1890, Brock Correspondence. Hobson, in *Tell About the South,* 11, 85–129, never mentions DuBose but discusses his more prominent contemporaries' fears and aspirations, which DuBose shared.

19. Robert D. Little, "Southern Historians and the Downfall of the Confederacy," *Alabama Review* 3 (1950): 243–62, and 4 (1951): 38–54; William J. Cooper Jr., *Jefferson Davis, American* (New York: Alfred A. Knopf, 2000), 623–24; William C. Davis, *Jefferson Davis, the Man and His Hour: A Biography* (New York: HarperCollins, 1991), 650.

20. Thomas E. Schott, *Alexander H. Stephens of Georgia: A Biography* (Baton Rouge: Louisiana State University Press, 1988), 346–47, 357, 365, 367–68, 382, 413, 420–21, 429, 433–35, 440, 471; Alexander H. Stephens, *A Constitutional View of the War between the States,* 2 vols. (Philadelphia: National Publishing Co., 1868–1870); Edmund Wilson, *Patriotic Gore: Studies in the Literature of the American Civil War* (New York: Oxford University Press, 1962).

21. Cooper, *Jefferson Davis,* 614, 615, 616–19; Blight, *Race and Reunion,* 259.

22. Cooper, *Jefferson Davis,* 658, 737, note 2; DuBose, *Yancey,* 621, note, on omission of Yancey's name by Davis.

23. See V[irginia] C. Clay to DuBose, October 13, 1887; P. G. T. Beauregard to DuBose, December 20, 1889; Robert Barnwell Rhett [Jr.] to DuBose, September 24, 1884; Dalton H. Yancey to DuBose, September 18, 1889; Reminiscences of Thomas H. Watts; A. K. Yancey to DuBose, March 12, 1891, all in John W. DuBose Correspondence, Alabama Department of Archives and History (hereinafter cited as DuBose Papers); DuBose to Ben Yancey, July 6, 1887, March 16, 1888, November 22, 1889, and December 10, 1889; William E. Yancey to Ben Yancey, February 24, 1889, all in BCY Papers. In his completed *Life and Times of William Lowndes Yancey,* in a note on 2:602, DuBose thanked Barnwell Rhett Jr. for the loan of his unpublished history, most likely the article by Rhett, "The Confederate Government at Montgomery," in *Battles and Leaders of the Civil War,* 4 vols. (New York: The Century Co., 1887), 1:99–110.

24. DuBose to Ben Yancey, July 6, 1887, and December 10, 1889, BCY Papers; Ben Yancey to DuBose (on Jefferson Davis and Benjamin Hill), September 8, 1889, DuBose Papers. See DuBose, *Yancey,* 586, note, for Beauregard's comment, originally in Beauregard to DuBose, December 20, 1889, DuBose Papers.

25. DuBose, *Yancey,* 441; Davis, *Davis,* 265; Lynda Lasswell Crist and Mary Seaton Dix, eds., *The Papers of Jefferson Davis,* vol. 6 (Baton Rouge: Louisiana State University Press, 1989), 200, note.

26. DuBose, *Yancey,* 584; Biographical Directory of the U.S. Congress, http://bioguide.con gress.gov/scripts/biodisplay.pl?index=D000113 (accessed August 14, 2012).

27. Walther, *Yancey,* 355–56, 357; *Richmond Dispatch,* August 1, 1863, reprinted in the *New York Times,* August 5, 1863.

28. Yancey to C. C. Clay, April 26, 1863 (typescript), Clement C. Clay Letters, Rare Book Room, Manuscript and Special Collection Library, Duke University, Durham, NC; Yancey to Davis, May 6, 1863, in Linda Lasswell Crist, Mary Seaton Dix, and Kenneth H. Williams, eds., *The Papers of Jefferson Davis,* vol. 9 (Baton Rouge: Louisiana State University Press, 1997), 166.

29. See C. C. Clay to Yancey, May 2, 1863; Yancey to Davis, May 6, 1863; Davis to Yancey, June 20, 1863; Davis to Clay, June 20, 1863; Yancey to Davis, July 11, 1863; Clay to Yancey, June 30, 1863; Clay to Yancey, July 25, 1863, all in DuBose, *Yancey*, 743–52; Walther, *Yancey*, 212–23, 368, 369.

30. Davis, *Jefferson Davis*, 442–44, and 739, note, and William L. Barney, "William Lowndes Yancey," in Richard N. Current, ed., *Encyclopedia of the Confederacy*, 4 vols. (New York: Simon & Schuster, 1993), 4:1747–50.

31. DuBose, "William L. Yancey in History," *Richmond Times*, October 31, 1899, reprinted in *Southern Historical Society Papers* 24 (1896): 98–101; "Confederate Diplomacy," *Charleston Sunday News*, July 17, 1904, reprinted in *Southern Historical Society Papers* 32 (1904): 102–16; "Alabama: The Relation of the State to the Birth of the Southern Confederacy," *Confederate Veteran* 24 (1916): 201–8, "Yancey: A Study," *Gulf States Historical Magazine* 1 (January and March 1903): 239–52, 311–24. Other reviews of DuBose's *Yancey* appear in Thomas McAdory Owen, ed., *Report of the Alabama History Commission* (Montgomery: Brown Printing Co., 1901), 1:190–91.

32. M. V. Moore to Benjamin C. Yancey, March 14, 1891; DuBose to Ben Yancey, March 18 and 23, 1891, BCY Papers; DuBose, *Yancey*, 2:739–43. Although Yancey's "Protest" clearly took issue with the actions against him taken by the senate, it sheds no light on the actual assault. For details of this violent incident, see Walther, *Yancey*, 357–60.

33. William Garrott Brown, *The Lower South in American History* (1902; reprint, New York: Greenwood Press, 1969), chapter 2, "The Orator of Secession," quotations from pages 117, 129–30; "John DuBose" in Bham Wiki, http://www.bhamwiki.com/w/John_Du (accessed August 11, 2012); Wendell H. Stephenson, "William Garrott Brown: Literary Historian and Essayist, *Journal of Southern History* 12 (1946): 313–44.

34. Joseph Hergesheimer, *Swords and Roses* (New York: Alfred A. Knopf, 1929), chapter 2, quotation from p. 63; John Tyrce Fain, "Hergesheimer's Use of Historical Sources," *Journal of Southern History* 18 (1952): 497–504.

35. McMillan, "Yancey and the Historians," 185; Wendell H. Stephenson, "A Half Century of Southern Historical Scholarship," *Journal of Southern History* 11 (1945): 15–17, and *Southern History in the Making: Pioneer Historians of the South* (Baton Rouge, 1964), 140; George Petrie, "What Will be the Final Estimate of Yancey" *Transactions of the Alabama Historical Society* 4 (1904): 307–12.

36. McMillan, "Yancey and the Historians," 185–86, and note 68; Ralph B. Draughon Jr., "William Lowndes Yancey: From Unionist to Secessionist, 1814–1852" (PhD diss., University of North Carolina, Chapel Hill, 1968), 151, note 68. Austin Venable's short monograph *The Role of William L. Yancey in the Secession Movement* (Nashville, 1945) was his most significant work.

37. Clement Eaton, *The Mind of the Old South*, rev. ed. (Baton Rouge: Louisiana State University Press, 1967), 267–87, quotes on pp. 268, 275.

38. In fact, several Yancey items have emerged as recently as April 1996 in the Dixon Hall Lewis Papers at the Sam Houston Memorial Museum, Huntsville, Texas. Lewis helped cement Yancey's transformation from unionist to an uncompromising states' sovereignty advocate. See Walther, *Yancey*, 83–84, 113–17, 124, 156.

39. See William L. Barney, *The Road to Secession: A New Perspective on the Old South* (New

York: International Thomson, 1972); John McCardell, *The Idea of a Southern Nation: Southern Nationalists and Southern Nationalism, 1830–1860* (New York: W. W. Norton, 1979); David S. Heidler, *Pulling the Temple Down: The Fire-Eaters and the Destruction of the Union* (Mechanicsburg, PA: Stackpole Press, 1994); J. Mills Thornton Jr., *Politics and Power in a Slave Society: Alabama 1800–1860* (Baton Rouge: Louisiana State University Press, 1978); Eric H. Walther, *The Fire-Eaters* (Baton Rouge: Louisiana State University Press, 1992), chap. 2.

40. Bruce Levine, in *Half Slave, Half Free* (New York: Hill and Wang, 1992), 190, merely noted that Yancey, with Barnwell Rhett, John Quitman, and James Hammond, "urged secession" in 1850. Also see James M. McPherson, *Battle Cry of Freedom: The Civil War Era* (New York: Oxford University Press, 1988) and Charles P. Roland, *An American Iliad: The Story of the Civil War* (New York: University Press of Kentucky, 1991).

41. Beauregard quoted in Blight, *Race and Reunion*, 159; DuBose to Alonzo Brock, November 8, 1890, Brock Correspondence.

AFTERWORD

Contingency and Continuity

William J. Cooper Jr., an Appreciation

Gaines M. Foster

"Yeah, a South Carolina boy goes off to Princeton and comes back putting on airs," I kidded Bill Cooper, as he drank a glass of Scotch. "I thought real southerners drank only bourbon?" I had been at LSU only a couple of months and was at my first departmental party. Bill replied, with his usual calm, "My father drank Scotch. You may not believe this, but very little about me changed after I left for Princeton."[1]

William J. Cooper Jr., grew up Kingstree, South Carolina, a small town in the overwhelmingly poor and rural Williamsburg County, where his father owned a substantial farm and a gin. Bill's wife, Patricia Holmes—who later helped with some of his scholarly projects, in particular his work on Jefferson Davis—also grew up in Kingstree; her father was a doctor. They both left for college, he to Princeton and she to Agnes Scott, and went on to marry. Both retained a lifelong southern gentility and graciousness. Bill represents the best of what it means to be a southern gentleman, not just the bow tie, seen most days, at conventions of historians, and in pictures on his book jackets, but a courtly demeanor, easy confidence, and especially a deep sense of integrity, duty, and honor.

Bill graduated from Princeton in 1962, and then went to Johns Hopkins University, where he worked with David Herbert Donald, who had previously taught him at Princeton. Bill completed his graduate work with a demanding mentor in an impressive four years, receiving his PhD in 1966. He then spent two years on active duty as an officer in the U.S. Army. In the fall of 1968, he came to Louisiana State University as a new assistant professor. He would remain at LSU his entire career, working his way through the ranks. From 1982 to 1989, he served as Dean of the Graduate School; he took the job because he saw an opportunity to improve the university. He did, reorganizing the graduate school to make it more professional and, through both new rules and personal leadership, helping improve the quality of many of LSU's graduate programs. In 1989 he returned full-time to the History Department. That same year, he was appointed by the LSU Board of Supervisors as a Boyd Professor, the highest academic honor LSU can bestow on a faculty member.

Bill managed the return to the faculty with uncommon ease, but his sense of responsibility to the institution as a Boyd Professor and therefore a leading member of the faculty did not diminish. He served on a host of significant committees, such as the University Planning Council, and worked on several searches to fill important posts, including two to find LSU's chancellor. He contributed in less formal ways as well and proved an ideal departmental member, willing to use his own stature in behalf of the department or a colleague. I knew his scholarship and reputation, and his presence in the department was one of the reasons I felt incredibly lucky to get a job at LSU. As a young historian in the same field, I could not have asked for a more supportive senior colleague. Three decades later, I realize even more how fortunate I have been to be at LSU at the same time as Bill.

Bill's sense of responsibility as a historian and as a faculty member extended to his teaching, at which he excelled. Even as a Boyd Professor, he continued to teach the introductory survey of U.S. history—the first half at least, he never could get too excited about the progressives. He also taught a very popular upper-level course on the Old South; many semesters, it drew well over a hundred students. Bill is a commanding presence in the classroom and a compelling lecturer; his students respect his knowledge of the field, embrace his vision of the Old South, and relish his presentation. Some thought his lectures sounded as if they came from the voice of God. Others, at least those of a certain time period, saw a resemblance to Sean Connery's character in the *Raiders of the Lost Ark* series. All praised and enjoyed his classes.

Along with his undergraduate teaching, Bill dedicated tremendous energy to working with graduate students and has mentored an impressive group of historians. Many came to LSU specifically to work with him; others discovered him when they arrived. Several pursued topics in his field of antebellum southern politics, but he directed dissertations on a wide array of subjects. With all of his students, Bill spent a great deal of time keeping them on track. I have always envied his authority. When he told his students to do something or to meet some deadline, they actually did it. He demanded excellence, and then, when they had completed their dissertations, pushed them to publish— at once. They, in turn, became fiercely loyal and very proud to be his students. Some relished the opportunity to house sit in his absence; others took to wearing bow ties in homage. All appreciated and respected his advice and support, as their publication of this volume attests.

The Enigmatic South also honors Bill Cooper's accomplishments as a historian. His students want to acknowledge and celebrate their mentor's professional stature and his substantial contribution to understanding the history of the South. The honors Cooper and his books have received testify to the respect with which he and his work are held. He has been selected as a fellow at the Institute of Southern History at Johns Hopkins and the Charles Warren Center for Studies in American History at Harvard University and has been awarded both a National Endowment of the Humanities and a Guggenheim Fellowship. He also held the Douglas Southall Freeman Professorship at the University of Richmond. He has twice won the Jefferson Davis Award, given by the Museum of the Confederacy for an outstanding narrative history of the Confederacy or Confederate period, once for *Jefferson Davis, American* and again for *We Have the War Upon Us*. The Davis book also won the prestigious *Los Angeles Times* Book Award for Biography in 2000. More recently, in 2010, Cooper served as the president of the Southern Historical Association, selected in recognition of his distinguished body of scholarship and efforts in behalf of southern history.

When called upon, Cooper has also felt a duty to accept a public role, just as he has within LSU. He has spoken to civic and other groups and appeared in several documentaries; he even had a lecture filmed and broadcast on the History Channel. He was a member of the Board of Trustees of the Museum of the Confederacy and the Advisory Board of the American Civil War Center at Historic Tredegar. In 1991, the U.S. Senate selected him as to serve for two years on the National Civil War Sites Advisory Council. Yet Bill has never been an "academic entrepreneur," as historian Theodore S. Hamerow once described historians who build their careers through networking, editing, organizing conferences, and the like. Cooper has, of course, done some editing and organized a conference. From 1979 to 1993, he edited LSU Press's distinguished Southern Biography Series, commissioning, in some cases, and guiding to publication twenty-six books. He helped organize one conference at Tredegar, which led to one of his coedited books, *In the Cause of Liberty*. In the end, though, Cooper attained his standing in the historical profession the old-fashioned way, through a substantial body of scholarship.[2]

Cooper first published in 1970; it was an article in the *Journal of Southern History*, on Jefferson Davis as a war leader—an auspicious beginning that hinted at things to come. He would write surprisingly few articles, although as his stature grew he contributed a few more essays to various edited volumes. Early in his career, he edited and wrote an introduction for a classic contemporary analysis of the Old South, Daniel Hundley's *Social Relations in Our Southern States*, and after his biography of Davis appeared, he was asked to prepare the Modern Library volume *Jefferson Davis: The Essential Writings*. In addition to *In the Cause of Liberty*, he coedited two other collections of essays: a festschrift to his advisor, David Donald, *A Master's Due*, and an extremely useful historiographical reference, *Writing the Civil War*. Cooper also published a textbook on the Old South, most of it initially written early in the morning before going off to campus to be dean of the graduate school. Thomas E. Terrill wrote the New South section, and together, in 1991, they published *The American South: A History*. Their text is now in its fourth edition. All these publications have contributed to Cooper's renown, but his reputation rests primarily on his steady production of five substantial works of narrative history and one collection of interpretative essays.[3]

They have much in common, beginning with the fact that they are all well researched. An "archival rat" of sorts—of the modern sort since he has quickly taken to the use of digitized collections—Cooper always grounds his interpretations in wide-ranging research in the personal papers of politicians, their speeches, and the newspapers of the time. His immersion in the primary sources gives his work tremendous authority, a richness of detail, and a very human quality. He lets people speak for and explain themselves. These characteristics also reflect Cooper's assumptions about the historian's task. Cooper is unabashedly a political historian, of a particular kind. He began his career when many had embraced the new political history, which emphasized quantitative analysis of voting behavior and ethnocultural interpretations of American politics, with their stress on religious affiliation as the source of political identities. At the same time, other historians focused less on political actors and more on ideological systems. Earlier and later, many in the profession turned to class to explain political divisions. Cooper never adopted any of these approaches, and one could make a case that many political historians have now come around to his way of thinking. He thinks politics are important, that ideas and interests drive politics, but so, too, does partisanship and personal ambition. To understand politics—and since politics are fundamental to society, to understand society—the historian has to interpret how people, particularly political leaders, think and act. What they said and wrote and did, within the constraints of the political situation they faced, provides the best means for the historian to understand politics and government; hence, all Cooper's archival work and his focus on the leaders who shaped political developments. He never, of course, ignores ideology, the attitudes of the voters, social realities, or the economic and racial interests that in turn influence politicians' behavior.

Cooper's approach to history rests first and foremost on a fundamental commitment to understanding the people of the past on their own terms and in the context of their own times. He seeks only to explain them and their actions, not to judge either by his or his era's standards. Cooper also has a deep appreciation for the importance of contingency in history. One of his favorite questions on graduate students' general exams was: When did the Civil War become inevitable? I always dreaded it, felt sorry for the student who picked an early date, and sympathized as Bill repeatedly challenged any answer short of the firing on Fort Sumter. (I always wanted to interrupt to offer "1619—with the introduction of slavery," but never had the nerve.) Linked with contingency in Cooper's view is the importance of individual actors in history, their ability to reshape the political landscape and the course of history. His analysis of the role of President John Tyler provides an example of his respect for the importance of both contingency and individual action. In *The Politics of Slavery*, Cooper writes that Tyler, when he became president in 1841 after William Henry Harrison's unexpected death, then changed the administration's policy, pursued the annexation of Texas, and thereby transformed the political debate. "More than any other man," Cooper explains, Tyler altered the campaign of 1844 and led the southern Whigs to abandon their emphasis on economic nationalism and return to the politics of slavery, in which the territorial issue then became paramount.[4]

For someone always open to contingency, however, Cooper's interpretation of the South's history incorporates a surprising amount of continuity. His work on the Old South stresses southern commitment to liberty and slavery from the late colonial period to the onset of the Civil War. His work on the New South emphasizes the continuity of political leadership across the cataclysm of the Civil War; writing in the mid-1960s, Cooper added that those post–Civil War leaders "successfully established the social and political mores which have governed Southern life almost to our own day." Indeed, Cooper displays significant interest in continuity as well as contingency, or to put it another way, continuity and change. He introduced one of his books as "a study of the counterpoint between continuity and change" and linked the two as a chapter title in another. The tension between them, along with Cooper's appreciation for complexity, gives his interpretation of the South much of its power.[5]

The resulting body of work has made him one of the most important historians of the South of his generation, and one of the best and most influential of a far smaller cohort of students of southern political history. His six major books—at least thus far—range across the nineteenth century. Their contribution, though, may be divided into four main areas: the nature of the New South, a portrait of the Old South, an analysis of the role of Jefferson Davis, and a narrative interpretation of why that far-from-inevitable Civil War finally came.

Cooper wrote his dissertation on his home state of South Carolina and focused on the years that followed the end of Reconstruction. As he would later push his students to do, he published it quickly, in 1968, only two years after he received his degree. At the time, C. Vann Woodward's vision of the New South reigned among historians. Woodward, the most important southern historian of his era, argued for a fundamental discontinuity from the Old South to the New. Rejecting the term *Bourbon* to characterize the Democratic politicians who took control of the South at the end of Reconstruction, Woodward called them, with considerable irony, the Redeemers. He portrayed them as a new leadership elite, drawn from the town middle class, rather than the planter elite, and from the ranks of the prewar Whig Party, not the Democrats. They led a New South open to industrialization and reunion with the North but riven by class conflict that exploded in the failed Populist revolt. Cooper, a brash and bold young historian, challenged Woodward on almost every point. In South Carolina, at least, Cooper found a very different story. *The Conservative Regime: South Carolina, 1877–1890* revived the term *Bourbon*, borrowed from French history and used to describe a line of kings that had returned to power and forgotten nothing. Cooper saw Wade Hampton and other leaders of South Carolina's postwar Democratic Party as the old planter elite and former Democrats returned to power. These Bourbon leaders "strove to restore the ante-bellum commonwealth that had nurtured them" and for the most part succeeded. They practiced "economy minded government," championed the rebuilding of the state's liberal arts university, and welcomed some industrial development but focused their aid on the state's agricultural economy, which remained the economic and social basis of postwar South Carolina society.[6]

The Bourbons, though, did not succumb to rabid racism or initiate the rigid racial repression that would characterize much of the twentieth-century South; on this point Cooper agreed with Woodward, who dated segregation to the 1890s. Cooper, in fact, found that Hampton, though not all Bourbons, reached out to blacks and adopted milder racial policies than many would have suspected or than the leaders who followed them did. In an interesting interpretation, he attributes that approach to the Bourbons' confidence that they knew how to lead blacks, rooted in their experience as slaveholders—yet another argument for continuity.[7]

Having drawn his portrait of the conservative Bourbon domination of South Carolina in the 1880s, Cooper turned his attention to Benjamin Tillman and his agrarian followers. Cooper dismissed any notion that Tillmanism, as close as South Carolina came to a Populist revolt, emerged from class divisions. It drew its support, Cooper counters, from across class lines, family ties, and economic backgrounds. The rebellious farmers, though, did more often come from the upcountry than the rest of the state. In explaining the rise of Tillmanism, Cooper offered an explanation rooted in what historians today would call memory. Where the Bourbons had appealed to the Lost Cause, a glorification of the Old South and their Confederate experience, Tillman and his new generation of followers "challenged the sanctity of Confederate gray." "With agricultural depression and political opportunism providing the catalysts, young men protested that neither service in the past nor appeals to its memory could any longer suffice as prerequisites for high office or as determinants for public policy."[8]

In an example of the complexity of Cooper's vision of history, *The Conservative Regime,* a book based in and best known for its emphasis on continuity, ends with an explanation rooted in generational and cultural change. Southern historians might well pay more attention to Cooper's analysis of that generational change, but his portrait of the Bourbons has become increasingly accepted in the years since *The Conservative Regime* first appeared, which may explain why it has been republished twice, most recently in 2005. Other historians. many of whom stress continuity in race and labor relations rather than politics, share Cooper's conception of the post-Reconstruction political and social order as a continuation of the Old South and his interpretation of the Bourbon's conservative approach to governmental policy. Probably more historians today refer to them as Bourbons than as Redeemers.[9]

Important as Cooper's early work on the New South is, his two books on politics in the Old South have become even more central to the historiography of the South. *The South and the Politics of Slavery*, published in 1978, offers an overview of what historians term the Second American Party System. In it, Cooper provides a relatively detailed discussion of the rise of the Democratic Party in the 1820s and 1830s, its challenge from a strong southern Whig Party, and finally the collapse of the Whigs in the wake of the Kansas-Nebraska Act. Save for a brief period that Cooper terms "The Great Aberration," when southern Whigs supported the creation of a bank and other economic measures to stimulate growth, southern Whigs and Democrats pursued a "politics of slavery." In other words, the two parties consistently competed on the basis of who could best protect slavery from outside intervention, which meant that southerners in both parties had to have the support of their northern counterparts. When a northern antislavery wing of the Whig Party had enough influence to restrict slavery in the territories, the Whig party in the South collapsed. Only five years after *The South and the Politics of Slavery*, Cooper published *Liberty and Slavery: Southern Politics to 1860*, a synthetic history that covered a much longer period of time. It begins with a brief discussion of southern society and attitudes in the colonial period and then carefully shows how during the Revolution and the writing of the Constitution white southerners remained committed to slavery and insisted on its protection. In the new republic, Cooper convincingly shows, the Federalists made little headway in the South; Thomas Jefferson's and James Madison's "Republican party controlled the southern political world." With it in power, southern politics embraced a strong nationalism. Support for the Republicans, Cooper astutely adds, showed that for "most southerners the identity of those holding power was far more important than the niceties of constitutional theory and political philosophy. Southerners trusted themselves and their own leadership not to endanger fundamentally either southern interests or southern liberty. After all, most southerners perceived the Republican party as the guardian of liberty and of the South in the nation." The Panic of 1819 and the Missouri Crisis, though, brought an end to the South's flirtation with nationalism and returned the politics of slavery to its centrality in the southern political world. It re-emerged as Whigs fought Democrats and the territorial issue became central to southern politics. The fight over slavery in the territories led eventually to secession, when southerners came to believe that Lincoln and the Republicans threatened their liberty to own slaves and their ability to control their own society and institutions, by which they meant slavery. Along with his biography of Davis, *Liberty and Slavery* may be Cooper's best work and one that will long continue to have considerable influence on historians' understanding of the region and its past.[10]

Together, *Liberty and Slavery* and *The Politics of Slavery* provide a compelling analysis of southern politics before the Civil War, as well as a coherent and convincing interpretation of the nature of the Old South, an interpretation built upon a few central concepts. Putting the word *slavery* in the titles of both books indicates how central its existence is to Cooper's view of the Old South. Indeed, few if any historians have made slavery, and as a part of it, race, more central to the interpretation of the South than has Cooper. He begins his book on southern politics in the antebellum period with a discussion of the Old South's "Colonial Antecedents." "Taut, powerful ties bound the nineteenth-century South to its colonial ancestor," he writes. "Plantation agriculture began in the seventeenth century; Negro slavery was already 150 years old in 1860." During the Revolution some white southerners questioned whether slavery should exist, troubled by the contradiction between championing liberty and practicing slavery, but no one acted against it. By the 1830s, white southerners' commitment to slavery had only intensified, and more and more they came to see, and defend, slavery as a positive good. Slavery, in Cooper's view, was both an economic institution and a basis for white unity. Southerners who owned slaves had a vested economic interest in its survival; whites who did not still benefited from their identification as white and free. "Standing 'one and indivisible' on slavery, white southerners of all political persuasions and all social classes built a massive fortress around it. None could touch it but them, and they never did because even those who disliked slavery believed it untouchable." Southerners defended the institution where it existed as well as their right to take slaves into the territories; indeed, they "equated their right to carry slavery into the territories with the existence of slavery itself." Not only was slavery central to the southern social and economic order, in Cooper's view, but it also shaped the other values he finds at the heart of politics and society in the Old South: democracy, liberty, and honor.[11]

Observers at the time and generations of historians since have disagreed about the nature of the political and social order of the Old South. Some have argued for a democratic South, others, particularly during the time Cooper began crafting his portrait of the Old South, contended that the huge inequalities of wealth brought by slavery left the South with a rigid class structure in which aristocrats dominated society and politics. The debate continues among professional historians. The numerous neo-progressives among them endorse the idea of an aristocratic South or, at the very least, a republican South where democracy never fully developed. Cooper, in contrast, has consistently made a strong case for a democratic South—one where democracy was valued and practiced and one in which slavery contributed to democratic sentiments.

In the colonial and revolutionary-era South, Cooper argues, a deferential political order dominated, though even that early he sees some democratic tendencies. After the Revolution, in the period between 1790 and 1810, deference still shaped southern politics, although political leaders had begun to appeal to the voters and to try to form some sort of identification with them. By the 1820s and 1830s, democracy reigned, save perhaps in a few localities. Southern states had adopted universal white, male suffrage and a very democratic style of politics. "Southern politicians did not live and campaign in ivory towers"; they "avidly" sought "the favor and votes" of the people. Their constituents, in turn, expected to be courted and, when convinced, voted in heavy numbers. Cooper even goes further in making his case for not just a democratic style but a democratic reality in the Old South. In the late antebellum period, Cooper points out, 80 to 90 percent of small farmers owned their land, which provided a great deal of independence. Taxes in most southern states were based more heavily on slaves than land, which Cooper cites as a good example of the political power of the yeomanry and as evidence that democracy worked. It worked in large part because of slavery and race. Yeoman and poor whites accepted the leadership of the planters because both were white and not slave; "racial identity became a powerful force for white unity." Slavery, therefore, fostered democracy—for white males only, of course—rather than upholding an aristocratic order.[12]

Slavery also shaped southern political values, or ideology, a word Cooper uses, albeit sparingly. Cooper acknowledges white southerners' commitment to strict construction and states' rights, although he also notes exceptions such as the nationalism during the Republicans' dominance or the Whigs embrace of Clay's national economic policy. In Cooper's South, the one constant and the central political value was liberty. Liberty evokes the concept of republicanism that many historians have used to interpret American politics from the eve of the Revolution to the Civil War. Cooper's interpretation of liberty, though it obviously has some similarities with the use of liberty among historians who see republicanism as central to American political ideology, differs significantly. Cooper does not write of a political order based on the need to balance liberty and power, and he never mentions republican virtue. Nor does he trace the South's fascination with liberty to the English dissenting country tradition or see, as most do who write about republicanism, the contagion of liberty emerging during the revolutionary crisis of the 1770s. In Cooper's account, liberty has somewhat older roots and a "palpable, not abstract" quality. It has almost as strong a psychological as philosophical basis.[13]

"Liberty," Cooper writes, "comprised the central idea of the colonial South," although he stresses it became even more influential during and after the Revolution. At its heart, southerners' conception of liberty lay in the right and ability to control "one's own affairs"; it constituted a "freedom from outside interference." It often took concrete form. During the coming of the Revolution, for instance, southerners made British taxation a major issue and rallying cry because they believed liberty was tied to property, and taxation was a way to take away one's property. If liberty rested most fundamentally in individuals' control over their own life and property, their independence, southerners' conception of liberty also took corporate form, "the absolute necessity of defending liberty by fending off any outside effort to control southern institutions and the destiny of the South." More than anything else, definitions of liberty rested, like so much in southern culture, in its relationship with slavery. Southerners saw slavery as the opposite of liberty, and rather than lead them to oppose slavery, the contrast made them hold liberty more dear and fight for it more ferociously. Since they saw nothing wrong with slavery and considered slaves property, they defined liberty as the liberty to own slaves. An attack on slavery therefore became an attack on their liberty.[14]

Both liberty and slavery became intertwined with the final characteristic of the Old South that Cooper stresses, a commitment to honor, which like liberty took both individual and corporate form. Honor plays a central role in Cooper's conception of the Old South, the territorial dispute, and the eventual onset of the Civil War, yet his contribution to historians' understanding of honor, perhaps not unlike his emphasis on the centrality of slavery, probably has not gotten the credit it deserves. He made honor central to an understanding of southern behavior, admittedly quite some time after Charles Sydnor (whose work Cooper acknowledges) yet before Bertram Wyatt-Brown's important book on the topic appeared. Wyatt-Brown's and Cooper's use of honor have much in common, but where Wyatt-Brown treats it as a deeply rooted cultural system, Cooper stresses its ties to liberty and slavery. "Southerners who counted themselves in the upper order of society fought duels to protect their honor, their reputation, their good name, "Cooper explains. "These qualities became extensions of the southern absorption with liberty and independence. They became two parts of one whole—an independent man was by definition an honorable man; a man who cherished his liberty could not allow anyone to besmirch his reputation, his good name." Honor became so important to white southerners "because in the South dependence and dishonor meant slavery. Only slaves had to accept assault on their reputation, their integrity, their honor . . . Thus, to underscore their distance from slavelike characteristics white southerners embraced the duel." Like liberty, though, honor had corporate as well as individual implications. Since almost no white southerners thought slavery evil, attacks on slavery, by the abolitionists and later the Republicans, became attacks on them and "mocked their honor."[15]

The South's overwhelming commitment to the intertwined conceptions of liberty and honor, in Cooper's view, explains much about the antebellum sectional crisis. Convinced of their need for independence and liberty, southerners could accept no interference with their right to control their property, their slaves. Any attempt to say that they and their slaves could not enter the territories threatened their liberty and, even more, their honor. The South's fierce defense of the liberty to own slaves and to expand slavery therefore helps explain their fear of Republican interference with slavery and threats to their rights in the territories. Cooper portrays secession as the logical result of such beliefs, a decision reached in a democratic society and made not in secret but with substantial public support. It constituted the final vote in the politics of slavery. In the act of secession, white southerners thought they acted as true Americans and claimed the mantle of the American Revolution. Although he does not develop the theme as strongly as he does those of democracy, liberty, and honor, Cooper's two books on antebellum politics seem to agree that the South should be thought of as fundamentally American.

In 2000, Cooper followed his studies of antebellum politics with a biography of one of the era's most important politicians, highlighting the theme of Americanism in its title, *Jefferson Davis, American*. It may well become Cooper's most important book. The Confederate president has been the subject of sixteen biographies when Cooper's appeared, but many scholars consider Cooper's the best—no mean scholarly accomplishment. Cooper conceived of it very much as a narrative biography in the grand style, as the 655 pages of text and roughly 75 pages of notes suggest. In elegant prose that any reader would enjoy (as the book's selection for the *Los Angeles Times* Book Award testifies), it tells the story of Davis's life as it unfolded. Cooper consciously let the interpretation rest in the narrative, rather than making it explicit, but several years after the biography appeared, he published a shorter book, *Jefferson Davis and the Civil War Era*. A collection of essays drawn from various talks he has given, it is far more direct in its interpretation of Davis's role and behavior. Historians concerned with historiographical and interpretive debates will find it an invaluable companion volume to the biography.[16]

Jefferson Davis, American provides a sympathetic but never uncritical portrait of its subject and movingly tells the story of his personal as well as his public life. It discusses Davis's relationship with his older brother Joseph, who became a surrogate father, as well as his marriages, the tragic early one to Sarah Knox Taylor, who died shortly after they married, and the longer, fulfilling, but often far from easy one with Varina Howell. The book also recounts the psychic pain caused by the deaths of four of Jefferson and Varina's children and explains how much physical pain Davis endured over the course of his life as a result of various illnesses. It chronicles his prewar life as a successful planter and a slaveholder, judging him concerned about the welfare of his slaves out of both self-interest and "Christian stewardship," and it describes Davis's far less successful postwar efforts to make a living.[17]

Even as he pays close attention to Davis's personal life, Cooper devotes much of the book to an astute account of Davis's public role. Cooper clearly wants his readers to understand that Davis was an important historical figure before he became the Confederacy's only president, which occurs roughly half way through the book. Before Davis's presidency, Cooper works hard to show, he had been an extremely able politician, "a superlative one," in fact. Cooper recounts Davis's efforts in the House and Senate, showing him to be a strong southern partisan, committed to strict construction and states' rights but also willing on behalf of national defense to support a stronger national government. Cooper considers Davis, who served as a colonel during the Mexican War, "an authentic war hero" and, later, a successful secretary of war.[18]

Davis opposed the Compromise of 1850, although Cooper argues he did so in hopes of preserving the Union to which he long remained loyal. Cooper also makes quite clear that Davis, like the white southerners he wrote about in his earlier works, saw nothing wrong with slavery, fervently opposed the abolitionists' attacks on it, and adamantly defended the South's right not only to maintain it but to expand it into the territories. Davis also contrasted slavery with liberty, which made him more determined to preserve white liberty. When, after the election of Abraham Lincoln, the final crisis of the Union came and a new compromise seemed necessary, Davis "desperately wanted a settlement on terms that would salvage southern rights and honor" and thought that "the Republicans had to take the initiative in finding a solution." His knowledge of William Seward "gave him reason to think a deal possible between the Republicans and the South."[19]

When no compromise emerged, the new Confederacy turned to Davis to serve as its president, and the South's independence and nationalism became his cause, if not obsession. "The failure of the old Union delivered a severe emotional and psychological blow" to Davis, Cooper argues in one of the essays in *Jefferson Davis and the Civil War Era*. "The new Confederacy must not fail, and to it he gave his absolute commitment." For Davis, the past had to be abandoned, and "the Confederacy had become 'the noblest cause in which man can be engaged.' . . . Such notions as ambition, greed, vanity, and selfishness had to be banished from this sacred crusade." He also believed "national survival or Confederate independence meant liberty, failure would mean slavery. Thus, national unity or defenses assumed primacy, and that view underlay his constitutionalism and advocacy of energetic government." Indeed, Cooper argues, his commitment to independence would lead eventually to Davis's support for arming the slaves and emancipating those who served in the military.[20]

Many students of the Civil War portray Davis as a failed war leader. David M. Potter, in an influential essay, contrasted Abraham Lincoln's success as a political leader at war with Davis's failure in the same role, making the difference in their performance and abilities a major factor in Confederate defeat. Cooper, in contrast, constructs a strong but equivocal case for Davis as not just "an aggressive commander in chief" but an able one who "personally directed the

Confederate military machine." Cooper thinks Davis was a "superlative" politician before the war and that he remained one as president of the Confederacy. "Concerning the political dimensions of his position, broadly construed," Cooper concludes, "he merits high marks." Cooper has reservations, though, about Davis's "mixed" abilities as a military leader. "Davis did comprehend the strategic situation facing his country, and his basic strategic decisions were reasonable and understandable," he observes. "But as a purely military commander in chief, he exhibited serious flaws. Too often he did not exercise appropriate command authority over generals or intervene effectively when crippling disagreements divided senior commanders . . . Simply put, Davis did not have the steel or ruthlessness to make absolutely essential command decisions." Nevertheless, throughout the war, Davis retained the support and respect of most Confederates. Davis's critics, whom Cooper finds to be a very small minority, come in for severe criticism in the biography.[21]

Jefferson Davis goes on to chronicle Davis's postwar fate—his time in prison, his stays abroad, his few postwar public appearances, and his writings. Davis, Cooper argues, "interpreted Reconstruction as an extension of Republican oppression the Confederacy had so stalwartly resisted" and always held to the belief that the South had done nothing wrong. Unlike Robert E. Lee and his brother, he refused to apply for a pardon. His postwar appearances and particularly his massive *The Rise and Fall of the Confederate Government* defended the South's position. Davis, Cooper maintains, played a central role in the creation of the Lost Cause, the South's postwar memory of the conflict. In a fascinating essay, Cooper explains that in Davis's ardent defense of the Confederacy, his postwar explanations of the South's cause differed from his prewar rhetoric. Before the war, he shows, Davis rarely referred to states' rights and openly proclaimed slavery central to the need for independence; after the war, states' rights became central, and the defense of slavery disappeared. At the end of his life, though, Davis combined his refusal to repudiate, even abandon, the past, with hopefulness about the future. He "talked proudly about the grandeur of the United States, its growing wealth and power." Jefferson Davis, for Cooper, had always been and remained an American. His biography and the collection of essays that compliments it make that point, and they offer a nuanced portrait of a complex man and a complex era. Both volumes make the case for remembering Davis's antebellum contributions to the republic and provide an important revisionist perspective on Davis's role as Confederate president, one with which Civil War historians will have to come to terms.[22]

Cooper's next major book, which appeared in 2012, is *We Have the War Upon Us: The Onset of the Civil War, November 1860–April 1861*. In some ways, it is Cooper's boldest book and may become his most controversial one. It is one thing to take on C. Vann Woodward or David Potter, quite another to take on Abraham Lincoln. Cooper interprets Lincoln's refusal to compromise on the territorial issue as crucial to the spread of secession beyond South Carolina and to the onset of the war. *We Have the War Upon Us* in some ways epitomizes Cooper's approach to the past, particularly in its close attention to the political goals and maneuverings of various leaders and the importance it places on such activities. It also exemplifies Cooper's insistence on contingency and the key role able political leaders can play. He never explicitly says so, but a reader could easily conclude that if William Seward and not Lincoln had been the president, a compromise might have been found and war averted. Some readers, though, may find that the latest book differs in subtle ways from his earlier work on southern politics. Cooper still sees slavery at "the core of southern society and the southern economy." White southerners in the latest book still believe nothing is wrong with slavery and still demand that the North not interfere with it where it exists nor prevent its spread in the territories. Yet the book does not put as much emphasis on southern insistence on liberty, independence, and honor as the earlier works do. In the latest study, the South—particularly the upper and border states that did not initially secede along with South Carolina—seem more open to compromise than in *Liberty and Slavery*. The earlier work stresses the continuity of the politics of slavery that led to secession; the new book raises the possibility of contingency through examining the political leadership that might have avoided it.[23]

The apparent difference may reflect the fact that *We Have the War Upon Us*, although it certainly includes the South, is more about the North than any of Cooper's previous books. It focuses on two interrelated stories, the attempts in Washington to find a compromise to prevent the war and the developments in Charleston Harbor, where the firing on Fort Sumter leads to war. Cooper provides a clear discussion of the various attempts to find a compromise, managing to provide sufficient detail and still have a sprightly narrative that holds the readers' attention and recreates the tension of the five months leading up to the war. He views the victorious Republican Party as a new development in American politics, a sectional party that had no political base in the South.

Nonetheless, he does not find it to be a unified party, certainly not one in which everyone sought to end slavery. Republican "hard-liners" or the party's "left," as Cooper terms them, were relentlessly antisouthern, totally committed to ending slavery, and determined not to compromise, particularly on the territorial issue, even if it meant the end of the Union. At the other end of the Republican spectrum, though, conservatives within the party wanted to find a solution and valued the Union above all else. "The great middle of the party never wanted to have to decide between slavery and the Union," Cooper maintains. With the states of the upper and border South hoping to preserve the Union and the conservative and moderate Republicans, not to mention conservative northern Democrats, open to compromise, Cooper believes some sort of agreement on the territorial issue would have been possible, as did William Seward, who becomes the central figure in the book. An experienced political leader, astutely aware of the likelihood and danger of war, Seward worked skillfully and steadfastly to prevent it. Cooper contrasts Seward and his efforts with Lincoln and his refusal to compromise. A president elected with a minority of the vote, Lincoln was also an "untried, inexperienced leader." Unlike Seward, Cooper argues, Lincoln did not at first understand the gravity of the situation, said relatively little about the growing crisis before his inauguration, and throughout it refused to compromise, turning his back on the heritage of one of his earlier heroes, Henry Clay. Lincoln rejected any concession on the territorial issue, Cooper argues, for three reasons. He did not know or understand the South, and therefore he underestimated the threat. He acted out of partisanship, determined above all else to preserve his young party by supporting its hard liners. Finally, Lincoln himself had a "visceral antislavery commitment."[24]

With no support from Lincoln, and despite Seward's best efforts, no compromise could be reached. The crisis then came at Fort Sumter. Lincoln informed South Carolina's governor that he would resupply the fort but not send arms or reinforce it, and then he sent a ship to do just that, a strategy that maneuvered the newly formed Confederacy into firing the first shot. Lincoln's response, a call for troops to put down the insurrection, constituted in southern eyes, "coercion," the one thing leaders of the upper South could not countenance. It, after all, violated their sense of liberty, independence, and honor. The war began.[25]

We Have the War Upon Us is Cooper's latest book but probably not his last.

He is already hard at work on a biography of John Quincy Adams, a shift in emphasis occasioned by a request to complete a biography his advisor, David Donald, had begun before his death. Cooper's agreeing to take on the task is entirely in line with his sense of duty. That he is hard at work in the Adams papers is also characteristic. Even after having written so much, Cooper has undertaken another book based on substantial work in the primary sources; by this point in their careers, not a few historians of his stature have abandoned the archives and offer up only book reviews and an occasional thoughtful essay, if that. Cooper's willingness to immerse himself in the sources, the elegance of his prose, and the rigor of his arguments give his work tremendous authority. His scholarship has ranged across the nineteenth-century South, and historians now and in the future will have to understand and address his arguments for the pre–Civil War roots of the post-Reconstruction political order, the nature and politics of the slave South, Jefferson Davis as antebellum politician and wartime president, and the onset of the Civil War. General readers will profit from his books as well. That he has produced such a distinguished body of work while remaining an excellent teacher and giving so much time to the welfare of his department and LSU makes what he has done all the more honorable. Bill has certainly earned a good Scotch.

NOTES

1. I have a very vivid memory of this interchange but cannot swear I have it exactly right. The following biographical details come from my memory of other conversations and a check of LSU records. Readers may find the remaining footnotes equally arbitrary and unhelpful. I provide citations to all quotes and to all of Cooper's books that I mention—along with a few to scholars referred to by name. I do not provide comprehensive notes for the works that form the scholarly context into which I place Cooper's work.

2. Theodore S. Hamerow, *Reflections on History and Historians* (Madison: University of Wisconsin Press, 1987), 134. William J. Cooper Jr. and John M. McCardell Jr., *In the Cause of Liberty: How the Civil War Defined American Ideals* (Baton Rouge: Louisiana State University Press, 2009).

3. Cooper, "A Reassessment of Jefferson Davis as War Leader: The Case from Atlanta to Nashville," *Journal of Southern History* 36 (May 1970): 189–204; Daniel R. Hundley, *Social Relations in Our Southern States* (1860), ed. Cooper (Baton Rouge: Louisiana State University Press, 1979); Cooper, *Jefferson Davis: The Essential Writings* (New York: Modern Library, 2003); Cooper, Michael F. Holt, and John M. McCardell Jr., *A Master's Due: Essays in Honor of David Herbert Donald* (Baton Rouge: Louisiana State University Press, 1985); Cooper and James M. McPherson, *Writing the Civil War: The Quest to Understand* (Columbia: University of South Carolina Press,

1998). Cooper and Terrill, *The American South: A History* (New York: Alfred A. Knopf, 1991; 4th ed., Lanham, MD: Rowman and Littlefield, 2008).

4. Cooper, *The South and the Politics of Slavery, 1825–1856* (Baton Rouge: Louisiana State University Press, 1978), 176.

5. Cooper, *The Conservative Regime: South Carolina, 1877–1890* (1968; reprint, Columbia: University of South Carolina Press, 2005), 15; *Politics of Slavery*, xii; Cooper, *Liberty and Slavery: Southern Politics to 1860* (New York: Alfred A. Knopf, 1983), 148.

6. C. Vann Woodward, *Origins of the New South, 1877–1913* (Baton Rouge: Louisiana State University Press, 1951); Cooper, *Conservative Regime*, 39, 40.

7. On Woodward's view of the origins of segregation, see Woodward, *The Strange Career of Jim Crow* (New York: Oxford University Press, 1955).

8. Cooper, *Conservative Regime*, 206.

9. The second, a paperback version from Louisiana State University Press, appeared in 1991, and the third from the University of South Carolina Press in 2005.

10. Cooper, *South and the Politics of Slavery*, 149; Cooper, *Liberty and Slavery*, 95, 106.

11. Cooper, *Liberty and Slavery*, 3; Cooper, *South and the Politics of Slavery*, 63, 64.

12. Cooper, *South and the Politics of Slavery*, 29; *Liberty and Slavery*, 80–90 percent, 248, 9.

13. Cooper, *Liberty and Slavery*, 117.

14. Ibid., 14, 15, 72.

15. Charles S. Sydnor, "The Southerner and the Laws," *Journal of Southern History* 6 (1940): 3–23; Bertram Wyatt-Brown, *Southern Honor: Ethics and Behavior in the Old South* (New York: Oxford University Press, 1982). Wyatt-Brown had already begun to talk about southern honor before Cooper's *South and the Politics of Slavery* appeared, although Cooper's book was published four years before *Southern Honor*. Cooper, *Liberty and Slavery*, 118, 180.

16. Cooper, *Jefferson Davis, American* (New York: Alfred A. Knopf, 2000); *Jefferson Davis and the Civil War Era* (Baton Rouge: Louisiana State University Press, 2008). I have read the two in conjunction with one another, and both shape my view of Cooper's interpretation of Davis that follows.

17. Cooper, *Jefferson Davis, American*, 233.

18. Cooper, *Davis and the Civil War Era*, 3; *Jefferson Davis, American*, 158.

19. Cooper, *Jefferson Davis, American*, 317.

20. Cooper, *Jefferson Davis and the Civil War Era*, 48; Cooper, *Jefferson Davis, American*, 463. Cooper also uses the "noblest cause" quote as a chapter title in *Jefferson Davis, American*, 372.

21. David M. Potter, "Jefferson Davis and the Political Factors in Confederate Defeat," in David Donald, *Why the North Won the Civil War* (Baton Rouge: Louisiana State University Press, 1960), 91–114; Cooper, *Jefferson Davis, American*, 353; *Jefferson Davis and the Civil War Era*, 89.

22. Cooper, *Jefferson Davis, American*, 657, 658.

23. Cooper, *We Have the War Upon Us: The Onset of the Civil War, November 1860–April 1861* (New York: Alfred A. Knopf, 2012), 20.

24. Cooper, *We Have the War*, 61, 148, 13; 73.

25. Cooper, *We Have the War*, 263.

CONTRIBUTORS

CHRISTOPHER CHILDERS is an assistant professor of history at Benedictine College in Atchison, Kansas. He is the author of *The Failure of Popular Sovereignty: Slavery, Manifest Destiny, and the Radicalization of Southern Politics*.

RICHARD FOLLETT is professor of American history at the University of Sussex in Brighton, England. He is the author of *The Sugar Masters: Planters and Slaves in Louisiana's Cane World* and *Slavery's Ghost: The Problem of Freedom in the Age of Emancipation*, coauthored with Eric Foner and Walter Johnson. He is currently writing a study of American slave revolts.

GAINES M. FOSTER is LSU Foundation Murphy J. Foster Professor of History at Louisiana State University. Among his publications are *Ghosts of the Confederacy: Defeat, the Lost Cause, and the Emergence of the New South, 1865–1913* and *Moral Reconstruction: Christian Lobbyists and the Federal Legislation of Morality, 1865–1920*.

SAMUEL C. HYDE, JR., is Leon Ford Endowed Chair, professor of history, and the director of the Center for Southeast Louisiana Studies at Southeastern Louisiana University. He is author or editor of eight books, including *Pistols and Politics: The Dilemma of Democracy in Louisiana's Florida Parishes, 1810–1899*, and screenwriter of six films, among them the award-winning *American Crisis, American Shame: The National Consequence of Coastal Erosion*, recipient of a Gold Medal at the New York International Independent Film Festival and a Special Jury Remi Award at WorldFest International Film Festival.

SARAH L. HYDE is an assistant professor of history at River Parishes Community College in Gonzales, Louisiana. She is the author of numerous articles on education in the antebellum Gulf South, including "Casual Neglect: Louisiana Legislators and Antebellum Public Education, published in the *Gulf South Historical Review*. She is the recipient of the William F. Coker Award, the T. Harry Williams Fellowship, and the LSU Graduate Dissertation Fellowship.

JAMES M. MCPHERSON is the George Henry Davis '86 Professor of American

History Emeritus at Princeton University, where he taught for forty-two years until his retirement in 2004. His books include *Battle Cry of Freedom: The Civil War Era*, which won the Pulitzer Prize in History in 1989, *For Cause and Comrades: Why Men Fought in the Civil War*, which won the Lincoln Prize in 1998, and *Tried by War: Abraham Lincoln as Commander in Chief*, which won a second Lincoln Prize in 2009. His most recent book is *War on the Waters: The Union and Confederate Navies, 1861–1865*.

JULIA HUSTON NGUYEN is a grantmaker and independent scholar in Washington, D.C., who has published articles in the *Journal of Mississippi History* and *Louisiana History*.

PAUL F. PASKOFF is professor emeritus of the Department of History at LSU. His recent publications include *Troubled Waters: Steamboat Disasters, River Improvements, and American Public Policy, 1821–1860* and "Measures of War: A Quantitative Examination of the Civil War's Destructiveness in the Confederacy," in *Civil War History*.

GEORGE C. RABLE is the Charles G. Summersell Chair in Southern History at the University of Alabama. His books include *Civil Wars: Women and the Crisis of Southern Nationalism*, *The Confederate Republic: A Revolution Against Politics*, *Fredericksburg! Fredericksburg!*, and *God's Almost Chosen Peoples: A Religious History of the American Civil War*.

JOHN M. SACHER is an associate professor of history and department chair at the University of Central Florida. His *A Perfect War of Politics: Parties, Politicians, and Democracy in Louisiana, 1824–1861* won the 2003 Kemper and Leila Williams Prize for best book on Louisiana History. His research focuses on nineteenth-century southern politics, and he is currently investigating Confederate conscription. He has published articles in *Louisiana History*, *Civil War History*, and the *Journal of Southern History*.

ERIC H. WALTHER worked as an editorial assistant with the papers of Jefferson Davis at Rice University and is currently a professor of history at the University of Houston. Walther is the author of *The Fire-Eaters* and *The Shat-*

tering of the Union: America in the 1850s. His *William Lowndes Yancey and the Coming of the Civil War* received the James Rawley Award from the Southern Historical Association, as well as the Jefferson Davis Award from the Museum of the Confederacy.